WITNESS IN A GENTILE WORLD

A Study of Luke's Gospel

by Eric Johns & David Major

The Lutterworth Press
Cambridge

ACKNOWLEDGEMENTS

Quotations from *New English Bible*, 2nd edition © 1970 by permission of Oxford and Cambridge University Presses.

The authors and publishers are also grateful to the following for permission to reproduce photographs: J. C. Allen Photographic Library; 50; Andes Press Agency / Carlos Reyes: 22, 34, 36, 51, 63, 66, 67, 72, 83, 123, 128, 138, 147, 160; Cephas Picture Library: 13/ W. Geiersperger, 116/ John Millwood, 16, 30, 38, 39, 120/ Mick Rock, 52, 95; Hulton Picture Company: 55; Alan Hutchison Picture Library/ Chandana Juliet Highet, 139/ Jenny Pate, 14/ Liba Taylor, 4, 70; National Gallery: 156; Jamie Simson: 157. Photographs on pages 11, 43, 61 were taken by David Major.

The Lutterworth Press
P.O. Box 60
Cambridge CB1 2NT

British Library Cataloguing in Publication Data

Johns, Eric, *1941 -*
    Witness in a gentile world.
    1. Bible N. T. Luke 2. Christianity. Scriptures
    I. Title II. Major, David
    226.406

    ISBN 0-7188-2802-X

First published 1991 by The Lutterworth Press

Cover illustration and line drawings by Anna Bakhnova

Printed in Great Britain at the Alden Press, Oxford

CONTENTS

INTRODUCTION

In many ways, Luke is the most modern of New Testament writers. The pace of his story-telling, the vividness of his characterisation and the structure he imposes on his material all serve to make us feel at home when we enter his world. This familiarity, however, can at times lead us to forget that he was a first-century writer and subject to the conventions of his age.

Luke combines in his writings both Hellenistic and Hebrew traditions. This fusion of cultures reflects the position in which he and the Church of his period found themselves. He wrote for a Church which was carrying to a Gentile world a message which had been born in a Jewish religious milieu.

Many of Luke's concerns - the meaning of discipleship, wealth, the role of women in the church, for example - are still relevant today. In order to understand Luke's account of the teaching of Jesus it is necessary to understand how Luke went about composing his gospel and the influences which acted upon him.

With this aim in view, we have tried to make available the latest theological scholarship in a form which people will find both interesting and intelligible. The emphasis of this book is on Luke as a creative writer who was attempting to present the truth about Jesus, as he saw it, in a way which would make sense to his readers. This is the task which every generation of Christians undertakes; and it is never finished.

The quotations used are from the New English Bible, but the book can be used alongside any version of the Bible.

NOTES FOR TEACHERS

This book has been written to meet the needs of students studying Luke's gospel for GCSE. The material has been divided into two levels of difficulty in order to accommodate the wide ability range of candidates. Text printed in larger type (single column) will be found suitable for the whole ability range; that in smaller type (double column) is designed for candidates able to pursue issues to a greater depth, or for use at the teacher's discretion. Our aim has been to extend the student's theological understanding as far as possible, and to provide a sound foundation for later A-level study.

The book takes into account the requirement of the National Criteria for Religious Studies that candidates should be aware of the relevance of sacred texts to the contemporary world. There are, therefore, sections which focus on the relevance of Luke's gospel to Christians confronted with the issues of today's world. These and the Notes sections, which add substantial background information, will be particularly useful for resource-based learning and for Contemporary Christianity syllabuses.

The questions at the end of each chapter aim to encourage responses in the three areas of knowledge, understanding and evaluation. Most questions are structured, and the more straightforward knowledge questions come first, followed by those requiring understanding and evaluation. We have not attempted to divide questions rigidly into these three areas since they are too closely related, and answers often display more than one skill. Many of the illustrations have questions attached to them which aim to provoke responses in one or more of these areas.

The present book employs the same approach as our *Witness in a Pagan World* which has become established as a standard textbook for Mark's gospel. We hope that this volume will prove equally successful in meeting the needs of teachers faced with the challenge of teaching Luke for GCSE.

E.J.
D.M.

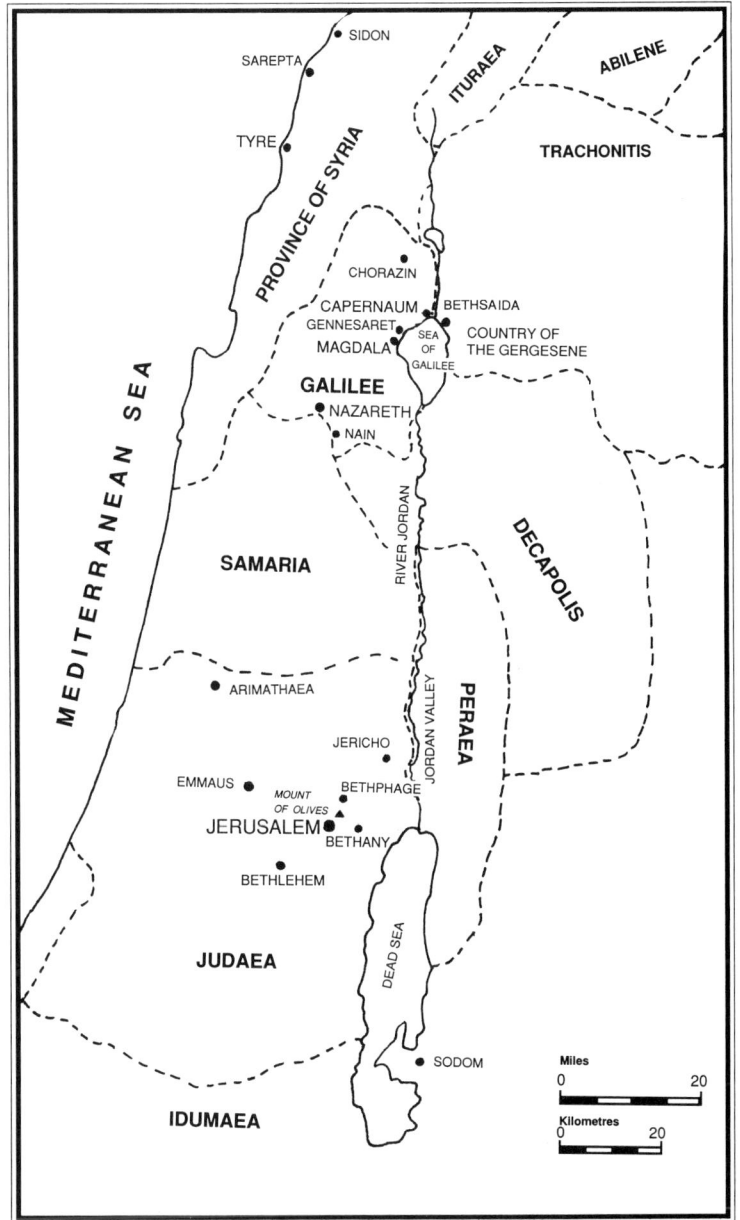

Map of Palestine at the time of Jesus

Notes on the political background

Palestine was part of the Roman Empire during the first century AD.
Herod the Great (37-4 BC) ruled Palestine with the permission of Rome. On his death, the kingdom was divided up between his three sons.

Herod Archelaus ruled Judaea, Samaria and Idumaea, but was deposed in AD 6.
From then on, Roman procurators were appointed. Pontius Pilate ruled from AD 26-36

Herod Philip ruled Iturea (4 BC-AD 34).

Herod Antipas ruled Galilee and Peraea (deposed by the Romans in AD 39).

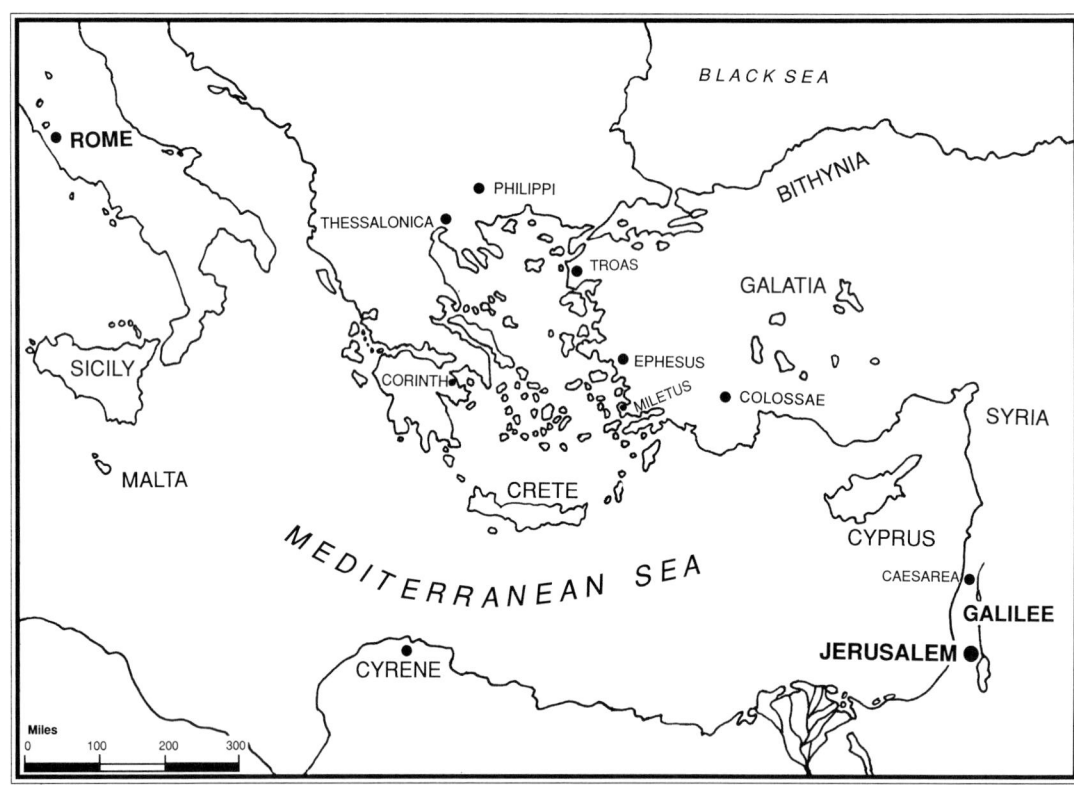

Map of the Mediterranean in the first century AD.
(See Chapter 2 section C for the names of some of the cities visited by Paul)

I.

The Background to the Gospel

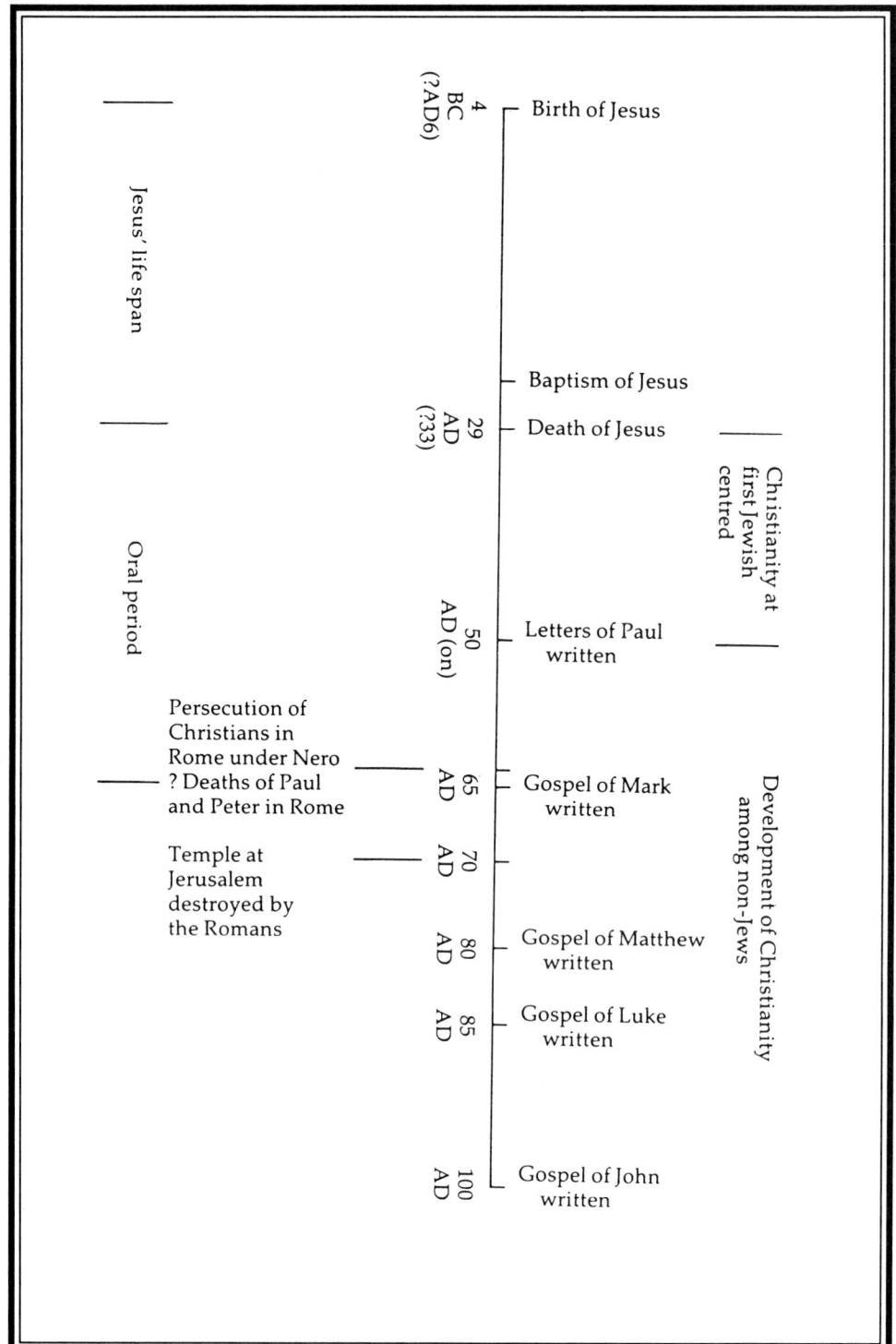

Time chart showing events of 1st century AD.
(Dates are approximate)

1
WHAT IS A GOSPEL?

Luke's gospel is as relevant to people today as it was to those who first read it. In the space of twenty-four quite short chapters, Luke provides Christians with guidance on how they should live, an account of God's plan for humanity and information about Jesus' life.

By the time Luke wrote his gospel more than fifty years had passed since the crucifixion of Jesus. Two generations of Christians had struggled to spread the gospel, been persecuted for their faith and yet had finally succeeded in establishing churches all around the Mediterranean.

Luke belonged to one of these churches. When he looked back to the events of Jesus' lifetime, he saw that everything had happened according to a plan. That plan had been prepared by God and its details had been revealed in the prophecies of the Old Testament. Jesus had carried out God's plan faithfully and had been raised from the dead. In due course, Luke believed, Jesus would return and set up his kingdom on earth. That was the climax towards which history was moving. But only God knew when that would be.

What was important to Luke was how people ought to live so that they could be sure of their place in the kingdom. Did it matter whether a person was poor or rich? What happened if someone did something wrong? Did prayer really help? What should be the role of women in the church? What would life be like in the kingdom? What had Jesus taught about repentance?

These are a few of the questions Luke tries to answer in his gospel. They are questions which Christians ask today. This book is about Luke's answers to these questions and to many more.

A. THE MEANING OF THE WORD 'GOSPEL'

Our word 'gospel' is made up of two Old English words, *god* and *spell*. These words have been combined and shortened to give us the modern word 'gospel'. The word *god* in Old English meant 'good' and the word *spell* meant 'news' or 'story'. So the word 'gospel' means 'good news'.

The Latin word for gospel is *evangelium* and from this we form our words 'evangelist' and 'evangelise'. Luke is an evangelist: that is, one who proclaims the gospel.

We can go back one step further. The Latin is a translation of the Greek in which Luke's gospel and the rest of the New Testament were orginally written. The Greek word for gospel is *euangelion*. Like the Old English this word also has two parts. The *eu* means 'good' and the *angelion* means 'news' or 'message'. It can be seen that when the translation into Old English was made, the words which came to form our word 'gospel' reflected very accurately the meaning of the original Greek.

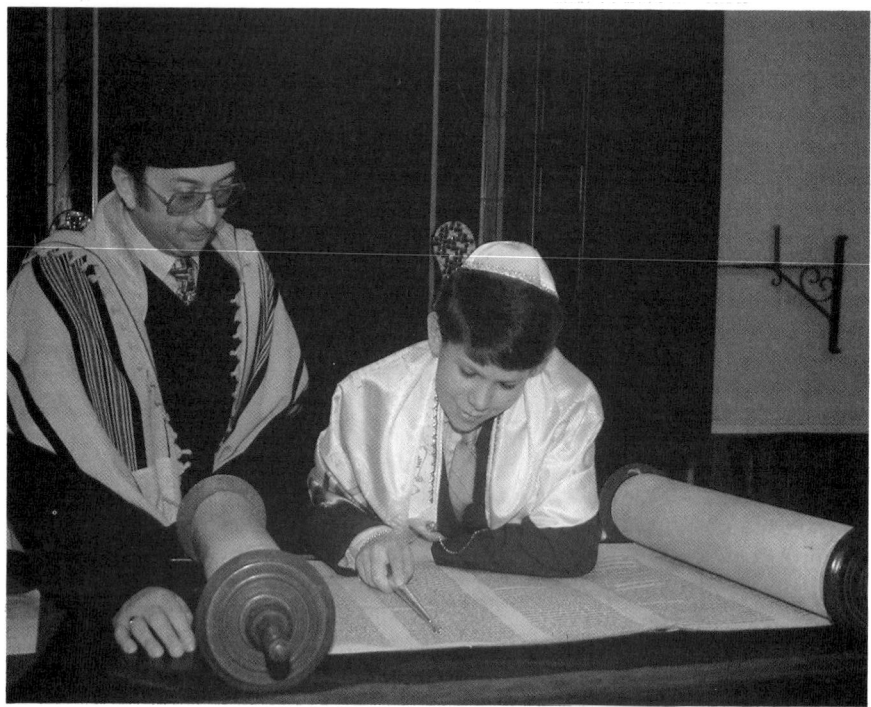

A Jewish boy learning to read the Torah - the first five books of the Jewish Bible
(Christians would call them the first five books of the Old Testament).
Torah scrolls are always handwritten on parchment in Hebrew.

B. THE *ORAL PERIOD* AND THE WRITING OF THE GOSPELS

i) The good news in the *oral period*

Jesus was crucified at some time during the years AD 29-33; Mark wrote his gospel, the first of the New Testament gospels to be written, at some time during the years AD 65-69. The period between these events is called the *oral period*. This simply means, the time when the gospel was passed on by word of mouth.

As far as we know Jesus himself had left no written teaching. He made up stories and rhythmical sayings which were easy to remember, and his disciples followed the custom of the time by memorising them. After Jesus' death his disciples continued his work using the same methods as their master. These methods were efficient. Until the invention of printing the quickest way to spread news was by speaking directly to crowds of people. Writing on papyrus scrolls was slow and, in a world where many people could not read, it was not an effective way of spreading urgent news.

There were Jewish communities in many cities in the countries bordering the Mediterranean and it was in the synagogues of these communities that Christian missionaries proclaimed the good news. They also preached in city squares and argued with passers-by (Acts 17:16-18). When anyone, Jew or Gentile, showed an interest in their message they taught them in small groups and prepared them for baptism. The story of the expansion of Christianity is told in the Acts of Apostles which was also written by the author of Luke's gospel.

During the *oral period* the early church faced opposition, engaged in argument, told how Jesus had been crucified and resurrected, developed ways of worship, and passed on Jesus' teaching to converts. In the course of these activities the material the church used underwent various changes. Some biblical scholars called *form critics*, claim that it is possible to tell from the *form* or *shape* of the units of material (principally those in Mark's gospel) how the material was used during the *oral period*. Form critics generally identify four types of material:

1. *Pronouncement stories* were used by the early church to provide a context for a saying of Jesus. What was important was the saying; the story served as a way of remembering it. E.g. Luke 20:19-25. The form of this pronouncement story is: v.19 context; vv.20-24 action; v.25 saying.

2. *Miracle stories* were used to show Jesus' supernatural power. E.g. Luke 4:33-37. The form of this miracle story is: vv.33-4 description of problem; v.35 miraculous action; vv.36-7 result/reaction of onlookers.

3. *Sayings of Jesus* were used to instruct. They have various forms from brief, easily remembered sayings which divide into two balanced parts, to long parables; but in all cases there is one main point being made. E.g. Luke 6:27-31; 15:11-32.

4. *Stories about Jesus* were used to inspire converts and to explain the basis of certain acts of worship. E.g. Luke 3:21-22; 9:28-36; 19:28-38.

Form critics have said that the material passed on by the church during the *oral period* served specific purposes and that was why it was preserved. The gospel-writers drew on this oral tradition when writing their gospels.

ii) The gospels of Mark and Matthew

The earliest complete gospel we possess is thought to be that of Mark. By examining the material in this gospel we can see how the needs of the Christians who belonged to Mark's church influenced him.

Mark almost certainly wrote his gospel for a church which was suffering persecution. This fact affected both his choice of material and the way in which he presented it. Jesus is shown battling with evil. He prophesies suffering for his followers, suffers himself and feels abandoned by God. But he rises from the dead and promises that his followers will too. Through Mark's account of Jesus, the members of his church could understand their own situation and find the strength to continue in their faith.

Matthew's gospel is often referred to as the 'church' gospel. This is because he is concerned with the needs of a developing church. When Matthew describes the Last Supper his description of it turns Jesus' words to his disciples into instructions to the church on how to perform a communion service. We can also see that Matthew appears to have been writing for people of a Jewish background.

When we come to Luke we shall see that he too has special interests which guide his choice of material and affect how he presents it.

Symbols of the evangelists Mark and Matthew

C. A GOSPEL IS NOT A BIOGRAPHY

There have been many attempts to write a biography of Jesus but none has been successful. The reason for this is that we do not have the sort of information about Jesus necessary to construct a modern biography.

For instance, the gospels do not contain any of the following information about Jesus: details of his family, of his education, of his likes and dislikes; what he did before his baptism by John; whether he was married; a physical description; and even the dates of his birth and crucifixion are not certain. We do not even know the order of events during the years of his teaching which the gospels describe.

Why did the evangelists omit all this fascinating material? The answer is that to them it was irrelevant. They set out to tell the good news of Jesus. In other words, to recount the teaching and actions of God's Messiah which their readers needed to know in order to gain salvation. They were more interested in the future than the past.

If Luke's readers asked whether striving to grow rich was a worthwhile activity they needed to hear the parable of the rich fool (12:13-21). If they wanted to know how to pray they needed to learn the Lord's Prayer (11:1-4). It did not matter where or when Jesus had delivered these teachings. What mattered were the teachings themselves and one's response to them.

Luke's gospel, therefore, is not a biography. Any information about Jesus' life which Luke includes is directly related to his presentation of the good news.

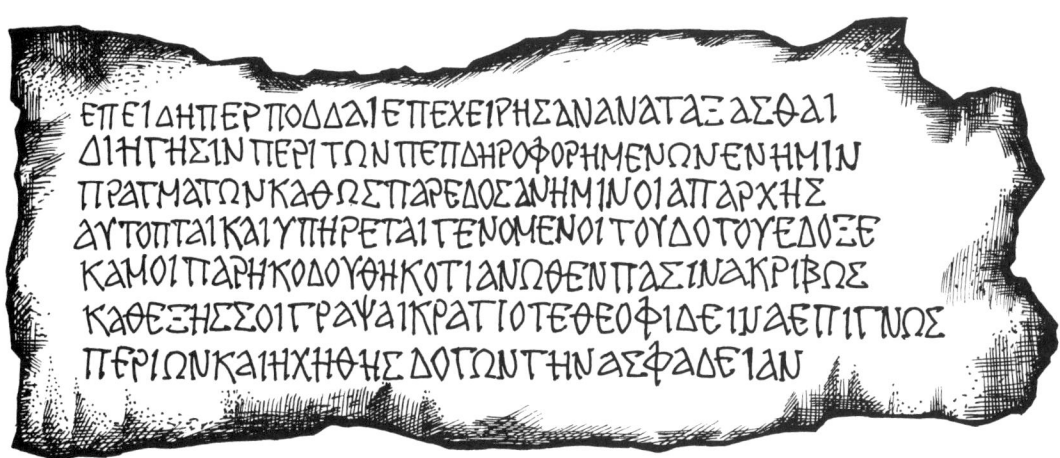

When Luke wrote his gospel all Greek writing was in capital letters. There was no punctuation and there were no spaces between words. This passage is Luke 1:1-4. What does it say in English?

Questions for chapter 1

1a. What words were combined to make our word 'gospel'?

b. What does the word 'gospel' mean?

c. What does an evangelist do?

d. Is 'gospel' a good translation for 'euangelion'?

2a. What does the phrase 'oral period' mean in New Testament study?

b. What, approximately, were the dates of the oral period?

c. What methods did the first Christian missionaries use to spread the gospel?

d. What different types of sayings or stories have form critics identified? Give an example of each type.

3a. Which New Testament gospel was the first to be written?

b. What was probably happening to the church for which Mark wrote?

Symbol of Luke the evangelist

2
WHO WAS LUKE?

There are three sources of information we can use to find out about the author of Luke's gospel.

1. There are sources outside the New Testament which record the traditions of the early church.

2. There is what Luke himself wrote: the gospel and the Acts of the Apostles. We can examine these and ask whether, intentionally or not, he tells us anything about himself.

3. There are the other writings in the New Testament which may shed some light on his identity.

On the basis of these three sources we have to try to answer the questions: *Who* was Luke? *When* was the gospel written? *Where* was the gospel written?

A. CHURCH TRADITION ABOUT LUKE

The name 'Luke' has been connected with the gospel and Acts since, at least, the first half of the second century. How did this name come to be associated with these books?

The simplest answer arises from the dedication which appears at the start of each volume. This suggests that the books were written for publication and not for private use. If they were for publication, the author's name would have been connected with the books from the start. But this gives us a name only and tells us nothing about the man himself.

Outside the New Testament, the earliest written sources which mention a 'Luke' as the author of the third gospel say that he was a doctor and a companion of Paul. This information is mentioned in passing which suggests that it was generally accepted.

We can trace this church tradition back to Irenaeus, who was the bishop of Lyons in about AD 180. He says that "Luke, the follower of Paul, set down in a book the gospel preached by his teacher". Another early source, the Muratorian Canon which listed the Christian books in use in Rome in the second half of the second century, states: "The third book of the gospel is that according to Luke. Luke, the physician, when, after the Ascension of Christ, Paul had taken him as travelling companion, wrote in his own name what he had been told, although he had not himself seen the Lord in the flesh. He set down the events as far as he could ascertain them, and began his story with the birth of John."

These quotations preserve the tradition of the early church, but we have to be cautious where such tradition is concerned. This is because there were disputes about the authority of the various gospels. An individual church which wanted a certain gospel to be accepted by the whole church would try to show that the teaching it contained had been passed down to it by one of the apostles and was therefore authoritative. The claims made by some churches for the genuineness of their traditions would today be called 'propaganda'.

In the case of Luke's gospel a good, if negative, reason for thinking that a 'Luke' was the author is that we know of no one of that name who was important in the early church in the period when Luke-Acts was written. This means that there was nothing to be gained by any group claiming authorship for Luke which would have been the case if he had been influential.

B. THE WRITINGS OF LUKE

i) The author of Acts of the Apostles

The gospel of Luke is dedicated to someone called Theophilus who is addressed as "your Excellency", 1:1-4[1]. This was the conventional way of beginning a book at the time that Luke wrote. An author would try to find an influential person who would be willing to accept the dedication. This helped to give a book respectability.

In the introduction to the gospel Luke says what he is setting out to accomplish by writing this book. He does not say that his is a two volume work, but Acts begins with the words "In the first part of my work, Theophilus," and there then follows a summary of the events which have been described in the gospel (Acts 1:1-5). The story is then continued in the book which follows.

There is very little doubt that the author of Luke's gospel and Acts is the same person. Even without the introductions to link them we could tell from the vocabulary and the style of Greek in which they are written that both come from the same author. In addition, both books are concerned with the same themes, for example, the importance of Jerusalem, the Holy Spirit, the Gentile mission. Also, there are similar patterns to events, such as the arrest and trial of Jesus in the gospel and of Paul in Acts.

We can say, with a considerable degree of certainty, that the author of Luke's gospel was also the author of Acts of the Apostles.

ii) A Gentile Christian in a Gentile world

Luke's conventional dedication at the start of the gospel shows him to be a well-educated man familiar with the literature of his day. His style of Greek reinforces this opinion. The introduction is in almost classical language, while at other places the gospel is written in the Hellenistic Greek which was used amongst educated people of Luke's time. In yet other passages he writes in the Greek of the Septuagint, a Greek version of the Old Testament.

What we find in Luke's writings is a combination of two very different cultures, the Jewish and the Greek. How did this come about in the works of a man who was almost certainly non-Jewish?

One possibility is that Luke was one of the people the Jews called 'God-fearing'. That is, they admired the Jewish religion with its high moral standards, they attended the synagogues but took no part in services, and they remained Gentiles. As Christianity spread and churches were established many of these people became Christians. Once the Christian church had broken away from Judaism and it had been decided that it was not necessary to become a Jew before becoming a Christian, many God-fearing Gentiles joined the new religion. It was a far simpler procedure to become a Christian than a Jew. If Luke had followed such a path it would explain not only his interest in the Gentiles, but also his detailed knowledge of the Old Testament.

In Acts, Luke is concerned with the spread of Christianity in the Gentile world, and in the gospel many of his interests suggest that he wrote against a Gentile background. He uses Mark's gospel as one of the sources for his gospel but omits such matters as Jewish laws which would have been of little interest to Gentile readers. By contrast he is constantly interested in people who are Gentiles and with the church's mission to the Gentiles.

In whatever way Luke's knowledge of both Jewish and Greek cultures came about, the evidence suggests that he was a Gentile writing for Gentile churches.

---

[1] The name Theophilus means 'God-lover'. It has been suggested that this name was used to disguise the identity of the person to whom Luke dedicated his books; or, alternatively, that it was a dedication to any God-lover. There is no evidence to support either suggestion.

C. THE COMPANION OF PAUL

In Acts, there are four passages where the author suddenly changes from describing the journeys of Paul in the third person to writing 'we', as though quoting from a diary he had kept while a companion of Paul. (See Acts 16:10-17; 20:5-16; 21:1-18; 27:1-28:16.)

These passages describe journeys from Troas to Philippi, from Philippi to Miletus, from Miletus to Jerusalem, and from Caesarea to Rome. They span several years. In the descriptions of the events which separate them Paul and his companions are referred to as 'they'. The companion of the 'we' passages does not seem to have been present between journeys.

One of the difficulties of these passages is that we cannot be sure that the 'we' does refer to Luke and Paul. It could mean Paul and some other companion. People in the ancient world certainly kept diaries of events and of journeys and it is possible that Luke might have copied such a record into his book. An argument against this, however, is that there is no noticeable change of style between the 'we' passages and the rest of the book.

In his letters Paul mentions his companion, Luke, three times. (See Col. 4:14; Philem. 24; 2 Tim. 4:11.) The difficulty again is that we cannot link the 'we' passages to these mentions of Luke. At Col. 4:14 Paul calls Luke 'the doctor'. This led people to look for signs of special medical knowledge in the two books, but there is only the sort of knowledge any educated person of Luke's time might possess. This means that the church tradition (mentioned in section (a) above) that Luke was a doctor is not confirmed.

The remains of an aqueduct at Caesarea. It was from Caesarea that Paul set out for Rome, possibly with Luke as his companion.

Another difficulty about connecting Luke with Paul is that the gospel and Acts display very different ideas and attitudes from those we find in Paul's letters. But this might be accounted for by the fact that Luke was writing at a different time, with different purposes in mind, and, even if he had been Paul's companion, he would not necessarily have put forward his ideas.

It has to be admitted that the internal evidence of the New Testament does not allow us to reach any firm conclusion about Luke's identity. We cannot be certain that the Luke mentioned by Paul in his letters was the companion on the 'we' journeys mentioned in Acts, and even if the same person is involved, we still cannot be sure that he is the author we know as Luke.

D. WHO WAS LUKE?

How can we answer our original question? Do we have enough evidence to identify Luke or to make some general statements about the sort of person he was?

Church tradition claims that the author was Luke the companion of Paul. If we approach the New Testament with this idea in mind, we can find evidence which might appear to support it. But sources outside the New Testament add nothing to what we can discover from the New Testament itself. Tradition also claims that Luke was a doctor, but the evidence of the gospel and Acts does not confirm this. Tradition preserves the claim of Luke's authorship, but offers no further evidence to back it up.

We must bear in mind what we said about the possibility that church tradition might have originated as propaganda. This means that we must approach it with caution but not dismiss it out of hand. There are several good reasons for thinking that the author really was called Luke.

1. The name Luke was connected with the two books from an early date, and Luke seems to have been generally accepted as the author.

2. The books were most likely written for publication and the author's name attached to them from the start.

3. Since Luke does not appear to have been important in the church no one would have gained by trying to make out that the books were written by him if that were not the case.

This does not identify the author very satisfactorily but more than that we cannot safely say.

We can, however, use the evidence of the New Testament and make some general statements about the sort of person Luke was. First, he is the author of both the gospel and Acts. Second, he is an educated man familiar with the literature of his day. Third, we can be reasonably certain that he is a Gentile, though one with a thorough knowledge of the Old Testament.

E. WHERE WAS THE GOSPEL WRITTEN?

To attempt to answer this question we have once again to look at what Luke tells us in his writings, what hints other New Testament sources give, and at sources outside the New Testament.

Luke does not tell us anything about himself directly. But we have been able to piece together some information. Since we think he was a Gentile Christian we should start trying to locate the place of writing by considering Gentile cities where there were Jewish synagogues and where Christian churches were established. Unfortunately this procedure does not narrow down the search very much. There were Jewish communities in many of the cities around the Mediterranean and churches were widely established within a very few years of Jesus' death.

If we assume for the moment that church tradition is accurate and that Luke was indeed the companion of Paul, we find that the first 'we' passage in Acts begins at the port of Troas in what is now Turkey. If Luke did come from that region he certainly did not stay there. His account of Paul's journeys ends with another "we" passage with Paul under arrest in Rome. According to church tradition Paul died there in the persecution of Christians by the Emperor Nero. Luke does not mention this.

Some early manuscripts of the gospel claim that it was written in Rome. Other manuscripts have what is known as the 'Anti-Marcionite Prologue' attached to them which says that Luke came from Antioch in Syria, wrote his gospel in the region of Achaea in Greece and died in Boeotia aged eighty-four. Other manuscripts claim Alexandria in Egypt as the place of composition.

None of these suggestions has conclusive evidence to support it and we can draw no firm conclusion about where the gospel was written or where Luke came from.

However, in the case of Luke, these questions are not so pressing as they are where Mark and Matthew are concerned, since they appear to have written for particular communities, while Luke aims at a wider audience. He dedicates his gospel to Theophilus but it is not intended for one man alone. Luke was most probably a Gentile Christian writing for other such Christians wherever they lived.

F. WHEN WAS THE GOSPEL WRITTEN?

One of Luke's sources was Mark's gospel which is usually dated between AD 65 and AD 69. This gives us the earliest possible date at which Luke's gospel could have been written, but we should expect Mark's gospel to have been in circulation for some years before it could come to be accepted and used as an authoritative source.

This leaves us with the question, 'How long after Mark did Luke write?' Those who favour a later date draw attention to the style of the work. It suggests someone sitting back and taking a long view of events; it does not read like the work of someone living through a time of persecution as does Mark's gospel. The author appears to be a member of a settled church, where women are important and the problems are those of wealth rather than pagan opposition. As a result the writing of the gospel is usually put between the years AD 75 and AD 85.

A celebration of Roman imperial power: the Arch of Septimus Severus in Rome.
Some early manuscripts of Luke's gospel claim
that it was written in Rome.

There are those who favour an early date for writing. They put forward two main arguments:

1. That Luke wrote a first draft of the gospel, known as Proto-Luke, at some time before Mark wrote, possibly during the two years that Paul was at Caesarea, and that later he inserted sections of Mark's gospel into it (see chapter 3 section (a)). This theory assumes that Luke was Paul's companion and that he stayed with him at Caesarea. The major objection to this is the gospel itself: if the sections which Luke took from Mark are removed from the gospel, we are left with a shapeless mass of material. Luke-Acts, in the way we have it today, gives every indication of having, from the start, been planned as a whole.

2. That if Luke had known of Paul's martyrdom in Rome in AD 64, he would not have ended Acts with Paul under arrest but would have recorded his death. This requires a very early date for composition, before Mark if one assumes, as appears likely, that the gospel was written before Acts. But an examination of Acts does not suggest a book written immediately after the events it records. Even knowing Paul's fate,

it would have been reasonable for Luke to end the book where he does since such an ending fits in with the pattern of the whole work.

There are those who argue for a date after AD 70. They cite four passages, all connected with the Jewish rebellion of AD 66 and the fall of Jerusalem in AD 70. At 21:20 Luke appears to have turned a vague prophecy from Mark 13:14 into a definite prediction about the destruction of Jerusalem. This suggests that he had knowledge of the events of AD 70 and so wrote after that date. Against this view it has been argued that Luke was not in this verse rewriting Mark, but was inserting words from another source which were more likely to reflect what Jesus actually said than did Mark's account. Two passages in Luke, 19:41-44 and 23:27-31, appear to reflect knowledge of the fate of Jerusalem with references to a siege and the sorrow which will come upon the people. Both of these passages are found only in Luke.

The fourth reference is to 6:15 where the list of the Twelve includes "Simon who was called the Zealot." In his parallel list Mark calls Simon the "Cananean"

Ruins on the summit of Masada where Jewish zealots made their last stand against the Romans.
The Dead Sea is in the background.

which means a zealous man. By calling him a Zealot Luke connects him with the Jewish religious fanatics who led the rebellion against the Romans between AD 66 and 70. Their final stronghold at Masada fell in AD 73.

If Luke wrote before this last date, it is argued, he would not have wanted to risk linking the Christians with the rebels. However, once the Zealots' power had been destroyed it could be seen that the Christians were a separate group and not a threat to Rome. This suggests a date after AD 73.

There have been some commentators who have argued that Luke had available to him a copy of Matthew's gospel.

Matthew is thought to have written between AD 80 and AD 85. If Luke did indeed make use of this gospel - and it is not generally agreed that he did - this means that he must have written after AD 85.

Others maintain that John used Luke's gospel in writing his own, though there is no general agreement on this. The date of John's gospel is usually put at AD 90-100. If he did use Luke this would give us an indication of the latest date possible for Luke.

A further, though not very convincing, reason for saying that Luke wrote very late in the first century is that he made use of *The Jewish Antiquities*, a book by the historian Josephus which was published in AD 93. This suggestion relies on Luke having obtained information from this source and on his having copied it wrongly. We have no reason to believe that Luke was careless, the opposite in fact, and it ignores the possibility that he may have found the information elsewhere.

Finally, there are the letters of Bishop Ignatius of Antioch which are dated between AD 97 and AD 117. There are phrases in them which suggest that Luke-Acts was known to him. This gives a limit to how late we can date the joint work.

As with much else about Luke the evidence is not conclusive. What there is tends to suggest a later rather than an earlier date.

Questions for chapter 2

1. What sources of information can we use to find out about the author of Luke's gospel?

2a. What do the earliest written sources which mention Luke say about him?

  b. What does Irenaeus say about Luke?

  c. What does the Muratorian Canon tell us about Luke?

  d. Why do we have to be cautious about accepting everything that church tradition tells us?

3a. Which New Testament book, besides the gospel, is Luke thought to have written?

  b. What evidence is put forward to support the argument that Luke wrote this book?

4a. What is there about Luke's gospel which shows the author to be an educated person?

  b. Why is Luke thought to have been a Gentile?

5. Was Luke the companion of Paul?

6a. Why is the date of the writing of Mark's gospel important for dating Luke's gospel?

  b. How long after Mark did Luke write?

7. What date would you give for the writing of Luke's gospel? Suggest what evidence supports your opinion.

Modern-day Jerusalem, looking towards the Temple Mount.

3
WHERE DID LUKE FIND HIS MATERIAL?

A. MARK'S GOSPEL

At the start of his gospel Luke says that "Many writers have undertaken to draw up an account of the events that have happened among us" (1:1). The word 'many' is vague but at least it tells us that Luke knew of other writings about the good news. The question which interests students of the gospels is, Were the other New Testament gospel writers among these 'many'? When we read the different gospel accounts of Jesus' ministry, we first notice many similarities then we become aware of numerous differences, some minor some major. How can we account for both the similarities and the differences? This difficulty is known as the *synoptic problem*.

If we compare Matt. 21:23-27, Mark 11:27-33 and Luke 20:1-8 we can see, even in English (and the similarities are greater in the original Greek), that at least one evangelist copied. The difficulty of knowing who it was arises because in the first century AD there were no copyright laws and anyone could make use of anything anyone else had written without admitting it. There are, therefore, no acknowledgements in the gospels of the evangelists' sources. All that we can do is to compare the gospel texts and draw our own conclusions.

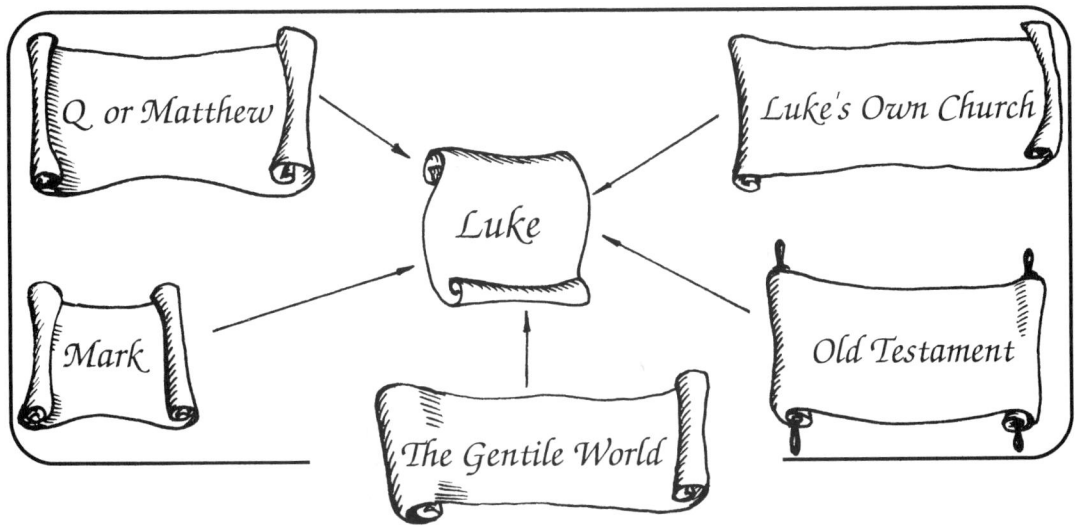

Diagram showing the influences which affected Luke as he wrote his gospel

MATT. 21:23-27	MARK 11:27-33	LUKE 20:1-8
He entered the temple, and the chief priests and elders of the nation came to him with the question: 'By what authority are you acting like this? Who gave you this authority?' Jesus replied, 'I have a question to ask too; answer it, and I will tell you by what authority I act. The baptism of John: was it from God, or from men?'	They came once more to Jerusalem. And as he was walking in the temple court the chief priests, lawyers, and elders came to him and said, 'By what authority are you acting like this? Who gave you authority to act in this way?' Jesus said to them, 'I will ask you one question; and if you give me an answer, I will tell you by what authority I act. The baptism of John: was it from God, or from men? Answer me.'	One day, as he was teaching the people in the temple and telling them the good news, the priests and lawyers, and the elders with them, came upon him and accosted him. 'Tell us', they said, 'by what authority you are acting like this; who gave you this authority?' He answered them, 'I have a question to ask you too: tell me, was the baptism of John from God or from men?'
This set them arguing among themselves: 'If we say, "from God", he will say, "Then why did you not believe him?" But if we say, "from men", we are afraid of the people, for they all take John for a prophet.' So they answered, 'We do not know.' And Jesus said: 'Then neither will I tell you by what authority I act.	This set them arguing among themselves: 'What shall we say? If we say, "from God", he will say, "Then why did you not believe him?" Shall we say, "from men"?' - but they were afraid of the people, for all held that John was in fact a prophet. So they answered Jesus, 'We do not know.' And Jesus said to them, 'Then neither will I tell you by what authority I act.'	This set them arguing among themselves: 'If we say, "from God", he will say, "Why did you not believe him?" And if we say, "from men", the people will all stone us, for they are convinced that John was a prophet.' So they replied that they could not tell. And Jesus said to them, 'Neither will I tell you by what authority I act.'

The word *synopsis* is Greek. It means 'to view at the same time'. The name Synoptic Gospels has been given to Matthew, Mark and Luke because they can be printed in parallel columns and viewed at the same time. The 'synoptic problem' is deciding what the relationship is between the gospels.

The most likely suggestion is that Matthew and Luke copied from Mark. The main evidence put forward to support this view is as follows:

1. Mark contains 661 verses; about 600 verses in Matthew and 300 in Luke are approximately word for word the same as in Mark.

2. When all three gospels have a passage in common, if there are any differences then either Matthew or Luke will agree with Mark against the other; Mark will not be the odd one out. (In the few cases where Matthew and Luke do agree against Mark, it is thought to be the result of copyists making Luke agree with Matthew.)

3. Matthew and Luke improve on Mark's Greek which is rough and uneducated.

4. The order of events in Mark is followed in Matthew and Luke. When Matthew and Luke include common material not in Mark they put it into Mark's narrative in different places. (*See* where Matt. 10:26-33 and Luke 12:1-10 are placed.)

5. Mark's gospel is thought to have been written in the years AD 65-69 against a background of persecution. Matthew and Luke appear to have been writing against different backgrounds, and their concerns suggest that by the time they wrote Christianity was becoming more established in the world.

6. Matthew and Luke remove repetitions in Mark. (Compare Mark 1:32; Matt.8:16; Luke 4:40.)

We cannot finally prove that Mark was copied by Matthew and Luke but the weight of evidence is overwhelmingly in favour of this conclusion.

B. LUKE'S SECOND SOURCE

(i) Q

A quick look at the lengths of Luke's and Mark's gospels tells us that if Luke used approximately half of Mark's material that still leaves the source of two-thirds of Luke to be accounted for. The reader of a synopsis will soon note that besides the material obtained from Mark, Matthew and Luke have a substantial amount of other material which is either identical or very similar. This has led to the suggestions that either they both shared another written source or that one of them copied from the other.

The first suggestion is the most popular with New Testament scholars. It is argued that one of the 'accounts of events' Luke mentions (1:1) is a collection of the sayings of Jesus. This source is called Q, from the first letter of the German word *Quelle* meaning source. If this written source did exist, no copy of it has ever been discovered.

Some of the Q material is: Luke 4:1-13; 6:20-23; 7:1-10; and Matt. 4:1-11; 5:3-12; 8:5-10. Compare these passages to see how closely they agree.

It is thought that Q was originally written in Aramaic (the language Jesus spoke), that it was even earlier than Mark and that it was written in Palestine - though, of course, none of this can be proved.

Some of the minor differences in Q material in Matthew and Luke are thought to have arisen because they possessed different Greek translations of Q. But there are larger disagreements which cannot be explained by this theory. There is no agreed explanation to account for the variations but some suggestions are:

1. There was more than one written Greek copy of Q available to Matthew and Luke.
2. There was more than one original document in Aramaic.
3. Some of the material was oral not written.
4. Matthew and Luke made alterations to the Greek in order to bring out what they thought was the real meaning of a passage.

(ii) Matthew

A theory supported by a minority of scholars is that Matthew and Luke did not have a common written source, but that Luke possessed a copy of Matthew from which he took the material we call Q. This theory has the advantage that it does not require us to 'invent' lost documents which can be an easy way out of a problem.

According to this theory, Luke transferred material which is similar in the two gospels almost without change, while the greater variations are the result of a process called midrash. This is a Hebrew method of retelling a story to bring out the underlying meaning and to account for apparent contradictions. In the Old Testament 1 & 2 Chronicles are a midrash of the books of Samuel and Kings. Luke's parable of the lost son (15:11-32) then becomes a midrash of Matthew's two sons (Matt. 21:28-32). This means that much of the material which is identified as 'special Luke' (L) is in fact Luke's midrash of material in Matthew and Mark. (See chapter 4 section (e) for an example of midrash.)

Those who argue against this theory point out that in places Luke's material appears to be earlier than Matthew's, not a midrash of it; that we are required to believe that Luke would dismantle Matthew's set speeches like the Sermon on the Mount; and that Luke used the material from Mark and Matthew in different ways: Mark in large blocks (e.g. 4:31-44; 8:4-9:50), while material from Matthew is mixed with Luke's own special material in a different way (*but see* section (c.ii) *below*).

The argument continues. However, you should remember while using this book that when Luke's source is given as Q some people would wish to substitute Matthew.

C. THE ORAL TRADITION OF LUKE'S CHURCH

i) Special Luke (L)

Mark and Q sources account for the majority of Luke's material, yet there is a substantial amount remaining. This includes the birth narratives (chs. 1 & 2), the story of Zacchaeus (19:1-10) and incidents which are inserted into Mark's passion narrative such as the trial before Herod (23:6-11). All such material is called 'special Luke' or L.

It is not known where this material came from though it is generally thought to have been oral material and to represent the stories preserved by Luke's own church, or the results of Luke's own research. Some scholars have suggested that Luke 1 & 2 come from a different source again because they are so influenced by the Old Testament. But Luke could well have adopted the style of Greek of the Septuagint when recounting these stories (*See* section (d) below).

ii) Proto-Luke [2]

It was mentioned in section (b.ii) above that Luke uses material from Mark in blocks. In contrast to this he mixes Q and L material together. Very little Q can be found in blocks of Mark. It is only in the Passion narrative that one finds Mark and L mixed. One conclusion drawn from this is that there was an early edition of Luke's gospel which is known as Proto-. Luke. This gospel, it is suggested, was made up of Q and L. Later, Luke obtained a copy of Mark and inserted Mark's material into Proto-Luke. This does not seem very likely because the gospel and Acts appear to be written to a plan, not haphazardly assembled, and Mark provides the basic structure. Q and L in isolation are an unformed mass of material.

D. THE OLD TESTAMENT

The Old Testament was vitally important to the early Christians. There was no New Testament in existence at that time. When Christians in their worship wished to hear the word of God they had two options. They could retell the stories and sayings of Jesus or they could read the Old Testament. The Old Testament was God's word delivered through the Law and the prophets. It was not something which was dead and finished with; God's word could never die. In the Christian view, Jesus had brought a correct interpretation of the Old Testament; more than that, he had fulfilled its prophecies. With a true understanding of Law and prophets, it was possible to understand God's plan for humanity and to see how Jesus had put it into effect.

The Old Testament also showed how God had acted in the past and recorded the words he had spoken through the prophets. When Luke wrote the two opening chapters of his gospel he wanted to emphasise that God was once again active in human affairs. To do this he used the language of the Septuagint and framed his stories so that they mirrored those of the Old Testament.

[2] Proto means 'first': so 'Proto-Luke' is the name given to a supposed first version of Luke's gospel.

When Luke wanted to show that everything was happening as had been foretold he quoted prophecy (e.g. 3:4f). When he wanted to tell people that Jesus worked with God's power he showed Jesus doing what God had done in the Old Testament (e.g. 8:22-25; Ps.89:9). When he wanted the appropriate words for Jesus to address to God he quoted the Psalms (23:46; Ps. 31:5).

E. HOW LUKE USED HIS MATERIAL

We have already noted that Luke mixes blocks of material from his sources alternately. E.g. 5:1-11 L; 5:12-6:17 Mark; 6:20-47 Q (with some L inserted). He follows Mark's order of events for Jesus' ministry. It might seem, looking at Mark, that there could be no other order. But it is not possible to tell from the units of material themselves (pericopes[3] is the correct word for these units) whether, for example, the feeding of the five thousand came before or after the telling of the parable of the Sower. We have to remember that in the oral period each pericope was separate and used as circumstances required.

Luke drops Mark's references to time (e.g. 5:18 see Mark 2:1). He also presents the disciples in a better light (e.g. 8:24 see Mark 4:38). In addition, he rewrites the beginnings and endings of pericopes more extensively than their central sections (e.g. 4:31-37 see Mark 1:21-28). It appears that he made fewer changes in Q material i.e. the sayings of Jesus. But if he used Matthew it is possible that we do not always recognise rewritten material. We can see from the above examples from Mark that Luke felt at liberty to impose his own style on material and to adapt it to his needs. (*See* chap. 4 section e.)

Questions for chapter 3

1. What evidence is there to support the view that Matthew and Luke copied from Mark?
2a. What does 'Q' stand for?
   b. What material is Q thought to have contained?
   c. Which evangelists are believed to have made use of Q?
3a. What is *midrash*?
   b. What arguments are used to support the view that Luke used Matthew?
4a. What does 'L' stand for?
   b. Which material in Luke's gospel is thought to come from source L?
5a. What is the Septuagint? (*See* also chapter 2 section (bii) for information.)
   b. In what way is Luke's gospel connected with the Septuagint?
   c. Why was the Old Testament especially important to the early Christians?
6. What sources do you think Luke used in writing his gospel? Give examples and, where possible, set out quotations from Luke and his sources in parallel columns to support your opinion.

---

[3] *Pericope* is a Greek word which literally means 'cut around'. The idea it suggests is that if one took a pair of scissors to a scroll and cut out the account of an event, story, saying, etc., one would have a unit of material which would be complete and made sense by itself. But it would give no idea of the time, place or circumstances in which the event occurred or the story was told.

*Dressed Torah scrolls. Each scroll is covered by a
mantle, and crowns with bells are placed on the top of
the rollers. A breastplate is hung over the front of the
scroll together with a hand-shaped pointer.*

4

THE MANY FACES OF LUKE

A. LUKE THE APOLOGIST

An *apologist* is not someone who apologises in the modern sense of saying sorry. He is more like a lawyer arguing a case for the defence. The apologist explains. In the case of Luke, he explains what Christians believe so as to give, as he says to Theophilus, "authentic knowledge about the matters of which you have been informed" (1:4).

The need for a Christian apologist arose because, as Luke saw it, the Romans had been *mis*informed about Christianity. He, therefore, aims to defend the Christian faith by correcting three misunderstandings about Jesus and his followers.

1. Jesus was called 'Messiah', or king, which immediately made Romans suspicious that he and his followers would be opposed to Roman rule. Luke, therefore, sets out to demonstrate that neither Jesus nor his followers seeks worldly power. The Messiah's kingdom is not of this world.

2. To make things worse, Jesus had been executed by a Roman procurator for treason against Rome. Luke, therefore, shows that Jesus was not guilty of treason but was the victim of a Jewish plot.

3. Luke wanted to make it clear that there was a division between Christians and Jews. By the time Luke wrote, the Jewish revolt of AD 66 had taken place and Jews throughout the empire were looked upon with suspicion. Luke wanted to show that Christians had never shared Jewish nationalistic ambitions.

The Jews of the diaspora (those who lived outside Palestine) had, for the most part, probably not shared the nationalistic ambitions of Palestinian Jews. They enjoyed special privileges under Roman law which, even before the revolt, made other groups resentful of them. These people too may have been in Luke's mind when he sought to explain Christianity (though the initial Christian mission to the Jews had ended a long time before he wrote). In Acts 28:22 Jewish leaders in Rome tell Paul, "We should like to know what your views are; all we know about this sect is that no one has a good word to say for it." The fall of Jerusalem would have appeared as a judgment by God on the Jews of Palestine and Luke sets out to explain why this happened.

If Luke's apologetics (explanations) were successful, Christians might be free from the threat of persecution by Rome and might be granted the same privileges as Jews. Also, if he could defend and explain the Christian faith successfully, perhaps the Jews of the diaspora would understand that salvation was now offered through Jesus.

B. LUKE THE HISTORIAN

Luke is generally regarded as the historian among New Testament writers. He places the events he records firmly in their historical context. For example, he starts his account of the good news by saying "In the days of Herod king of Judaea" (1:5). When Jesus is to be born, Luke notes that Augustus was emperor and Quirinius governor of Syria (2:1-2). He anchors his account of God's activity as accurately as he can in human history.

Luke, by his own admission, sets out to write "an account of the events that have happened among us" (1:1). But this account was not written primarily as history as we should understand it. Luke's purpose was to provide a firm foundation for Christian faith. If a modern historian set out to describe the same events as Luke, he would account for them in terms of human actions and emotions, of politics, of economics and so on. Luke does not do this. He sees events occurring because of the activity of the Holy Spirit and in fulfilment of God's plan for humanity.

This makes us aware of an obvious point but one which it is all too easy to forget: Luke is not a modern writer. He is an historian, but one who lived in the first century AD and who shared the ideas of his time. Anyone who approaches Luke's gospel as though it were a modern piece of writing will fail to understand it.

Luke was influenced by two cultural traditions: the Hellenistic and the Jewish.

Hellenistic is a term used to refer to the Greek culture which dominated the eastern Mediterranean. Luke's way of writing history resembles that of Hellenistic historians in several ways.

1. The good Hellenistic historian was expected to collect material from various sources and not simply make use of what others had written. Luke appears to be conscientious in this respect. He uses written sources (Mark and Q) and adds other material (L). He also tells us that he "has gone over the whole course of events in detail" (1:3).

2. It was the custom for historians to explain the importance of the events they were describing by providing their central characters with speeches which commented on what was happening. Luke does this with Mary and Zechariah (1:46-55; 1:67-79).

3. Historians were not expected to be impartial. They were expected to praise good behaviour and condemn bad. Luke is firmly against the Jewish authorities (23:1-5). He would have thought it wrong to be otherwise: they were, in his view, on the side of evil.

4. Historians were expected to be accurate, and where we can check on Luke he is usually reliable. His comments on Roman law, administration, politics and geography are generally correct. He also tries to place the events surrounding Jesus in their precise historical setting. But he is not always successful: the dates of Quirinius and the census are confused (2:1-2).

5. Some historians of Luke's time felt that it was acceptable to describe the same incident differently on two occasions if that served their purpose. This is what Luke appears to do with the Ascension (24:50-53; Acts 1:3-11).

The second and greater influence on Luke was the Old Testament. This was the basis of Jewish culture as well as religion.

1. The books of the Old Testament show God working through historical events to guide his people and to demonstrate his plan for humanity. In the gospel and Acts, Luke shows this process under way once more on account of the Holy Spirit, which is active in Jesus and the church.

2. Luke works like the historians of the Books of Kings, selecting incidents from previous records and using them to demonstrate that God is in charge of history and is guiding humanity towards the goal he has chosen for it.

3. His purpose in writing is the same as that of the historians of the Old Testament. It is to write a history of God's dealings with humanity.

Luke uses the techniques of Hellenistic historians, but he sees himself writing in the tradition of the Old Testament. The result is that he produces a history of God's activity which is rooted in Jewish soil but written for a Gentile world.

C. LUKE THE THEOLOGIAN

A theologian is one who writes about God. This is what Luke does. He tries to explain how God acted in and through Jesus to save humanity.

i) Salvation and kingship

Salvation and the kingship of Jesus are twin themes in Luke's theology.

A. Keywords to look for in connection with salvation or deliverance are:

saviour/deliverer,
good news,
forgiveness,
peace.

Salvation means being saved from the powers of evil and death and being given a place under God's rule in his kingdom. The ideas connected with salvation all come from the Old Testament and can be found particularly in Isaiah 61:1-2. Luke quotes this passage at 4:18-19, and it sets out the programme for Jesus' ministry:

This Orthodox bishop's head-dress is called a 'crown'. It symbolises that the Church has taken over the authority of the emperors of the Eastern Roman Empire and rules in the name of Christ.

1. Jesus is filled with the Holy Spirit (3:22);
2. He announces the good news (4:43; 6:20-23);
3. He proclaims release for prisoners i.e. from evil:
   a. by forgiving sins (7:47-49),
   b. by freeing people from slavery to evil (13:10-17),
   c. by defeating death (8:49-56);
4. He proclaims the year of the Lord's favour i.e. peace between God and humanity (2:14; 19:38). Jesus is announced as the deliverer and he shows, by his own resurrection, that salvation has been achieved(24:26).

B. Keywords to look out for in connection with the kingship of Jesus are:

Messiah/Christ,
Son of God (or: of the Most High),
Son of Man,
Holy Spirit,
kingdom of God.

The birth of Jesus is the result of the activity of the Holy Spirit which is God's power in the world (1:35). The kingship of Jesus is announced to Mary by the Angel Gabriel (1:32). Jesus' mission and the type of king he is to be are gradually revealed. A new meaning is given to the titles which are used early on in the gospel (1:32, 35). The healings and the feeding of the five thousand which lead up to Peter using the title 'Messiah' indicate that Jesus is to be a king who defeats evil and offers his followers a place in the kingdom of God. When Peter calls Jesus 'Messiah', Jesus immediately adopts the title 'Son of Man'. The use of the title 'Son of Man' shows that Jesus is not to be a nationalistic king but a heavenly one who is glorified after suffering (9:22; 24:26). This teaching is followed by the Transfiguration, which reveals the heavenly nature of Jesus' kingship (9:29). His glory is not of this world. The truth of what Jesus has taught is shown by his resurrection. His kingship will not only be of the Jews but of all who repent (24:47). The Holy Spirit which was in Jesus will continue to work through the church (24:49).

These themes will be referred to frequently in the main part of this book.

ii) Salvation-history

It has been suggested that Luke was interested in history because he saw salvation as an historical process. God's plan for humanity's salvation started in Old Testament times. Salvation was offered to the Jews. They misunderstood God's word and Jesus was sent to reveal the true meaning of the Law which had been given to Moses, and of the prophets who had warned the people of their wrong behaviour.

For Luke, the 'Jesus-event' was the centre of history. He saw the Old Testament leading up to it. The time of the Christian church led from it to some unknown point in the future when Jesus would return. The time of the church was, therefore, one of preparation. This was why Luke wrote. He wanted to convince his generation of the correctness of his views and so prepare them for Jesus' return.

As far as we can tell, there was not, in Luke's view, going to be any immediate end to the world. The prophecies of Jesus which seemed to imply this had, perhaps, been misunderstood and needed reinterpreting. The end-time, judgment, and the establishing of the kingdom of God would happen, but one could never know when, so one had to be constantly prepared.

This, for Luke, linked salvation to history and explains why he went on to write about the early years of the church. The Holy Spirit was working through the church just as it had through Jesus. Now, in Luke's day, just as in Old Testament times, God's plan was unfolding through history to its appointed end at some time in the future.

D. LUKE'S OTHER INTERESTS

Luke illustrates his theology of salvation and the kingship of Jesus through various *themes* and *topics* to which he keeps returning throughout his gospel.

(i) Themes in Luke's gospel

There are four major themes between which all the teaching of Jesus in Luke's gospel can be divided. They are:

1. True and false religion.
2. Seeing things clearly.
3. Getting ready for the kingdom.
4. Life in the new order.

These are treated in detail in chapter 10.

(ii) Topics in Luke's gospel

There are ten main topics which are of special interest to Luke and to which he returns frequently in his presentation of the good news. They are:

1. *Repentance* This is the first step on the way to salvation so, not surprisingly, it is a constantly recurring note in Jesus' teaching. It is the theme of John the Baptist's preaching and the message Jesus gives the church to proclaim (3:8; 24:47). It means completely changing one's life so that one lives as God requires.

2. *Forgiveness* Repentance brings forgiveness (7:47). Jesus has the right to forgive sins and this he does freely to those who show faith (5:21; 23:43).

3. *Prayer* In Luke's gospel Jesus is shown to pray at all important moments. For example, it is during prayer that the Holy Spirit descends (3:22); Jesus prays before choosing the Twelve (6:12); and he prays for strength before crucifixion (22:39-44).

4. *Reversal* Luke emphasises the contrast between the situation in this world and what will happen at the day of judgment (6:20-26). (See **5** below also.)

5. *The poor* Jesus brings the promise of the kingdom to the poor. It is part of Luke's presentation of the theme of reversal that the poor will be rewarded for their faithfulness and the rich will suffer (6:20-26).

6. *The lost* Because the Law was interpreted with great rigidity, large sections of the population were considered by the Pharisees to be beyond hope of salvation. Luke shows Jesus challenging this view of the Law and offering hope to the lost (19:1-10).

7. *Women* Stories and incidents concerning women occur frequently in Luke. Widows represent the poor and helpless members of society (18:1-8); women are disciples (8:1-3; 10:38-42); women weep for Jesus (23:28). The birth narrative is told from the point of view of Mary rather than Joseph (Luke 1 & 2; compare Matt. 1 & 2). In giving women a prominent place in his gospel, Luke is following the Old Testament where women play an important part in events. (See: Judges 4 & 5; the books of Ruth and Esther.)

8. *Wealth* The gospel contains warnings against the dangers of wealth (12:13-21), and contrasts it with true wealth which can only be found in the kingdom of God (12:33).

9. *The Temple* The gospel begins and ends in the Temple. It is the centre of Judaism and the house of God on earth. It is there that Jesus is hailed as deliverer (2:25-38), and as such Jesus has a special right to occupy it (2:49; 20:1-8). He foretells its destruction (13:35), and at the crucifixion the torn curtain symbolises this (23:45). The Temple sacrifices maintained the relationship between God and his people. Once the Temple was destroyed the only means of salvation was through Jesus: this is why the Temple and its fate are so important to Luke.

10. *Jerusalem* The Temple was in Jerusalem. In Jewish thought the city was the centre of the world and when God established his kingdom it would be ruled from Jerusalem. Luke sees Jerusalem not as the centre of God's kingdom, but as the centre from which the good news was sent to the Jews and, when they refused it, the centre from which it was sent out to the whole world. The gospel begins in Jerusalem and with Jesus' crucifixion ends there; Acts of the Apostles begins there and ends in Rome, the capital of the world. The significance of this pattern for Luke is that it shows God's plan of salvation for all humanity revealing itself through historical events.

E. LUKE THE STORYTELLER

Luke is an outstanding writer. He varies his style according to his subject-matter. For example, the prologue is in classical Greek, the infancy narratives in the Greek of the Septuagint and the majority of the gospel in Hellenistic Greek (i.e. the everyday language of ordinary people). He is also an excellent storyteller. The most popular parables are found in his gospel, e.g. The Good Samaritan and The Lost Son (10:25-37; 15:11-32). He uses his skill as a writer for one purpose only: to present the good news in the most effective and memorable way possible.

Those who support the idea that Luke used Matthew's gospel as a source, claim that he used his skill as a writer to produce a midrash of Matthew's gospel. That is, he rewrote material from Matthew to remove what he saw as inconsistencies, and to bring out more clearly what he believed to be its real meaning.

To see how Luke worked we need to understand that he saw the events in Jesus' journey to Jerusalem (9:51-18:14) as a mirror image of the events which befell the Israelites on their journey to the promised land as described in Deuteronomy. God had been active in the history of the Israelites, now he was active again in the life of Jesus. In order to know how God acted one had only to look at the Old Testament. Since God was active again, one could say either that he would act in the same way as before, or

that similar incidents could be used to illustrate what was happening and so bring out the full meaning of events.

We can see how this midrashic method works if we compare Luke 14:15-24 with Matthew 22:1-10 and Deuteronomy 20:1-7. In Matthew two excuses are made for not attending the feast. Luke sees Deuteronomy 20 as the parallel for this point in Jesus' journey and uses Deuteronomy 20:7 to provide a third excuse for not attending the feast. Luke, according to this view, has used his storytelling gifts to produce a more effective and restrained story than Matthew and to clarify what he saw as the important point in the teaching. (*See* chapter 3 section (b.ii) for a description of midrash.)

Questions for chapter 4

1 a. What is an apologist?
   b. Why was a Christian apologist needed?
   c. Why might the Romans have been suspicious of Christians?
   d. Why would Luke want to show that Christians were different from Jews?
2 a. Why is Luke regarded as an historian?
   b. In what ways is Luke different from a modern historian?
3 a. What does the word 'Hellenistic' refer to?
   b. How does Luke resemble a Hellenistic historian?

   c. In what ways is Luke influenced by the Old Testament?
4 a. What is a theologian?
   b. What does 'salvation' mean?
   c. In what sense is Jesus a king?
   d. List the ten main topics in which Luke is interested.
   e. Why is Luke said to be a good storyteller?
5. Compare Luke 14:15-24 with Matt. 22:1-10. Which story, do you think, is better told? Give your reasons.

II.

The Contents of the Gospel

*The shepherds receive the good news of the birth of Jesus
from an angel. This painting is in the church
at Shepherds' Fields, Bethlehem.*

5
THE BIRTHS OF JOHN AND JESUS

A. JOHN'S BIRTH IS ANNOUNCED
(1:5-25)

Luke begins his gospel by telling of the circumstances surrounding the birth of John the Baptist. The setting is the Temple at Jerusalem. Here Zechariah was performing his duties as a priest. He was offering incense at the altar in the Court of the Priests. For Zechariah this would have been a great occasion. He had been chosen for it by 'lot' (1:9, *and see* Note on Priests), which was a method used to find out whom God wanted to offer the incense. Zechariah was, therefore, seen by Luke to have been specially chosen.

According to Luke, there must also have been sadness in the life of Zechariah and his wife Elizabeth. They were childless, which was regarded as a shameful thing in the world of the first century AD. Luke makes the point that the ageing couple were good people and loyal to God. However, their childless state would have been interpreted by the people of their day as a sign that God did not favour them. Such an interpretation, though, is shown by Luke to be entirely wrong. Zechariah and Elizabeth are greatly favoured by God. The message from the angel Gabriel to Zechariah is that Elizabeth will have a child whose purpose will be to prepare the way for the Messiah. It is almost as if the whole of their lives had been a preparation for this most important birth.

In his speech to Zechariah, Gabriel says that John will be a great man of God. Like some of the famous prophets of the Old Testament, John will not drink wine or strong drink. He will be filled with the Holy Spirit and his only loyalty will be to God. The power of John is compared by Gabriel to the power of Elijah. In the Old Testament, Elijah is said to be the prophet who will prepare the way for the Messiah (*see* Malachi 4:5).

The story of Zechariah and Elizabeth is similar to a number of stories of the Old Testament where childless couples are granted children in their old age. There is the story of Abraham and Sarah (Genesis 16-21), of Elkanah and Hannah (1 Samuel 1), and the same theme is evident in the story of Samson's birth (Judges 13).

These stories would have been familiar to Luke and may have provided him with ideas for his own story. In each case what was important was that God was seen to be active in people's affairs. Luke shows, in this opening scene of his gospel, how God is active again in history. In the first place God chooses Zechariah to offer the incense through the drawing of lots. Then comes the message from Gabriel. Immediately the reader is made aware that God is starting to put his plan for the salvation of humanity into effect.

NOTE ON PRIESTS

There were approximately twenty thousand priests in the Palestine of Jesus' day. This large number was because being a priest was a matter of birth rather than choice. Any male descendant of Aaron (the great priest of the Old Testament and brother of Moses) was a priest and had the right to serve in the Jerusalem Temple. The priests were divided into sections or 'divisions' (1:8) and each division had a turn in conducting the Temple rituals. The priests drew 'lots' in each division to find out who would serve in the Court of the priests. Those who were chosen carried out this particular duty only once in their life-time, whilst some priests never achieved this honour. The specific duties of the priest in the Court of the priests included prayer and the burning of incense as an act of devotion to God. Following the instruction given to Aaron (Exodus 30:7-8), this took place every morning and every evening.

NOTE ON ANGELS

Angels are good spirits, as opposed to the evil spirits which play such a prominent part in Luke's gospel. Their main function, according to the Bible, is to bring messages from God to people. Belief in angels probably developed in Judaism some time after the Exile of Jews to Babylon, from the 6th century BC onwards.

Those people today who reject the idea of evil spirits may also reject the idea of angels. They may regard them as best confined to a particular time in history when people thought of good and evil as spirit forces sent by God to help people (angels) or by the devil to hinder them (demons).

Gabriel is regarded in Christian tradition as an archangel or 'chief' angel. He appears in the Old Testament book of Daniel as well as in the New Testament.

B. JESUS' BIRTH IS ANNOUNCED
(1:26-38)

The setting for the announcement of Jesus' birth changes from that of the great and holy city of Jerusalem to the small and unimportant town of Nazareth in Galilee. Here the angel Gabriel visits Mary, who is betrothed to Joseph. Joseph is described as a descendant of David and at 1:32 Gabriel says that Jesus will be given "the throne of his ancestor David".

It is worth considering why these references to David are so important to Luke. David was the best known and most revered of all of Israel's kings. He was chosen by God to unite the Israelites as one people and to establish Jerusalem as the holy city. His home was Bethlehem, and it was here that many Jews believed the Messiah would be born (*see* Micah 5:2). A popular view of the Messiah was that he would be a great king like David, once again uniting Israel and setting the nation free from oppression. By linking Jesus with David, Luke is making the point that Jesus is the Messiah and king of Israel, though not in the earthly sense, for "his reign shall never end" (1:33).

Gabriel tells Mary that she is to have a child who is to be named Jesus and whose title will be "Son of the Most High". God is the "Most High" and, as "Son", Jesus has the closest possible relationship to God and will act with his power and authority. Mary will conceive through the Holy Spirit and the power of the Most High, " . . . and for that reason the holy child to be born will be called 'Son of God'" (1:35). The reader is left in no doubt about the special father-son relationship which exists between God and Jesus.

NOTE ON BETROTHAL

Betrothal was much more binding than engagement is today. It was for a definite period of time (one year), at the end of which marriage would take place. Betrothal, like marriage, could only be ended by divorce.

C. STORIES OF THE BIRTHS OF JOHN AND JESUS

(i) Similarities and differences in the two births

As you read the first two chapters of Luke's gospel, note how the action switches from events to do with John's birth (1:5-25 & 57-80) to events to do with the birth of Jesus (1:26-38 & 2:1-40), and how the two stories come together when Mary visits Elizabeth (1:39-56). It takes a skilful writer to do this successfully, and Luke certainly makes the method pay off. By setting the birth stories side by side, Luke is able to point more easily to both the similarities and the differences between the two events.

What are these similarities and differences which Luke uses to make comparison between the two births? First, the news comes to the prospective parents in a similar way. Both Zechariah and Mary are confronted by the angel Gabriel, who announces to each that they will have a child. Both are naturally afraid at the appearance of the angel, but that is quite understandable. Both question the angel's words and seemingly with good cause. Zechariah asks: "How can I be sure of this? I am an old man and my wife is well on in years" (1:18). For that unbelieving attitude Zechariah is given a period of dumbness so that he is left in no doubt that this is God's doing.

Gabriel's whole approach to Mary is much more respectful. He greets her as "most favoured one" (1:28). Though Mary questions the angel's word by asking how she can have a child when she is still a virgin, the angel explains that the child is to be the son of God. To confirm that God is involved, Gabriel tells Mary that her cousin Elizabeth (known to be unable to have children and in any case now too old) is to have a child. On hearing this, Mary responds obediently, saying: "Here am I; I am the Lord's servant; as you have spoken, so be it" (1:38).

A difference is also apparent between John and Jesus in the brief description which Gabriel gives concerning the role and function of each. Despite the great importance of John's work, it is made clear that he is the forerunner, whilst Jesus is to be "Son of the Most High" and "king over Israel for ever" (1:32).

A further difference is to do with the way in which the respective babies are conceived. Though Elizabeth's conception is remarkable in that both she and her husband are old, there is no suggestion that it occurred other than through the means of a normal sexual relationship between two married people. Whereas in the case of Mary, Luke says that she was a virgin when she conceived and that conception took place as a result of the action of the Holy Spirit. Now whatever doubts you may have on biological grounds concerning the ability of a virgin to conceive, it must be stressed that no such problem worried Luke. He was concerned with theology, not biological science, and what was important to him was to show that Jesus really was God's son. As at the creation of the world, so in the creation of new life, God can make something or someone out of nothing. Mary's conception was nothing short of a miracle, a new creation by God, and that is the point Luke wishes to establish.

After the separate annunciations (announcements) to Zechariah and Mary, Luke brings the two stories together by having Mary pay Elizabeth a visit. Luke does not miss the opportunity to make

*The Annunciation: a carving from Aylesford
Priory showing the Angel Gabriel greeting Mary
and the Holy Spirit descending.*

a further comparison between John and Jesus. Elizabeth's baby, we are told, leaps for joy inside her womb when the two women meet. And Elizabeth herself acknowledges Mary's superiority and speaks of Mary's baby as her Lord (1:42).

The stories separate again for the respective births to take place. In the case of John, attention is focused on a family argument as to the child's name. The matter is settled by Zechariah who follows the instruction given to him by Gabriel (1:13) and names the child John. Zechariah is immediately released from his dumbness. Those who hear of the events surrounding John's birth realise that something unusual has taken place and they wonder, "What will this child become?" (1:66).

At this point the comparison between the births of John and Jesus comes to an end (2:21 makes it plain that there was no argument over Jesus' name as there was with John). After all, the story is about Jesus and so for most of the remainder of the chapter the significance of Jesus' birth is further illustrated - the shepherds have a vision of angels and come to pay homage, and Simeon and Anna recognise Jesus as the Messiah.

NOTE ON CIRCUMCISION

Following Jewish custom, both John and Jesus were circumcised on the eighth day after their respective births. In Judaism, circumcision (the cutting of the foreskin of the penis) is traced back to Abraham where it is a symbol for the special relationship which God has with his people. The circumcision of Jewish boys is as important in Judaism as the baptism of infants is to many Christians. It is during the ceremony of circumcision that a Jewish boy is given his name. This provides another parallel with Christian baptism.

NOTES ON LUKE'S SONGS (PART 1)

At certain points in chapters one and two of his gospel, Luke gives the reader a break in the action - the narrative or story-line gives way to a theological summary (placed on the lips of one or other of the main characters) so that the reader is made fully aware of the real significance of what is going on. This happens three times in all: with Mary (1:46-55), with Zechariah (1:68-79), and with Simeon (2:29-32). These summaries are written in the style of the Psalms of the Old Testament and can, therefore, rightly be called songs. They are sometimes used as part of church worship and then they are usually referred to as: Magnificat, Benedictus, Nunc Dimittis. (These names are taken from the first words of the Latin text.) It is not, however, in style alone that these songs remind us of the Old Testament but also in their content. Each is rich with quotations from the Old Testament which suggests that Luke wants his readers to understand that Christianity is a continuation of the old Jewish religion, because all the hopes and promises of the Old Testament period have been fulfilled in Jesus.

The Magnificat (1:46-55)

The song of Mary is based on a number of Old Testament texts and, in particular, on the song of Hannah in 1 Samuel 2:1-10. Two main themes are interwoven in this song. There is the particular theme of what God has done for Mary, and the general theme of what God has done for his people. Luke links Christianity into the whole of Jewish history by showing how the promise to Abraham has been fulfilled. In basing much of this song on Hannah's words, Luke is reinforcing this idea, because Hannah was the mother of Samuel (who was a model figure and a most important leader of the Old Testament period) and Mary is to be the mother of Jesus (who will be the leader of the new Israel). There is a continuity of the old order with the new and it is the same God who is responsible for both. This, then, is a song of triumph because God has acted, as he promised he would, to save his people.

The Benedictus (1:68-79)

The song of Zechariah, like the Magnificat, is full of Old Testament quotations. It is about the way God has acted in history on behalf of Israel and how the promises God made through the prophets have been fulfilled - the new is continuous with the old. It is also about the part which John has to play in God's plan of salvation. At 1:76 Zechariah refers to John as the "Prophet of the Highest" who "will be the Lord's forerunner, to prepare his way". The song praises God for being true to his promises and makes clear the important but subordinate role of John the Baptist.

A carving showing Mary greeting Elizabeth. How does
Luke show that Jesus is superior to John when he
describes this meeting? See 1:38-45.

(ii) The birth of Jesus: a momentous event in world history (2:1-40)

There are problems over Luke's introduction to Jesus' birth which cannot be resolved except by acknowledging that historically Luke got it wrong. No evidence can be found of a registration (census) having been taken at this time and Quirinius, it seems, was not the governor of Syria[4]. However, these inaccuracies are of little importance when compared with Luke's purpose in recounting this information. He wants to set the scene, and to stress the great significance of the birth of the son of God, setting it all in a historical context - a context which embraces the whole world (see 2:1).

The registration (and in particular the instruction that everyone should go to his home town to be registered) also provides Luke with an opportunity to get Joseph and his pregnant wife from Nazareth to Bethlehem. (In Matthew's gospel, Bethlehem appears to be the home of Joseph and

---

[4] Quirinius became governor in AD 6.

Mary.) For Luke, their home is Nazareth but Joseph's ancestral home is Bethlehem and so he must go there for the census. Luke, like Matthew, knows the prophecy concerning the Messiah being born in Bethlehem, though he does not spoil the flow of his story by quoting it.

Hardship is evident in the story in that "there was no room for them to lodge in the house" (2:7), and the child is laid in a manger[5]. From these few details given by Luke, it has subsequently been assumed that Jesus was born in the filth of a stable with a variety of animals gathered around as witnesses. There is, of course, no evidence for this from Luke himself. He simply gives a hint of that possibility, and later writers developed the theme, so that the stable has become the traditional Christmas scene.

NOTE ON HOUSES IN PALESTINE, 1ST CENTURY AD

In Palestine many of the houses of poor people consisted of only one room. At night the family would gather any animals they possessed into the house for safety. The family themselves would sleep on a raised platform, usually above a stone-built oven.

NOTE ON SHEPHERDS' VISION OF ANGELS

An angel brings a message to the shepherds just as Gabriel had done to Zechariah and Mary. Like Zechariah and Mary the shepherds are afraid at this encounter. It is one thing to believe that good and evil come from the spirit world, but quite another to meet those spirits face to face! But, for Luke, this scene fits well with what has gone before. From Jesus' humble birth in a crowded and unwelcoming town, the picture switches dramatically, just for a moment, to one of heavenly splendour. Heaven and earth become one and angels and people talk to each other. The "heavenly host" are the representatives of God's court. Their presence emphasises that what has happened is good news for the whole world. Their song is about "peace". Peace in this context is not simply the opposite of war and strife but refers to a perfect way of living which can come only from God. This is the peace which the angels say God is offering to all people through Jesus.

NOTE ON JOSEPH AND MARY'S SACRIFICE (2:22-24)

Luke shows Joseph and Mary obeying the rules and traditions of the Jewish religion, following the birth of Jesus. They go to the Temple at Jerusalem to present Jesus to God and to make the necessary sacrifice. According to Luke, they make the sacrifice for poor people: two pigeons rather than a lamb and a pigeon (see Leviticus 12:1-8).

If the rules in Leviticus were being followed this event occurred at least thirty-three days after Jesus' circumcision. Following childbirth (and at menstruation) women were regarded as ritually impure. Indeed blood of any sort was thought to bring about impurity both to the individuals concerned and to any persons with whom they came into contact. (*See* Notes on the Good Samaritan p.102 and the Woman with the haemorrhage p.90).

Impurity lasted for a period of forty days following the birth of a male child, and during that time the woman remained at home. After forty days a sacrifice had to be made in order to return her to a state of ritual purity. This is presumably what Luke is referring to at 2:22 when he speaks of "their purification". Strictly speaking it was Mary alone who would require purification.

Although Luke's Gentile readers would not have been impressed with details about Jewish ritual, Luke presumably wishes to emphasise that Jesus was brought up in accordance with the rules of the Jewish religion.

---

[5] A manger is a trough from which animals eat their food.

A traditional nativity scene from the church at Shepherds' Fields, Bethlehem.

NOTES ON LUKE'S SONGS (PART 2)

Nunc Dimittis (2:29-32)

The song of Simeon makes use of Old Testament quotations in speaking of the fulfilment of God's promise and of a new future which is being opened up. Simeon, who represents the very best of the old Israel (as 2:25 makes clear), acknowledges the new order which has significance for the whole world as well as for Israel. Thus, at an early stage in his gospel, Luke prepares the reader for what is eventually to come, namely the mission to the Gentiles - the main subject of Luke's second book, Acts. Simeon's further comment at 2:34-35 should not be overlooked. Luke has already told us that Simeon is "guided by the Spirit" (2:27) which means that, like the prophets of old, he speaks the word of God. In the Old Testament God is the one who foresees coming events and at 2:34-35 a glimpse into the future is given. The message which Jesus brings divides people and brings suffering and judgment. It may be that the "prophecy" at 2:34-35 is actually something that Luke's readers were already experiencing.

iii) Old religion and new religion meet

Why does Luke set the birth stories of John and Jesus side by side and why does he need to point to similarities and differences between the two events? It could be that what was firmly in Luke's mind was the need to blend the new (Christianity) with the old (Judaism). He achieves this partly through his use of Old Testament language, style and story-form in his opening chapters (see section g. below). He thus shows Christianity's link with Judaism in a rather subtle way. There is perhaps a need to make the point more forcefully and so Luke links the birth of John who, as the forerunner (1:17) of the Messiah, brings Old Testament prophecy to its final and its highest point, with the birth of Jesus, the Messiah, and founder of the new order. The theme of the birth of a child is the same, but in every case Jesus is shown to be more important than John, despite the wonder of events surrounding John's birth. The new is superior to, and supersedes, the old and that is perhaps the message which Luke wants to make absolutely clear to his readers. Christianity is the rightful heir and successor to Judaism and is better than the old religion. Put another way, Luke is trying to show

The town of Nazareth today.

that there is *continuity* between Judaism and Christianity - hence the similarities between the two birth stories. But with the coming of Jesus a new way of understanding God and the world is required. The ways of the old religion must change - hence the differences between the two events.

D. "THE HUMBLE HAVE BEEN LIFTED HIGH"

In chapter 4 section (d.ii), we saw that a favourite theme of Luke's is the reversal of fortunes. Nowhere is this theme more apparent than in the first two chapters of Luke's gospel. The idea of reversal is basically about the difference between the way people think and act and the way God thinks and acts. Three examples may help to make the idea of reversal clearer.

1. People would expect that if God intended to have a son by a human mother he would choose at least a princess to bear him. But, according to Luke, he chose an unknown girl from a small town which, because of its mixed population of Jews and Gentiles, was treated with some suspicion by Jews from Judaea. What God does is the *reverse* of people's expectations.

2. People would expect that God would choose a place of some comfort and dignity where his son would be born - a royal palace perhaps. Yet, according to Luke, there was not even room for Mary "to lodge in the house" and a manger had to be used for a cot. What God does is the *reverse* of people's expectations.

3. People would expect that if God wished to announce the birth of his son he would do it either to one of the highest religious officials of the day, such as the chief priest, or perhaps to kings, princes, or governors. But, according to Luke, he makes the announcement to a group of humble shepherds. Shepherds were in some ways the most unlikely people to choose because, by the nature of their job, they were on the fringe of civilised society and were unable to keep the religious rules in the way that most Jews were expected to. The Pharisees, for example, referred to them as sinners. What God does is the *reverse* of people's expectations.

These three examples show how Luke uses the idea of reversal as an underlying theme of the story he tells in the first two chapters of his gospel. (We shall come across the idea again, especially in chapter10.) He also brings the whole idea of reversal of fortunes to the surface in the song of Mary where we read at 1:52-53:

he has *brought down monarchs* from their thrones,
but the *humble* have been *lifted high*.
The *hungry* he has satisfied with *good things*,
the *rich* sent *empty away*.

According to Luke, God's standards are not the world's standards. Those who hold positions of power and appear to be secure are laid low by God, whereas those who are weak and appear to be insecure are lifted up. God is the one who up-ends human standards, turning apparent disadvantage into advantage.

The "humble who have been lifted high" in Luke 1 and 2 include:

Zechariah and Elizabeth - two aged and respectable people who had no children and, contrary to expectations, became parents of the Messiah's forerunner;

Mary, who was an unimportant Jewish girl, yet gave birth to God's son;

the shepherds, who were on the fringe of civilised and religious life, yet were the first to be told of Jesus' birth and the first to visit the child and recognise who he was (note that in Matthew's gospel this privilege is given to the wise men);

Simeon and Anna - two humble and devout old people, representing all that was best in the Jewish religion, are the ones privileged to see Jesus - the high religious officials of the Temple are not so honoured.

E. THE BIRTH OF JESUS TODAY

How essential is it that Christians today should believe in the virgin birth? Many people today - including some Christians - find the idea hard to accept. It is an issue which, from time to time, causes conflict within the church.

Some Christians will argue that it is absolutely essential to hold to the virgin birth, otherwise how could we understand Jesus to be God in any real sense? They are prepared to accept that a miracle did occur.

Other Christians may affirm their belief in the Incarnation (that is, the idea that God took on human form), without wishing to specify exactly how this was achieved. They may accept the stories as being attempts by first century Christians to convey something of their belief that Jesus was the Son of God. However, they do not necessarily feel that belief in the virgin birth is absolutely essential to that position. They are of the view that Jesus can still be thought of as God even without that belief.

There are also Christians (though perhaps those who hold to the view of the virgin birth and Incarnation would not wish to call them that!) who would prefer to regard Jesus simply as a man, albeit a very special and extraordinary man, who displayed God-like qualities and showed people what it meant to lead a good life trusting perfectly in God. In that sense he could truly be described as God's Son. But they prefer not to think of him as God who came to live on earth. For them, belief in virgin birth and Incarnation is not essential to their Christian faith.

There are, of course, many non-Christians who know of the stories of the virgin birth and reject them for all sorts of reasons, perhaps often because they believe them to be inconsistent with a scientific view of the world.

Having thought about the issues, what do you believe?

F. JESUS AT THE AGE OF TWELVE
(2:41-52)

Luke is the only New Testament writer to include any information about Jesus as a child. (There are some other gospels, not included in the New Testament, which do tell stories about this period of his life.) The age of twelve is significant for a Jewish boy; it is when he prepares to become a son of the Law (Bar Mitzvah)[6], which means that he must accept, as an adult, the responsibilities and duties of his religion. It would seem that Luke uses this incident to show how Jesus is becoming aware of the special role he must fulfil. This awareness develops at the festival of Passover in Jerusalem (the holy city to which all Jews were expected to come on great festal occasions, if they were able). In other words, it occurs at the heart of the Jewish religion at a time when all Jews look forward with *hope* to a future of *freedom*. (Freedom is the great theme of Passover.) In a subtle way, Luke is perhaps suggesting that Jesus is the new heart of religion and that he offers the Jewish people freedom. (This same idea, of course, is repeated at the end of the gospel when Jesus returns to Jerusalem, again at Passover-time, and is crucified. His resurrection three days later offers that freedom to all who choose to accept him.)

Luke notes that it was "after three days" that Jesus' parents found him. This would remind the reader of the death of Jesus - the other time when Jesus left his wider 'family' - and that it was after three days that he returned to them at the resurrection.

According to Luke, Jesus' parents are naturally anxious about him. By contrast, Jesus is calm. His parents do not understand the answer Jesus gives to their question about his treatment of them. Luke presumably wants his readers to see that even at this early age Jesus realises what his mission and purpose is to be whereas, even those closest to him, do not. However, it is not yet time for Jesus' ministry to begin. He has wisdom, but he is still learning (he listens to the teachers and puts questions to them 2:46), and so he returns home and continues to be under his parents' authority (2:51).

STUDY NOTES ON ORIGINS OF BIRTH STORIES

G. THE TWO ACCOUNTS OF THE BIRTH OF JESUS

Luke and Matthew are the only two New Testament writers who tell us anything at all about the events surrounding the birth of Jesus, and they each present a very different account. It is Luke who records the Christmas story that most people know and remember. The angel Gabriel, the long journey from Nazareth to Bethlehem because of the Roman registration, the lack of room in the house, and the shepherds, are all features of Luke's story and are not found in Matthew's account. Here, we find clear evidence of Luke's ability to tell a story in an interesting and memorable way. In contrast to Matthew's account, which is full of terrible and terrifying events, Luke's story is rather pleasant, though it is far from sentimental and there are a number of features we may consider to be harsh: for example, the journey from Nazareth for a pregnant woman, the lack of proper accommodation, and a manger for a cot.

It is true that Matthew gives us information about the wise men and the star, but these are the only two features from that story which are usually remembered. We tend to forget the fear which overcame Herod when he was asked by the wise men: "Where is the child who is born to be king of the Jews?" (Matt. 2:2). This fear for his own and his family's position led Herod, according to the story, to use deception and then violence of the most outrageous kind ("the massacre of all children in Bethlehem and its neighbourhood, of the age of two years or less." (Matt. 2:16). Because of Herod's evil actions, the child Jesus and his parents were forced to become refugees and seek exile in Egypt, eventually return-

---

[6] Nowadays there is a ceremony called 'Bar Mitzvah' which marks a boy's passage from childhood to adulthood at the age of thirteen. This ceremony did not exist in its present form at the time of Jesus.

ing to Palestine after Herod's death. Even then, Matthew tells us, it was not safe for them to stay in Judaea so they moved to a town in Galilee called Nazareth.

Two questions are of obvious interest here:

1. Why do the other New Testament writers tell us nothing at all about Jesus's birth?

2. Why do Matthew and Luke tell such different stories?

1. A likely answer to the first question is that there was either very little information about Jesus' birth in the oral tradition of the early church or none at all. We can appreciate that stories about Jesus' ministry would have been passed on to the early church by the disciples; but who would have been the eye-witnesses to the events which Matthew and Luke describe in their birth stories?

Presumably Mary and Joseph are the only two real possibilities. There is a tradition that Joseph was an old man when he married Mary and it is generally assumed that he was dead before Jesus began his ministry, which would rule him out as a possible source. We do not know how long Mary lived but it seems likely that her death occurred some considerable time before Matthew and Luke wrote their gospels. It also seems quite possible that neither of them even knew Mary, let alone collected information from her.

If Mary had been known to either Matthew or Luke, either directly or through reliable third parties, it seems likely that only one story about Jesus' birth would have existed. Because of the differences between the two accounts, it is clear that Mary could not have been the source for both stories. If she had been the source for one of the stories, and this was generally known to be the case, the other story would have been discredited.

Given the situation where both stories seem to be equally acceptable to the early church, it would seem likely that if any information about Jesus' birth did exist it was very thin indeed. Another answer to the first question may be that the focus of attention of the earlier New Testament writers was very much on the future (the Second Coming) rather than on the past (the First Coming). The early Christians, as far as we can tell, believed that Jesus had been raised from the dead, was now in heaven, and would very soon return. When he did so, the whole world would be changed. As a past event, the birth of Jesus may have been of little interest to them, and it was only with the passing of time that later writers (like Matthew and Luke) became interested in events surrounding Jesus' birth.

2. The answer to the second question ('Why do Matthew and Luke tell such different stories?') follows from the answer to the first. In the absence of definite historical information about Jesus' birth, Matthew and Luke had to construct their own stories.

Where they are similar it may have been because of a common tradition in the early church (for example, Mary and Joseph's betrothal, an angel announcing the birth, conception through the Holy Spirit) or because Luke had access to Matthew's gospel.

The differences may result from the creative story-telling abilities of each writer. Or, to put it in stark terms, Matthew and Luke may have made up the stories. Many Christians today find this idea difficult to accept. They feel that if this is the case it is tantamount to saying that Matthew and Luke were frauds, deliberately out to deceive by presenting fiction as historical fact. (*See* Notes on Ancient Writers *below*.) This is to misunderstand the motives of the gospel writers. They were most definitely not out to deceive anyone. Their concern was to tell the good news in the most convincing way possible. Writing history was not their main concern anyway. Their prime intention was to write about God. To do that they must have felt that they had all the information they needed ready to hand. First, they had the experience of the risen Jesus in their own lives. Like all Christians, they had accepted for themselves that Jesus was the Messiah and Son of God who, through his life, death and resurrection, had given them, and all who accepted him, salvation. Second, they had their Bible (the Old Testament) in which they believed that God, through the prophets, had promised the Messiah and had actually given quite precise details about him (for example, that Jesus' mother had been a virgin when she conceived (Isaiah 7:14[7]) and that Jesus was born at Bethlehem (Micah 5:2).

From their knowledge of Jesus and their knowledge of the Old Testament, Matthew and Luke had a basis for telling about Jesus' birth. Each then had to construct a story which would convey to their readers the full impact of this momentous event. With few, if any, traditions about Jesus' birth to hand, they were free to use their creative skills as story-writers and theologians.

Different stories emerged because each writer was anxious to make his account as relevant as possible to the needs of the people he was writing for. Each writer also used the Old Testament differently. As well as the prophecies about the Messiah, the Old Testament also yielded other important ideas for their stories. For example, Matthew seems to be inspired by some of the events surrounding the story of the Israelites in Egypt and the Exodus, whereas Luke uses the idea of childless couples having children in their old age, and passages from scripture to build up his own songs.

NOTE ON ANCIENT WRITERS

Writers in the ancient world were not tied to the sort of conventions we expect authors to comply with today. For example, we have the broad division in our libraries of Fiction and Non-Fiction. Then, we further subdivide each category so that we know what type of literature we are dealing with. Authors in the ancient world were quite free to mix fact with legend and to add their own ideas and interpretations to events. This was not thought to be deceitful or unscholarly because people did not observe our modern conventions. So if Matthew and Luke did not have historical information about Jesus' birth available to them, it did not matter much. They would not have been concerned to work like modern historians, trying to uncover what really happened. It was sufficient for them that in Jesus prophecy had been fulfilled. In a sense, the scriptures were a more valuable guide than anything anyone might have remembered hearing about Jesus' birth anyway.

The prophecies about the Messiah are there for all to read, but they are open to interpretation. Jews, for example, do not share the Christian interpretation and do not accept that Jesus was the Messiah. In a similar way, Matthew's and Luke's interpretations of prophecies led them to different conclusions about the course of events connected with Jesus' birth.

Model of Jerusalem Temple

---

[7] It is sometimes argued that the Hebrew word translated as 'virgin' can also be translated 'young woman' and, therefore, the prophecy itself does *not* necessarily imply a miracle.

H. LUKE'S PURPOSE IN TELLING OF THE BIRTH OF JESUS

(i) A 'bridge' between Old and New Testaments

Why did Luke find it necessary to tell the story of Jesus' birth? This is an important question because it could be that Luke added Chapters 1 and 2 some time after he had written both the gospel and Acts. (The way Chapter 3 begins is similar to the opening of Mark's gospel and may have been Luke's original starting-point.)

It seems most probable that, whether Luke wrote the birth story before or after the rest of the gospel, his intention was to provide a 'bridge'

between the Old Testament and the New Testament. We saw at section (c.iii) above how he achieves this partly by setting the birth of the representative of the old order (John the Baptist/ Judaism) against the birth of the representative of the new order (Jesus/Christianity). Luke wants to show how the New Testament (that is, the period of Jesus and the church) does follow on naturally from the Old.

(ii) The developing picture of Jesus

Perhaps we can detect in the New Testament writings themselves a developing picture of Jesus. It may have been that the very first Christians thought of Jesus as a special person whom God had chosen to be the Messiah. They may have thought of him as originally being an ordinary man whom God decided to set apart for special work. Some groups of Christians seem to have believed that Jesus was made the Messiah at his *resurrection*,

while a reading of Mark's gospel might suggest that it was at his *baptism* that Jesus became Son of God.

Matthew and Luke are, in a sense, through the birth stories, objecting to this idea. One of their purposes in constructing the birth stories, was perhaps to show how God had 'sent' Jesus - the miraculous nature of Jesus' conception is designed to demonstrate this point. Jesus was God's Son in a special sense and not just by adoption.

NOTE ON JESUS AS GOD AND MAN

Later on in the early church this picture became even more developed so that by the time of the writing of the creeds in the third and fourth centuries AD, Jesus had become equated with God. It eventually became accepted teaching, though not without much argument, that Jesus had, in fact, been both God and man. He was man, in that he experienced what it was like to live on earth with its temptations and sufferings; and he was God, in that he existed before and after his earthly life, and even while on earth had been sinless.

(iii) The sinlessness of Jesus

Another issue which may have arisen in the early church was the sinlessness of Jesus (*see also* page 49.) This belief points to his uniqueness and the difference between him and ordinary people. The view was held among the people of Jesus' day that, since the Fall (that is, the events of the Garden of Eden involving Adam and Eve - *see* Genesis 2-3), every human being was born in sin. It was a

commonly held view that this sinful nature was transmitted through sexual intercourse. So, if Jesus had been conceived in the normal way he too would have been in sin. Perhaps, then, this is another reason for the virgin birth. It is interesting that James, a later gospel-writer, whose work is not in the New Testament, may have spotted another problem to do with the sinlessness of Jesus - that unless Mary herself had been conceived by miraculous means, she would have been conceived in sin and, therefore, passed on sin to Jesus. James therefore includes, in *his* story, the miraculous conception of Mary, in order to break the chain.

(iv) Founders of religions

A final point might also be made. If you look at the history of religions, you will discover that it is common for legends to develop, especially around the figure of the founder. Miraculous births often form part of the legendary material. It is also not uncommon to find in ancient religions, stories about gods becoming human. To look at Matthew and Luke in this wider context may help us to understand something of what they were trying to achieve through their stories of the virgin birth.

Questions for chapter 5

1:5-25

1a. What are the names of John the Baptist's parents?

  b. Why was it surprising that John's mother should become pregnant?

2a. Where was John's father when he encountered the angel?

  b. Why was he in that particular place?

3a. What did the angel say to Zechariah?

  b. What, according to the angel, was to be John's special role?

  c. What was Zechariah's response to the angel?

  d. What happened to Zechariah for doubting the angel's words?

1:26-56

4a. In which town did Mary and Joseph live?

  b. Why do you think Luke makes the point that Joseph was 'a descendant of David'?

5a. What did Gabriel say to Mary?

  b. How at first did Mary react to the angel's words, and what was her final response?

6a. What happened when Mary and Elizabeth met?

  b. What does Elizabeth say which suggests she already knows that Mary is pregnant?

7a. What other name is given to the song of Mary?

  b. What is the song about?

1:57-80

8a. Why was there confusion at John's naming ceremony?

  b. What Latin name is given to the words spoken by Zechariah?

  c. Who is to be called 'Prophet of the Highest'?

2:1-40

 9a. Why, according to Luke, did Joseph and Mary have to travel to Bethlehem?

  b. Why was it important for Luke that Jesus should be born at Bethlehem?

10a. What information does Luke give about the conditions under which Jesus was born?

  b. Make a list of the items usually included in the typical Christmas crib. How many of these are specifically mentioned in Luke's gospel?

11a. Who, according to Luke, were the first people to be told about Jesus' birth?

  b. How did they react to the presence of the angel?

  c. What did the angel say to them?

  d. What action did they take following the angel's visit?

12a. To which city did Mary and Joseph take Jesus after his birth?

  b. What offering were Mary and Joseph required to make?

13a. Whom did Mary and Joseph meet in the Temple?

  b. What promise had been given to this person by God?

14a. To what does the term 'Nunc Dimittis' refer?

  b. Why might the Nunc Dimittis be regarded as a prophecy?

15. What did Simeon mean when he said to Mary: "This child is destined to be a sign which men reject; and you too shall be pierced to the heart"? (2:35)

16 a. Who was Anna?

   b. Why did she give thanks to God for Jesus?

17. In which town did Jesus grow up?

18. Where do you think Luke got his information about the birth of Jesus?

19. What important teaching is Luke attempting to give his readers through the story of the virgin birth?

20. Do you think it is essential to believe in the virgin birth to be a Christian today?

21 a. What does the term 'Incarnation' mean?

   b. Do you think that a person can believe in the Incarnation without believing in the virgin birth?

22. Can a person be a Christian, do you think, without believing that the human Jesus is also God?

2:41-52

23 a. To which city did Jesus go at the age of twelve?

   b. What was the purpose of the visit?

   c. What does the term 'Bar Mitzvah' mean?

24 a. How did Jesus' parents react when they found Jesus was missing on the return journey?

   b. Where did they eventually find him?

   c. What was he doing?

   d. What importance, do you think, did Luke see in this event?

25. In the context of the incident at 2.41-52, what significance might the following have had for Luke: (i) Jerusalem, (ii) Passover, (iii) 'after three days'?

6
THE WAY IS PREPARED

A. THE MINISTRY OF JOHN THE BAPTIST
(3:1-17)

In the previous chapter we noted how Luke spends a significant amount of time in telling the story of the birth of John the Baptist, and we pointed to some of the possible reasons why he was so concerned to do this. One of the main reasons was to do with the relationship between the old order (Judaism) which John represents and the new order (Christianity) represented by Jesus. The way in which Luke presents the story indicates clearly that, for him, the new religion is superior to and replaces the old.

When Luke again picks up the story of John in Chapter 3 of his gospel, we see that this same idea is never very far from his mind. Yet, as we saw in the previous chapter, it would be quite wrong to assume that Luke has a low opinion of John. Quite the reverse is true in fact. Not only does Luke introduce John in the context of world history (see 3:1-2, where he names the Roman Emperor together with the political and religious leaders of Palestine, so suggesting that the beginning of John's ministry is a moment of great historical importance), but clearly he wants us to see John as a prophet in the very best traditions of the Old Testament - and no higher honour than that can be given to him.

At 3:2 Luke tells us that "the word of God came to John". Time and time again the books of the Old Testament prophets begin with the same sort of comment. For example, at Ezekiel 1:3 we read, "the word of the Lord came to Ezekiel" (*see also* Micah 1:1 and Zechariah 1:1 for further examples). That "the word of the Lord" comes to a person is a sure indication in Old Testament terms that the person is a prophet - it is one of the characteristic marks of a prophet. So, in making this comment about John, Luke is reinforcing in the minds of his readers the idea that John is a prophet of the Old Testament order. Again, it is characteristic of the Old Testament prophet that once he receives "the word of the Lord" he is compelled to speak it openly. And so John immediately goes about his work of "proclaiming a baptism in token of repentance for the forgiveness of sins" (3:3). Like the prophets of the Old Testament, his message is not a gentle one. John perceives a need to shake Israel out of its complacency, just as the Old

Testament prophets before him attempted to do. He describes the people who come to him for baptism as a "vipers' brood" and asks who it was who had warned them "to escape from the coming retribution" (3:7), that is, the punishment they will receive on the day of judgment. The warning is issued that they should take no comfort in their being able to say: "We have Abraham for our father", meaning that because they are God's 'chosen people' they are guaranteed a place in the kingdom of God. This, in fact, only heightens the problem for them, in that because they are 'chosen' they should know better and, therefore, their punishment will be that much more severe. John urges them to repent (that is, to have a complete change of heart, signified by their undergoing the symbolic act of baptism). Their repentance will be shown in their positive actions (producing "good fruit" in John's language). Only through repentance will they avoid the disaster spoken of in 3:9. Then, in a passage which is found only in this gospel (3:10-

14), Luke has John the Baptist offer sound advice to various groups of people who ask, "Then what are we to do?". The offering of such good advice is typical of Luke whose characters, when in a tight spot, reflect on their best course of action (compare the lost son 15:17 and the dishonest steward 16:3, among others). Here John tells the various groups (the people, tax-gatherers, soldiers) what they must do. Again, his advice is similar to much of the advice given to Israel by the Old Testament prophets (for an example, have a look at Jeremiah 7:1-7), and reflects his own concern for the poor and lowly (*see* p121). It stresses the need for social justice - the giving of food and clothing to the poor, not exploiting people by demanding more tax than is required, and not oppressing people who are unable to defend themselves.

This high opinion of John which Luke holds must, of course, be kept in perspective. John is not the Messiah, but, for Luke, the whole of Israel's history has been leading up to this point. In John, the very best traditions of the Old Testament come to the forefront. John is himself the last of the prophets and in him Old Testament prophecy is brought to a climax (Luke has Jesus himself acknowledge this at 16:16). Not only is John a prophet, but he is himself a fulfilment of prophecy, as Luke, following Mark (Mark 1:2-3), makes clear when he quotes Old Testament prophecy concerning the Messiah's forerunner (3:4-6). Luke adds to the prophecy quoted by Mark in order to stress the significance of the coming of the Messiah for the whole world (*see* 3:6 and *also* 2:29-32). This is how the status of John is kept in perspective, for John is the one who has come to "prepare a way for the Lord" (see 7:27). In order to reinforce John's subordinate role to that of Jesus, Luke notes the reactions of the people (3:15-17), how they were excited about John, wondering whether he was the Messiah. John quickly points to the difference between his water baptism and the baptism of the Holy Spirit which the Messiah will bring, and so brings into perspective his own role and function.

It is clear that Luke is very anxious to make sure that his readers understand that John the Baptist is the forerunner whose ministry ceases when Jesus arrives on the scene - the old order is both fulfilled and replaced with Jesus. As in Chapter 1, so in Chapter 3, Luke establishes beyond doubt what is the connection and the difference between John and Jesus.

B. THE END OF JOHN'S MINISTRY
(3:18-20; 7:18-35)

For Luke, as for Mark and Matthew, the arrival of Jesus on the scene signals the end of the ministry of John the Baptist. Once the Messiah has arrived, the work of those who prepared the way comes to an end. Luke has a sense of history and he feels the need to tie up any loose ends so, at 3:18-20, he explains why it was that John disappeared so suddenly. In fact he does not do as thorough a job as we might expect, and it is to one of Luke's main sources - the gospel of Mark - that we have to turn in order to make more sense of Luke's rather vague comment. Mark, at 6:14-29, informs us of the events surrounding John's death. Apparently, John had fallen foul of Herod Antipas (tetrarch or ruler of Galilee) by speaking out against his marriage. Herod had divorced his first wife and then married Herodias, his brother's wife. There were Old Testament rules which said this was wrong, and John had told Herod so. Mark tells us that it was out of spite that Herodias persuaded her daughter to ask Herod to have John beheaded.

Though Luke does not recount the incident of John's execution, he does, in passing, mention it (see 9:7-9) but only in the context of Herod wondering who Jesus was. This, and the other references to John which Luke makes (7:18-35 and 20:1-8), suggest that Luke is only interested in the Baptist in so far as he can be compared and contrasted with Jesus. Luke uses John like a reference point to establish who Jesus really is. John, as Luke sees him, was a heaven-sent prophet (*see* 1:13-17) whose job was to prepare the way for the Messiah (7:27) "He is the man of whom Scripture says, 'Here is my herald, whom I send on ahead of you, and he will prepare your way before you'". Jesus has shown himself to be the Messiah through the works which he performs (*see* 7:21-23), but both he and John have been despised and misunderstood, as 7:31-35 makes clear.

NOTE ON THE INFLUENCE OF JOHN THE BAPTIST

The attention given by Luke to John suggests the possibility that John still had quite a following even after his death. At 7:18 it is apparent that he still had disciples even though in prison, and at 20:1-8 it would seem the influence of John is still too strong among ordinary people for the priests and lawyers to speak against him. Earlier in the gospel (3:15), Luke notes that the people are wondering whether John was the Messiah.

It seems quite possible that, during the early years of the Christian church, followers of John the Baptist were still in evidence (see Acts 19:1-7). Perhaps the early Christians even regarded them as rivals. If this is correct, it may go some way towards explaining Luke's treatment of John. Whilst John is crucial to the Christian position as forerunner to the Messiah, he must be kept in perspective. Luke does this in Chapters 1-3, as we have seen, and at 7:18-35 this is still his concern. John's question, "Are you the one who is to come, or are we to expect some other?" (7:19), is an indirect confirmation from John that he does not think of himself as Messiah. In the same passage, Luke has Jesus give John high praise when he says that he is "far more than a prophet" (7:26) and that "there is not a mother's son greater than John" (7:28). But this is soon modified with the comment that "the least in the kingdom of God is greater than he" (7:28). What this means is not entirely clear, but it could be a further way of keeping John in perspective. The kingdom of God comes in Jesus, according to Luke, so does he mean that, as John comes before Jesus, he is not part of that kingdom? John, in Luke's view, belongs to the old order, that is, the time *before* Jesus. Even the most exalted person of that order comes below the followers of Jesus who are already in the kingdom of God.

According to this way of thinking, any following that John still had in the early days of Christianity was misguided. In Luke's view, there is only one person to follow and that is Jesus.

C. THE BAPTISM OF JESUS (3:21-22)

The way in which Luke presents the baptism of Jesus suggests that he was either less certain of the event's significance than was his predecessor Mark, or he felt it needed more cautious treatment than Mark had given it. For the earlier writer, the baptism is the point at which the story of Jesus begins. Jesus simply arrives on the scene without further comment, is baptised by John and, as he emerges from the water, the heavens open and there is a voice from heaven which says, "Thou art my Son, my Beloved; on thee my favour rests" (Mark 1:11). These words are similar to those found in the Old Testament at Psalm 2:7. This psalm is about the coronation of one of Israel's kings. When a person became king he was thought to be adopted by God and from then on would be treated as if he were God's son. As such he was God's representative on earth. In using these words, Mark is telling his readers that Jesus is God's new representative on earth. He is the Messiah whom the Jews have so long awaited. Luke has already made this point quite clear to his readers through the story of Jesus' birth so, in that sense, the baptism is not as essential to his gospel as it is to Mark's. Yet there is a need to mark the commencement of Jesus' ministry in some way and the baptism is an ideal way of doing this.

Mark's account, as it stands, seems to present Luke with some problems, and he feels the need to modify it. Even during the early decades of Christianity's existence, ideas about Jesus were changing. Writing later than Mark, Luke is probably more consciously aware of the idea that Jesus in his earthly life had been sinless. So, Luke is faced with a problem which Mark seems to have overlooked, namely, why was it that the sinless Jesus needed to be baptised when the purpose of baptism was to cleanse people from their wrong-doing and their old style of life and give them a fresh start? Matthew too seems to have recognised this problem, and he solves the matter by introducing a short dialogue between John and Jesus to give the reason for Jesus submitting to John's baptism. Luke does not do this. He chooses to play down the significance of the actual baptism by mentioning it almost in passing. "During a general baptism of the people, when Jesus too had been baptised and was praying" (3:21). Note that John is not mentioned as the one who is doing the baptising, and Luke immediately puts the baptism in the context of Jesus at prayer (Jesus at prayer is a favourite theme of Luke's which he uses to mark significant moments in Jesus' life, *see* page 118), so that what follows - the heaven opening and the Holy Spirit descending on him "in bodily form like a dove", and the voice from heaven - is more to do with prayer than baptism. Perhaps Luke is emphasising that it is through prayer that one is filled with the Holy Spirit. (A similar point is made when Jesus is at prayer in Gethsemane (22:39-46) and an angel brings him strength.)

Placing the baptism of Jesus within the context of a general baptism also enables Luke to show how Jesus identified himself with the ordinary people.

NOTE ON LUKE'S PRESENTATION OF JOHN THE BAPTIST

In Mark and Matthew, John the Baptist is presented very much as an Elijah-type figure. Their description of John's appearance and diet coincides with the appearance and diet of Elijah in 2 Kings 1:8. There are obvious reasons for this because, according to Malachi 4:5-6, Elijah would return before God's final intervention. Luke, however, prefers to present John as a prophet in the Old Testament tradition without especially identifying him with any one particular prophet, and so he leaves out the description of John's food and clothing, which would identify John with Elijah. As will become apparent later (*see* page 89), Luke prefers to show a close connection between Jesus and Elijah rather than between John the Baptist and Elijah.

*The River Jordan. John the Baptist "went all over the Jordan valley
proclaiming a baptism in token of repentance for the forgiveness of sins" (3:3).*

Infant baptism. The priest pours water over the baby's head and baptises in the name of the Father, Son and Holy Spirit.

D. BAPTISM TODAY

Since the very early days of Christianity, baptism has been the means by which people begin their lives as Christians. The first Christians were converts to the faith. They were adults who made a conscious decision to become members of the church. As a symbol to show commitment to their new faith, they underwent baptism. The baptism service would probably have been carried out on the banks of a local river. After making their promises, the converts would have been completely immersed in water. Through this symbolic act, the new members were thought to be made clean of their past wrong-doings and their old style of life, and so given a fresh start.

Some churches today still retain this form of baptism. They use the method of full immersion, and only baptise adults who have been taught about the responsibilities of becoming a Christian and honestly feel that they want to commit themselves to the Christian way of life. Some of the churches which follow this practice call themselves 'Baptist' to emphasise the importance they attach to this form of initiation into the Christian faith. In their church buildings, they may also have a tank (called a baptistry), set into the floor, which is large enough and deep enough for a minister to perform baptisms. There are even congregations who prefer to continue the tradition of baptisms in the open air, using a river, a lake, the sea, or even the local swimming baths.

The method of baptism just described is sometimes called 'believers' baptism', to contrast it with 'infant baptism' (sometimes called 'christening'), which is practised by other churches (including Anglican and Roman Catholic). As small children are clearly not able to make up their own minds about Christianity, their parents, together with godparents (sometimes called sponsors), make the promises on their behalf. The priest, or minister, standing at the font, baptises the child by pouring water over its head. He then makes the sign of the cross on the child's forehead, and a lighted candle is given to the parents as a symbol of the new life in Christ which the child has just received. When children are old enough to decide for themselves if they really accept the claims of Christianity, they can be prepared for Confirmation or full church membership. At this service, they make promises on their own behalf in the presence of a bishop (in Anglican and Roman Catholic churches) and the full congregation.

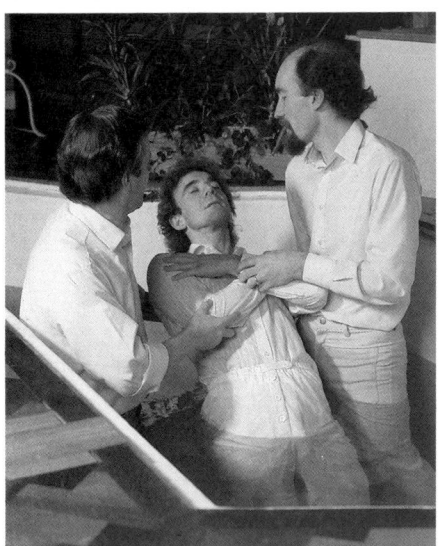

Baptism by full immersion. Adult, or believers' baptism is practised by a number of Christian denominations, most notably the Baptists.

NOTE ON THE GENEALOGY OF JESUS (3:23-38)

Why does Luke present his readers with Jesus' family tree? A lengthy list of near unpronounceable names seems to interrupt the flow of his story. But it should not be dismissed or passed over too quickly. It provides Luke with a further opportunity to make it clear to his readers who Jesus is. The story of Jesus' baptism which has gone immediately before, and the story of his temptation which comes immediately after do the same thing.

Genealogies were very important in Jewish life and examples can be found in the Old Testament (see the ancestors of Abraham listed in Genesis 11:10-32). Priests in particular had to be able to prove their descent from Aaron if they were to hold office (see Ezra 2:61-63 for an example of would-be priests who could not prove their pedigree).

Perhaps in a similar way, Jesus' family tree is meant to show that Christian claims about Jesus are entirely justified. His line is traced back through David, to support the view that Jesus is the Messiah the Jews have been waiting for. Luke goes further in his treatment of Jesus' genealogy than does Matthew, who traces Jesus' descent from Abraham, the father of the Jewish race (see Matt. 1:1-17). For Luke, Jesus has significance for all people, and so he traces the genealogy back to Adam, the father of all humanity and ultimately back to God, the true father and creator of all.

It may seem a little odd that Luke, who emphasises the divine conception of Jesus (1:35), traces his descent through Joseph. He is not unaware of this apparent irregularity as 3:23 shows (Jesus is said to be the son, 'as people thought', of Joseph). But Luke wants to stress Jesus' continuity with the Old Testament and the Jewish religion. Yet in tracing Jesus back to Adam he opens up the significance of Jesus for his Gentile readers as well.

Luke, like Paul, may also have had in mind the idea of Jesus as a second Adam. The first Adam, described by Luke as son of God, sinned and so spoilt the perfect relationship he had originally enjoyed with God. The second Adam, Jesus, was the true Son of God. He did not sin and opened up the possibility for people to enjoy once again that perfect relationship with God which the sin of Adam had previously denied them.

It is worth noting that Luke is the gospel writer who tells us how old Jesus was when he began his ministry. According to 3:23 he "was about thirty years of age". In the Old Testament book Numbers this is the earliest age at which a priest could take up his duties (Numbers 4:1-3 - though later, at 8:23-24, the lower age limit is given as twenty-five). It is possible that the thirtieth year at Ezekiel 1:1 is a reference to the age of the prophet, though this is by no means certain. If Luke did not know how old Jesus was when he began his ministry, these Old Testament references might have provided him with an answer.

E. CONFLICT AND OPPOSITION

We can read a lot further into Luke's gospel than we can in Mark or Matthew before we come across the more unpleasant side of things, namely the opposition which Jesus faced at every stage of his ministry. In Mark we cover only twelve verses before Jesus' temptation and then, hard on the heels of that, we have from 2:1 to 3:6 a series of 'conflict' stories in which the opposition to Jesus is very apparent. Matthew too does not delay in warning his readers of the opposition to Jesus which existed even at the time of his birth - when Herod heard from the wise men about the birth of the "king of the Jews" he set about trying to kill Jesus (*see* Matthew 2).

Luke, in characteristic style, warms more slowly to the task, and it is not until Chapter 4 of his gospel that the reader is really made aware of the problems which Jesus will have to face. First, Luke tells of the temptations of Jesus, then of Jesus' rejection by his own people at Nazareth (see page 57), and then he recounts a number of healing miracles where the demons oppose Jesus (see chapter 9). As the gospel progresses, so open conflict and opposition to Jesus become more apparent. He soon falls foul of the religious leaders of the day (5:21), and then it is not long before they are discussing among themselves what they can do to him (6:11).

As we study the temptations of Jesus in the next section, we need to be aware how this marks the commencement of an important aspect of Jesus' ministry, namely the opposition he had to face. (The theme of opposition will be taken up again in chapters 10 & 11 on the Teaching of Jesus and the Passion Narrative.)

F. THE TEMPTATIONS
(i) The fight against evil (4:1-13)

What lessons did Luke intend to teach his readers through the incident of Jesus being tempted by the devil? Luke gives us a clue by placing this event immediately after the genealogy. Jesus is the new Adam (*see* Note on p. 52) but he does not give in to temptation as did the first Adam (Genesis 3).

The incident also makes the point that if the Son of God is subjected to temptation then no one who has been baptised a Christian can hope to escape being tested. Even the disciples of Jesus will undergo severe testing at the hands of Satan (see 22:31).

A warning is also given that no one can expect to conquer evil at one go. At 4:13 Luke notes that the devil "having come to the end of all his temptations . . . departed, *biding his time*." The fight against evil will continue throughout the ministry of Jesus, and so it will throughout the life of the Christian.

(ii) What will the Messiah be like?

The temptations help the reader to see at the outset what sort of Messiah Jesus will be. In Jewish thought there was no *one* generally accepted picture of the Messiah: different groups expected different things of him. Would Jesus be the sort of Messiah who would meet the material needs of the world by turning stones into bread? The poor would undoubtedly welcome a Messiah of this sort. Or would he be a glorious king with great power and authority ruling over the whole world, presumably having first defeated the Romans? The zealots (Jewish nationalists) would undoubtedly welcome a Messiah of this sort. Or would he be a Messiah who would prove, through signs, like jumping from the top of the Temple, who he was? Such demonstrations of power would leave people in no doubt: they would not need faith to recognise him. Those who were always looking for a sign (compare 11:29) would undoubtedly welcome a Messiah of this sort. In his response to all these temptations, Jesus indicates that his idea of messiahship is totally different and is one based on true obedience to God.

(iii) Where Israel failed, Jesus succeeds

Luke is concerned to show that Jesus, the founder of the new order (Christianity) does not fall into error in the way that the old order (Judaism) had done in the past. To demonstrate the point, Luke clearly has in mind a particular period of time in Israel's history (the wilderness period), which was in a way a time of testing and temptation. (Deuteronomy describes the purpose of this period of time as God's opportunity to find out whether the Israelites "would keep his commandments, or not" (Deut. 8:2 RSV).) Following their escape from Egypt under Moses' leadership, the Israelites spent some *forty* years in the *wilderness* on their way to the Promised Land. It is worth noting that Luke following Mark, says that Jesus spent *forty* days in the *wilderness* (4:2). This should alert us to the comparison which he presumably intends his readers to make. The number forty itself is a symbol indicating that God himself is active in human affairs as in the past.

During their time in the wilderness things did not always go well for the Israelites. When temptation occurred, they often gave in to it. *Three* occasions in particular from Israel's past may have been in Luke's mind as he told of the *three* temptations of Jesus. He was perhaps anxious to make the comparison in order to show that where Israel failed Jesus succeeds.

Bread

At Exodux 16:2-3 the hungry Israelites complained bitterly that God had brought them into the wilderness to die. Although God provided bread (manna) from heaven for them, Deuteronomy makes the point that he let them hunger in order" to teach you that man cannot live on bread alone" (Deut. 8:3). These are the very words that Luke places on the lips of Jesus when Jesus is tempted to turn a stone into bread in order to satisfy his *physical* hunger. Jesus, who is "full of the Holy Spirit" does not give in to temptation.

Devil worship

At Exodus 32 the Israelites are restless and want a god they can see. This was clearly against all the teaching they had been given. (When they did eventually arrive in the Promised Land they were constantly tempted to worship other gods.) The writer of Deuteronomy reminds them, "You shall fear the Lord your God: serve him alone" (6:13). When Jesus was tempted to worship the devil, he replied in words similar to Deuteronomy 6:13: "You shall do homage to the Lord your God and worship him alone" (4:8). Where Israel failed Jesus succeeds.

Testing God

At Exodus 17 the Israelites are thirsty and ask, "Is the Lord in our midst or not?" (Exodus 17:7). In other words, they put God to the test. (Presumably if water is provided they will continue to believe in him.) The writer of Deuteronomy, referring to this 'test', warns, "You must not challenge the Lord your God" (6:16). In a rather different way, Jesus is challenged by the devil to *test* God by throwing himself from the parapet of the Jerusalem Temple. The devil, we are told, even quotes scripture (Psalm 91:11-12) at Jesus to reassure him of God's protection. Significantly Jesus, in his reply to the devil, uses the words from Deuteronomy which we have just quoted: "You are not to put the Lord your God to the test" (4:12).

Where Israel failed by giving into temptation time and time again, Jesus overcomes it. For Luke, his success is yet another way of expressing the belief that Jesus is the Messiah.

G. THE TEMPTATIONS TODAY

What are people today to make of a story in which someone has a conversation with the devil? Did this event really take place? In the study of the gospels the question, 'Did it really happen?' is not always the most profitable question to ask. The evidence available to us is not sufficient for us to be able to know with any degree of certainty about the history of any of the gospel events. All we can do is to focus attention on how Luke uses the material he has and to try to assess something of its significance for him.

However, this particular incident of Jesus in conversation with the devil does require some comment from the point of view of history. It is a story which clearly relates to a time in the past when the devil was thought of in real terms. In Luke's world, people had a strong belief in the existence of demons (*see* chapter 9) and presumably in the leader of the demons, the devil. But some beliefs are best confined to the particular period of history in which such thinking was common. In the case of belief in a devil and demons, this may have been a commonly held view of the first century AD, but it is *not* consistent with the thinking of most people living today. This is not meant in any way to minimise the evil which is extremely apparent in our world today in all sorts of ways. But it is not necessary to think in terms of all evil coming ultimately from the power of the devil. As a poetic device to represent evil, the devil is invaluable in the temptation story of Luke 4:1-13, and this is probably the best way to view him.

With the recording of the temptations of Jesus, the scene is set for Jesus' ministry to commence - 'the way is prepared'.

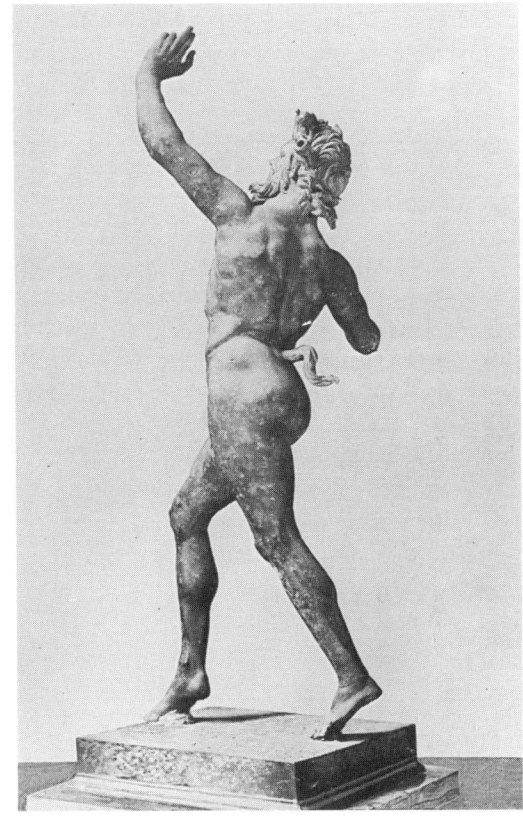

Dancing faun from 'The House of the Faun', Pompeii. A faun was a Roman rural deity with goat horns and tail. Christians came to think of Satan as looking something like this.

Questions for chapter 6
John the Baptist (3:1-20)

1 a. Where did John work?
  b. What did John proclaim?
2 a. What is meant by "the coming retribution"?
  b. How, in John's view, can those he has baptised show their repentance?
  c. Claiming descent from Abraham was of no use, according to John. What privileges might the Jews who came to him have expected from God, do you think?
3. What do you understand by the saying at 3:9: "Already the axe is laid to the roots of the trees; and every tree that fails to produce good fruit is cut down and thrown on the fire"?

4. What advice did John give
  (i) to the people; **(ii)** to the tax-gatherers; **(iii)** to the soldiers?
5. What do you think is meant by **(i)** the wheat; **(ii)** the chaff, in the saying at 3:17?
6. In what ways does Luke present John the Baptist as a prophet?
7. How does Luke show that John himself is a fulfilment of prophecy?
8. What is the purpose of John's work?
9. In what ways does John himself make a distinction between his work and the work of the Messiah?

10. How does Luke show that John's work comes to an end when Jesus arrives on the scene?

11a. What was John's fate, according to Luke?
  b. What other information is available to us about John's death and in which gospel can it be found?

Baptism
(3:21-22)

12. Describe the events of Jesus' baptism as told by Luke.
13a. What words are spoken from heaven?
  b. What is the significance of these words?
14. Why do you think Luke puts Jesus' baptism in the context of a "general baptism of the people" and does not mention John in connection with it?
15. Why do you think Luke emphasises that Jesus was *praying* when the Holy Spirit descended on him?
16. Look at the picture 'Infant baptism' on p.51

a. List the people you would expect to be present at an infant baptism.
b. In whose name is the child baptised?
c. Why would the child have godparents or sponsors?
17. Look at the picture 'Baptism by full immersion' on p.52
a. What is happening in this picture?
b. What does this symbolic action mean?
c. Name a denomination where you might see this ceremony.
d. Which is preferable, infant or adult baptism? Explain your opinion.

Genealogy
(3:23-38)

18a. According to Luke, how old was Jesus when he began his ministry?

b. What would have been the significance of (i) David, (ii) Abraham, and (iii) Adam, in the family tree of Jesus which Luke presents to his readers?

Temptations
(4:1-13)

19. How does the temptation story act as a warning to Luke's readers that the path Jesus is   to follow will not be a smooth one?
20. Where did the temptations of Jesus take place?
21. Describe the *three* temptations Jesus underwent.
22. What is threatening about the comment, " . . . the devil departed, biding his time"?
23. How might the temptation story be seen as a warning to a newly baptised Christian?

24. In what way might the temptation story help Luke's readers to clarify their thinking about the sort of Messiah Jesus is?
25. How far do you think Luke was contrasting Jesus, who does not give in to temptation, with the Israelites who did?
26. How would you explain the meaning of the temptation story to people today?
27. Is the idea of the "devil" helpful to Christians today faced with temptation?

7

THE MISSION OF JESUS AND THE MISSION OF THE CHURCH

A. THE TWO MISSIONS ARE LINKED: JESUS IN THE SYNAGOGUE AT NAZARETH
(4:14-30)

Jesus' teaching at Nazareth marks the beginning of his ministry in Luke's gospel. To understand why Luke started at this point we must look carefully at the order of events in this incident and see how they relate to the events of Jesus' life and to the mission of the church.

Luke emphasises that Jesus is the Messiah doing God's work. He does this by stating that Jesus was 'armed with the power of the Spirit' (4:14). He is the Messiah who, as promised in the Old Testament, has come to the Jews, God's chosen people.

Jesus' audience does not recognise who he is. All they see is 'Joseph's son' (4:22). The people of Nazareth stand for the Jews who reject Jesus. They demand proof of what he claims, a demand which echoes the third of Jesus' temptations. The only response by Jesus, which Luke records, is to refer to Elijah and Elisha the Old Testament prophets who brought relief from suffering to Gentiles, even though their own people were also suffering. (See 1 Kings 17; 2 Kings 5.)

This reply indicates what will happen to Jesus and his church. The Messiah will be rejected by the Jews and salvation will then be offered to the Gentiles and a new people of God will arise consisting of anyone who can see who Jesus really is. This is of particular interest to the Gentile members of Luke's church. (See: Parable of the Dinner Party 14:15-24.)

The final event in this section parallels the final event of Jesus' ministry. The congregation of the synagogue throw Jesus out of the town and attempt to hurl him over the brow of a hill, just as, at the end, Jesus is taken outside a town and crucified. How Jesus escapes on this occasion is not clear. The point appears to be that Jesus cannot be harmed until he has completed God's work of salvation.

Luke's placing of the incident of Jesus in the synagogue at Nazareth at the start of Jesus' ministry is clearly deliberate. He knew of other events before this (4:23) with which he could have begun, and Mark, who was Luke's source for this incident, puts it later in his gospel (Mark 6:1-6).

The events in the synagogue tell us a little about how services were conducted. But whether Jesus would have chosen the passage he read for himself, or whether the readings for the day would have been specified in a lectionary, is not known, and not the point as far as Luke is concerned. Luke quotes the passage from Isaiah 61:1-2 because it is a prophecy about what will happen when the Messiah appears. It is thus, for Luke, a description of Jesus and his mission: the spirit of the Lord is upon him, he has come to announce the good news (gospel), to heal and to proclaim God's care (salvation) for his people. It is another opportunity for Luke to show that there was continuity between the Old Testament and the mission of Jesus.

NOTE ON THE TITLE 'MESSIAH' OR 'CHRIST'

Both these words mean 'the anointed one'. 'Messiah' is Hebrew and 'Christ' is Greek. The reason Jesus has titles in both languages is that his first followers were Jews, but the international language of the first century was Greek and it was in that language that the New Testament was written.

In the Old Testament anointing meant having oil poured over your head (e.g. 1 Sam. 10:1). It was equivalent to being crowned and showed that the person had been adopted by God as his son, and chosen to be king of God's people. The king had the duty of representing the people before God and of conveying God's will to the people. Among the Hebrews the king performed duties which would today be thought more appropriate to a priest.

It was believed by the Jews of Jesus' day that God would send his Messiah to free them from oppression by the Romans and set up a kingdom which would be ruled according to God's laws. Many thought this would be accomplished by force. Luke is careful to correct this idea and to make clear the type of Messiah he believed Jesus to be. There are five main elements in Luke's presentation of Messiahship:

1. Jesus uses the title Son of Man - not Messiah -of himself, so as to avoid misunderstanding about his mission until his type of Messiahship is made plain (9:20-22).

2. Jesus rejects the idea of any kingship in this world by refusing the second of the devil's temptations (4:5-8).

3. It had been anticipated by the prophets of the Old Testament that the kingdom of God would be centred on Jerusalem; Jesus destroys this belief when he weeps over the city and prophesies its destruction (19:41-44).

4. Jesus reinterprets the Old Testament to show that death was an essential part of Messiahship (24:44-46).

5. Jesus shows that the old nationalistic idea of the Messiah had been transformed into that of a universal saviour (24:46-47).

References: 2:11, 26; 4:41; 9:20; 20:41; 22:67; 23:2, 35, 39; 24:26, 46.

B. THE MIRACULOUS CATCH OF FISH
(5:1-11)

In this short passage Luke exercises all his skill to combine several themes. He begins by presenting Simon Peter, who is to become the leader of the church after Jesus' crucifixion, as the one closest to Jesus. Jesus teaches the crowd and it is Peter's response to Jesus which illustrates how those who hear his words should respond. They should recognise that Jesus is the Messiah filled with the spirit of God, they should understand that they are sinners and, when called by Jesus, they should leave everything to follow him.

While Luke is describing the call of Peter he is also picturing the work of the church. Among the early Christians a favourite image for the church was a boat, and Christians were frequently represented by the symbol of a fish. The sea was seen as a place where evil powers lay in wait for people, so netting fish represented the missionary activity of the church: people were brought into the church where they could find salvation.

When Jesus appears the fishermen have worked all night. They were in darkness. Night/dark symbolise evil and the fishermen accomplish nothing while evil reigns. In the morning Jesus arrives. Morning/light symbolise good. With Jesus' help good triumphs and a huge catch is made.

The catch of fish is a sign (miracle) pointing to the true identity of Jesus. Luke makes this clear by the way he shows Peter addressing Jesus. Before the catch he says 'Master', which is a title used of a rabbi; after it he says 'Lord', which was a title used in worship in the early church. Peter has realised that he is in the presence of the divine.

Peter says, 'Go, Lord, leave me, sinner that I am.' This is Peter's first act of repentance (*See* p.146). He feels unworthy to be near Jesus but is nevertheless called to be Jesus' closest follower. The incident teaches that faith in Jesus is all that is needed to gain salvation. Peter represents the church which is made up of people everyone of whom is unworthy of salvation. It is only God's grace, which is freely given, that saves them.

Peter occupies the central position in the passage but is linked at the end with James and John. These disciples make up an inner group who are with Jesus at important moments in his ministry. Their reaction to his call demonstrates another teaching which Luke emphasises: a person's response to Jesus must be immediate; no one can afford to put off following Jesus until tomorrow because *today* may be the day of judgment (see 12:13-21).

The way in which Peter, James and John leave everything to follow Jesus is an example to everyone. They were not necessarily poor since the fishing industry on Lake Gennesaret was successful and even sent pickled fish to Rome. So leaving everything to follow Jesus meant making a considerable sacrifice. But true wealth could only be found in the kingdom of God and the only way to gain that was to follow Jesus.

Luke has taken the call of the first disciples from Mark 1:15-20. He has illustrated the saying, 'I will make you fishers of men', by combining it with the story of the miraculous catch of fish. A parallel story, but without the saying, can be found at John 21:4-8 where it is presented as a post-resurrection appearance of Jesus.

Peter's call hints at another of Luke's favourite themes: Jesus will not take no for an answer. His mission is to the lost, and like a shepherd he goes out after his sheep and brings them back (15:3-7). This is the task which Jesus passes on to Peter and the church. The Greek word translated as 'catching' (5:10) literally means 'taking alive', in the sense of saving people from danger. Bringing salvation to the world is the job of the church.

NOTE ON THE TITLE 'SON OF MAN'

The title 'Son of Man' is the most common messianic title in Luke's gospel, as it is in Matthew and Mark.

The words 'son of man' were to start with a Hebrew expression which meant 'man'. This was how the phrase was first used in the Old Testament, for example, at Psalm 8:4.

It gathered new meaning when it was used in Daniel. This book was probably written during the second century BC, a period of persecution for the Jews, and was intended to encourage them to remain faithful to their religion.

In Chapter 7 Daniel tells of a vision he experienced. In it he saw four terrible beasts, an old man, and one like a son of man. The interpretation of the vision explains that the beasts were the kingdoms which oppressed God's people, the old man (the Ancient in Years) was God, and the son of man was one who represented the saints of the Most High (God).

The vision foretold that the saints of the Most High would suffer for a time under the rule of the kingdoms, then judgment would be given by God in favour of those who had remained faithful in spite of persecution, and "kingly power, sovereignty, and greatness of all the kingdoms under heaven" would be given to them (Dan. 7:27). The son of man was a representative of the faithful people of God.

Luke uses the title 'Son of Man' in three ways:

1. The 'Son of Man' was an *apocalyptic* figure who would appear at some time in the future, establish the kingdom of God on earth and sit in judgment on the world (18:8). In the years immediately after the crucifixion, the appearance of this figure was identified in the Christian mind with Jesus at his Second Coming, which was expected at any moment. By the time that Luke wrote, it was realised that one could not predict when judgment would be, so his coming was put at some unspecified time in the future. This is why Luke emphasises that one has to be constantly prepared for judgment.

2. The Son of Man was one who had to suffer and die before being raised again (9:22). The son of man in Daniel suffered but remained faithful to God and was rewarded as a result. But Daniel does not say that the Son of Man was the Messiah. The idea that the Son of Man and Messiah were the same person does not seem to have existed before the time of Jesus. The idea of a Messiah who suffered was something new.

3. The Son of Man also referred to one who was present and announcing the good news of the kingdom of God. It was the title Jesus used of himself. He preferred it to Messiah, which was associated with traditional ideas of kingship. Luke calls the Son of Man a sign (11:30). Jesus appeared as a man, but those who had faith could see the presence of God to which his ministry pointed. As Son of Man, Jesus combined the roles of representative of God and representative of the faithful people of God.

By the time Luke wrote his gospel the three aspects of the title were seen as three elements in Jesus' mission. The gospel writers could present Jesus saying either 'I' or 'Son of Man' when referring to himself. (Compare Matt. 10:32 with Luke 12:8.) The title sums up Luke's and the church's beliefs about Jesus.

References: 6:5, 22; 7:34; 9:22, 26, 44, 58; 11:30; 12:8, 10; 17:22, 26, 30; 18:8, 31; 19:10; 21:27; 22:22, 48; 24:7.

C. THE FOUNDING OF THE CHURCH: THE MISSION OF THE TWELVE
(6:12-16; 9:1-6)

Before Jesus chooses the Twelve he goes into the hills to pray. Prayer again indicates that an important event is about to take place and this time it is emphasised even more strongly by the statement that Jesus "spent the night in prayer" (6:12). The symbolic pattern of night and day (darkness/light; evil/good) repeats the pattern of the miraculous catch of fish. Jesus is in communion with God throughout the night and, when day comes, offers salvation to a new people of God. Perhaps Luke also intends to emphasise that anyone who spends the night in prayer to God cannot be touched by evil.

The way Luke sets the scene suggests that he again has in mind events in the Old Testament. In this case his description reflects the time when Moses went up the mountain to receive the Law and then brought it to God's chosen people, the twelve tribes of Israel. This time Jesus goes into the hills (a place thought of as being near to God), prays, selects twelve from among his many disciples and descends to give his teaching to the people. (Compare Exod. 19.)

The Apostles are the first members of the New Israel. It is not by chance that Luke says that Jesus "named them Apostles" (6:13). 'Apostle' is one of Luke's favourite words. It means 'one who is sent'. Jesus himself has been sent to spread the gospel (4:43). The Apostles are to be sent to exorcise, to heal and to proclaim the gospel (9:1-2).

They are given strict instructions about how they are to behave on their missionary journeys. They must take nothing with them and accept what is offered wherever they stay. Luke is making one of his familiar points: the way to gain salvation is by having faith that God will provide for you - not by weighing yourself down with lots of possessions and always seeking more.

On one level Luke is writing about Jesus and the Apostles. On another level he is writing about the people in his church. His message to them is that they are now the people of God and that they should live in imitation of Jesus and the Apostles.

Finally, if the Apostles, or perhaps the Christian missionaries of Luke's own church, were rejected by any town, they were to shake its dust off their feet. It was an act which symbolised that the town had rejected salvation and it was a judgment on it.

In the early years of Christianity many groups claimed to offer salvation in the name of Jesus. Luke is at pains to stress that Jesus speaks to his church and the rest of the world only through the Apostles and their successors. They were appointed by Jesus and given his power and authority and in Acts of the Apostles Luke shows them continuing this work and appointing successors. 'Apostle' means not only 'one who is sent', but also 'ambassador' or 'delegate'.

The act of shaking dust off their feet reflects the Jewish practice when they left Gentile areas to return to their own land. Other lands were considered ritually unclean, so the act symbolised the division between God's people and those who would not enter the kingdom of God.

Luke's source for 9:1-6 is Mark 6:7-13. Luke makes the demands on the Twelve more severe by not allowing them, as Mark does, to have a staff, neither does he say that they were to travel in pairs. Luke probably makes the alterations to fit in with his Q source (compare Matt. 10:5-15) or to make their difference from other missionaries, who were identified by bag and staff, more marked. Some non-Christian missionaries made a very good living out of their preaching and Luke would not have wanted Christian missionaries to have been identified with them.

The Sea of Galilee (Lake Gennesaret - 5:1) seen from the west shore.

D. THE TRANSFIGURATION (9:28-36)

There is no other event in Luke's gospel which is like the Transfiguration. It is unique and of great importance both for the gospel and for the church. It confirms that Jesus speaks with God's authority and that he replaces the Law and the prophets as the way to know what God requires from humanity. It confirmed for Luke's church that they were the true people of God.

Luke leads up to the Transfiguration by a series of carefully chosen events each of which reveals something about Jesus, but leaves a question in the minds of those who read about them.

1. Jesus calls the Twelve to be a new people of God (6:12-16). Is Jesus a new Moses?

2. Jesus gives the Twelve power over demons (9:1). Who has the power to defeat evil?

3. Herod hears about Jesus but does not know what to make of him (9:7-9). Is Jesus one of the Old Testament prophets come back to life, or has Elijah reappeared?

4. Jesus feeds the five thousand (9:12-17). Who could give a banquet such as the Messiah would give in the kingdom of God?

5. Peter confesses that Jesus is God's Messiah (9:20). Can it be right that the Messiah must be rejected by the Jewish authorities?

With the Transfiguration Luke answers all these questions.

The Transfiguration is of central importance and, once again, Luke alerts us to this by telling us that Jesus goes into the hills to pray. He takes with him his inner group of Peter, John and James.

These three disciples see Jesus transfigured. This means that his face and clothes changed in some way and radiated a heavenly light. It was a vision of how Jesus would appear at some time in the future, after his resurrection and ascension, when he returned to rule his kingdom. Some Jews believed that at the day of judgment those who were to enter the kingdom of God would be given radiant new bodies. This is how Jesus is pictured.

Jesus is seen to talk with Moses and Elijah. These two figures from the Old Testament represent the Law (Moses) and the prophets (Elijah). They talk to Jesus about his "departure, the destiny he was to fulfil in Jerusalem" (9:31). This refers to Jesus' crucifixion and resurrection, which will bring salvation to his followers. But Peter misunderstands what is happening. Perhaps we are to believe that Peter, seeing the radiant figures, thought the kingdom had arrived and for that reason offered to build shelters for them. This reflects the Jewish belief that when God established his kingdom on earth his people would again live in shelters or tents just as they had in the wilderness centuries earlier when God had lived with them.

Then the cloud covers them and the disciples are afraid. The cloud symbolises the presence of God, and the voice which speaks is God's. At the baptism of Jesus the voice from heaven addressed him personally and said: "Thou art my Son, my Beloved; on thee my favour rests." Now these words are echoed but changed slightly because they are addressed to the disciples: "This is my Son, my Chosen; listen to him."

The message is for the three disciples who hear it and for the church which they represent. The words answer the questions Luke has raised. Jesus is not just another Moses or Elijah. He is greater than the Law and the prophets, he replaces them, and anyone who seeks salvation should listen to his teaching.

The Transfiguration of Jesus. Who, besides Jesus, is shown in this picture?

Luke has used Mark 9:2-13 as his source for the Transfiguration and has expanded Mark's account by adding to it themes which are central to his gospel.

. Mark makes no mention of prayer, but for Luke when Jesus prays he is speaking to God and such prayer is followed (or answered) by some momentous event. Mark says that Jesus was 'transfigured'. Luke does not use this word at all but refers particularly to Jesus' face. He perhaps had in mind Exod. 34:29f when Moses' face shone after speaking to God.

Luke has also added the information that Moses and Elijah were talking to Jesus about his departure. This is another important theme for Luke because what is being discussed is the salvation Jesus is to accomplish. The Greek word for departure is 'exodos'.

'Exodus' has two meanings: death, and deliverance. The word therefore points forward to Jesus' death in Jerusalem and suggests that there Jesus will accomplish a deliverance which will parallel *the Exodus* of the Israelites from slavery in Egypt. In this case it will be the freeing of humanity from slavery to the power of evil.

In Mark's account, Peter says what he does because he is terrified (Mark 9:6). Luke says, "he spoke without knowing what he was saying" (9:33), which could suggest that he was divinely inspired. Peter's words confirm that he is seeing a vision of Jesus as he will appear when he is in the kingdom, but he does not realise that it is not yet time for the kingdom to be established, just as he still does not understand what Jesus told the disciples at 9:22: the Son of Man has to suffer.

The command of the voice from the cloud seems to be especially appropriate to Peter. Listen to what Jesus tells you: the Messiah must suffer rejection and death before he can accomplish his work. It is not yet time for the kingdom to be established.

The Transfiguration links the baptism, which was the start of Jesus' mission, with the resurrection which was its completion. The voice from the cloud is heard at the baptism and at the Transfiguration. At the Transfiguration two men appear, Moses and Elijah, and at the empty tomb two men again appear (24:4). We are almost certainly expected to see them as the representatives of the Law and the prophets bearing witness to the resurrection and the fulfilment of the Old Testament promises to Israel.

The miraculous catch of fish and the Transfiguration are useful as reminders to us that the order of events in the gospels has been decided on by the evangelists themselves. John (21:4-8) makes the miraculous catch of fish a post-resurrection story because that suits his purpose. It has been suggested that the Transfiguration of Jesus was, originally, a post-resurrection vision of Jesus which Mark placed in the centre of his gospel (9:2-8), and which Matthew and Luke, who followed him, kept in the same place.

The point we must keep in mind is that for the evangelists Jesus' activity did not end with the crucifixion. Therefore, it did not matter whether an event occurred before or after the crucifixion. They were all events in Jesus' continuing relationship with his followers, and the evangelists placed them in their gospels wherever they thought that they best illustrated the meaning of the good news.

NOTE ON THE TITLE 'SON OF GOD'

In Hebrew to call someone 'a son of (something)' meant that he had that characteristic. (In Mark, James and John are called sons of thunder, Mark 3:17.) The title 'Son of God' indicates that Jesus had the characteristics of God, he was like God. Jesus does not refer to himself by this title.

In the Old Testament the title was given to the people of Israel and to their kings, and it meant that they were chosen by God for the special task of upholding his covenant and so showing the world what God was like. It did not imply a father-son relationship in a human sense. In Luke, however, the title is extended to mean son in an almost human sense (1:35-36). The birth of Jesus is the result of God's creative act by means of the Holy Spirit and the virgin birth. It therefore parallels the creation of Adam who is called 'son of God' (3:38).

The voice from heaven (i.e. the voice of God) at the baptism and the Transfiguration of Jesus calls him 'my Son'. This is probably intended as an echo of the words of Psalm 2:7 which were spoken at the coronation of an Israelite king, at which time God adopted the king as his son. Jesus is Son of God in a deeper sense than this, but the use of these words identifies Jesus as the Messiah whose task is to bring salvation to mankind. It was quite possible to be called Son of God without being the Messiah, so Luke wished to emphasise that both titles applied to Jesus in a unique way.

References: 1:32, 35; 3:22; 3:38 (of Adam); 4:3, 9, 41; 8:28; 9:35; 22:70.

E. THE EXPANSION OF THE CHURCH: THE MISSION OF THE SEVENTY (10:1-20)

Why does Luke's gospel contain accounts of both the mission of the Twelve and the mission of the seventy? Matthew and Mark only mention the mission of the Twelve. Why should Luke be interested in this second and larger mission?

The answer lies in his interest in the Gentile church. The whole of Luke's second book, the Acts of the Apostles, is concerned with how the gospel was taken to the Gentiles.

When we examine the number symbolism in the mission of the seventy we find that the message is that the gospel of Jesus is to be offered to the whole world. It is the number seventy which gives us the clue. According to the Jewish interpretation of Genesis 10 there were seventy[8] nations in the world. In sending out seventy disciples Jesus was saying quite clearly that his gospel was for all nations. Just as the Twelve symbolised a new Israel, so the seventy make it clear that membership of this new Israel is not limited to those who were members of one of the twelve tribes of the old Israel. The mission of the seventy makes it plain that the early church was quite right to offer the gospel to the Gentiles. It was what Jesus had intended. (There had been arguments in the early church about whether this was the right course to follow.)

The seventy are to perform the same tasks as the Twelve: to heal the sick and preach the gospel in this case emphasising the nearness of the kingdom.

In Luke's account of this mission there are three sayings of Jesus which give more instructions for missionaries.

---

[8] Or seventy-two: there was disagreement about numbers which modern translations still reflect. The New English Bible speaks of the mission of the seventy-two. Both Matthew and Mark contain accounts of two feedings, of five thousand and of four thousand people. Luke contains only the feeding of the five thousand. When we examine the symbolism in the feeding of the four thousand we find that the message is the same as that of the mission of the seventy. It is, that the gospel is for the whole world. Luke has dropped the feeding of the four thousand (which was in his source, Mark) and replaced it by the mission of the seventy, which makes the same point but in a way that is more appropriate to his interest in the Gentile mission.

1. When they enter a house they are to offer a greeting of peace. (In some present-day churches there is the exchange of peace at, or during, the Communion service.) Peace was the message which the angels brought to the shepherds at the time of Jesus' birth. It was for those on whom God's favour rested (2:14). If there is such a person there they are to stay, but if not the greeting will return to the missionary (10:5-7).

2. When a town makes them welcome they are to heal the sick and say that the kingdom of God has come close. This appears to echo Jesus' saying at 11:20 that when he drives out devils by the finger of God then the kingdom of God has come upon the person healed (10:8-9).

3. When a town does not make the missionaries welcome, they are to do as the Twelve were told to do and shake off the dust from their feet. This time the meaning is made very clear. The town has rejected the kingdom and at Judgment Day will suffer as a result (10:10-15).

The final words of Jesus in sending out the seventy make their importance clear and sum up the belief of Luke and his church. To reject the church's mission is to reject Jesus himself, and to reject Jesus is to reject God (10:16). There is no hope for those who do that.

The towns which will be condemned on the Day of Judgment, Chorazin, Bethsaida and Capernaum (10:13-15) are Jewish. They are condemned for failing to repent after seeing the miracles which were performed in them. The miracles are signs pointing to Jesus' identity (as Messiah), and to the nature of the power which works through the seventy (God's power). Tyre and Sidon are picked out as towns which will suffer less and they are Gentile towns.

Later in the gospel, at 22:28-30, the status of the Twelve (to be exact, eleven of the Twelve since Judas has gone to betray Jesus) is confirmed. They are to feast at the Messianic banquet in the kingdom and to sit as judges.

There is no possibility of doubt: Jesus' followers are the true people of God.

There are two warnings in the gospel to missionaries about the opposition they will face. The first, at 10:3, contains the striking image of lambs being sent among wolves. But the Seventy return jubilant. It is as though, until Jesus has completed his mission, the opposition can do nothing. (Remember the devil biding his time, 4:13.) The fall of Satan, 10:18, is a symbolic way of picturing the defeat of evil. Jesus' mission and the mission of the seventy give a foretaste of the final defeat which will take place at the time of judgment. Hence the jubilation of the seventy, 10:17.

The second warning comes immediately before Jesus' arrest, at 22:35-38. Jesus makes it clear that his followers will, from then onward, face violent opposition, just as he is about to. He, perhaps mockingly, suggests that the disciples should arm themselves. When they produce two swords Jesus' comment is, "Enough, enough." Faith in God is what is required. He demonstrates this by preparing for his arrest and crucifixion by prayer. When one of the swords is used, Jesus heals the victim (22:50f.) and goes with his enemies in obedience to God's will: an example to his followers of the sort of faith they should display.

F. MISSION TODAY: CHRISTIANITY AND OTHER RELIGIONS

The majority of the population of the world is not Christian. Does this mean that God has so arranged things that most of humanity will not find salvation? Are all other religions really inferior to Christianity? Has there been only one revelation of God, that of Jesus? Has God shown himself to other people at other times and in other forms?

You will find Christians who will answer yes to these questions and others who will say no. What is new in our century is that the questions cannot be ignored. This is because we live in a *pluralist* society. This is a society in which people who follow many different religions live side by side. Your neighbour is quite likely to be of a different religion from yours, or to be a Humanist or an atheist

Exchange of peace at Eucharist. In some churches the peace is a handshake, in others a kiss on the cheek.

- or perhaps you are the non-religious one. Whatever the case may be, we have to accept that Hindus, Muslims, Jews, Humanists and the followers of all other religions believe as strongly in their religion as do Christians in theirs.

So how are Christians today to view other religions?

The Roman Catholic church set out its views at the Second Vatican Council (usually known as Vatican II). The Council declared that all men were created by God, belonged to a single human community and that the aim of man was to reach God. It recognised that people were seeking God through different religions and that truths about God could be found in them; but *complete truth could be found only in Christianity*. Vatican II ruled out all discrimination on the grounds of race, colour, class or creed (religion), because all men were created in the image of God and discrimination was not compatible with Christ's aim of reuniting all mankind with God.

This is the *official* view of *one* church. Other churches have different views, and the followers of other religions certainly do not agree that complete religious truth is found only in Christianity.

How does this situation affect Christian mission today? The easiest way to understand how the work of present-day missionaries has been affected is to compare their activities with those of missionaries in the past.

In the eighteenth and nineteenth centuries almost all Europeans regarded all other religions as inferior to Christianity and their followers were looked upon as having only a childlike understanding of spiritual matters. When European countries were building empires in Africa and Asia, it was common for their merchants and armies to be followed by missionaries. It was seen as a Christian duty to 'civilise' other people by making them Christian.

Today most missionary activity takes place in Third World countries. But the contrast with the past is so great that missionaries of a century ago would hardly recognise it as a continuation of their work. Before going overseas most missionaries today would study the language, culture and religion of the people they were going to. They would go first to offer help in hospitals, in schools and on development projects. Mostly, they have to hope and pray that their example of Christian discipleship will lead those they help to ask for information about Jesus. If they are not asked, they do not turn away and shake the dust off their feet. Neither do they look upon those they help as spiritually inferior. The situation has changed since a century ago and changed even more since the time of Luke. As a result the rules which guide missionary activity have also changed.

We should not think of missionary work as being something that happens only in other countries. There are large numbers of people in this country who were baptised as Christians but do not practise their religion. Most churches carry on some form of mission which aims to bring these people back into the Christian family. There are also missions to non-Christians and missions which aim to encourage Christians themselves to be more active in spreading the gospel. Just as churches send missionaries overseas, so they also send workers into the most deprived areas of this country. The people living in such areas are as much outcasts from mainstream society as were those who were considered sinners at the time of Jesus. Part of the modern-day church's mission is to help such people and to spread the gospel whenever the opportunity arises.

Missionary in Ethiopia. Christian missionaries do not always face hostility from those they try to serve. The evil they face is often that of innocent suffering in a world which could prevent it.

The question, therefore, remains as relevant in today's world as it has ever been: How should Christians go about spreading the gospel?

Questions for chapter 7

4:14-30

1a. How does Luke tell us that Jesus is acting with God's authority?

b. From the book of which prophet does Jesus read?

c. What is the message of the prophecy?

d. Why does the mention of Elijah and Elisha anger the congregation?

e. How do the events in this passage relate to Jesus' mission?

f. Why would the way the people of Nazareth treated Jesus be of particular interest to the Gentile church?

5:1-11

2a. On which lake does this incident take place?

b. Whose boat does Jesus get into?

c. What other name is usually used for 'Simon'?

d. What does Simon say when he sees the size of the catch of fish?

e. What did the call of Simon have to teach about a person's response to Jesus?

f. What is the connection between this incident and the work of the early church?

6:12-16

3a. What does Jesus do before calling the Twelve?

b. List the disciples who make up the Twelve.

c. What does the word 'apostle' mean?

d. What is the significance of the number twelve?

9:1-6

4a. What tasks does Jesus give the Twelve?

b. What are the Twelve told to leave behind when they go on their journey?

c. How are the Twelve to behave i) when admitted to a house, ii) when not received?

d. What is Luke's message for the missionaries of his own church?

9:28-36

5a. Who accompanies Jesus into the hills?

b. What is Jesus doing when the appearance of his face and clothes change?

c. With whom does Jesus talk?

d. What does the voice from the cloud say?

6a. What is the connection between the Transfiguration and the kingdom of God?

b. What do Moses and Elijah represent?

c. Explain the importance to Luke's church of the words spoken by the voice from the cloud.

d. How does the Transfiguration link the baptism with the resurrection of Jesus?

7a. Compare Mark 9:2-13 with Luke 9:28-36. What differences are there in the two accounts?

b. What significance do you see in the changes Luke has made to Mark's account?

10:1-20

8a. What instructions does Jesus give the seventy (-two) about how they should equip themselves for the journey?

b. How are the seventy (-two) to behave

i) when admitted to a house,

ii) when a town does not welcome them?

c. Why would the number seventy (-two) be important to Gentiles?

d. What was the result of the mission?

e. Why did Jesus say that the seventy (-two) should rejoice?

9a. What is significant about the towns most strongly condemned by Jesus? (10:13 & 15)

b.. How should missionaries react to opposition (10:1-11; 22:35-38)? Does Jesus contradict himself?

10a. What is the Roman Catholic view of the relationship between Christianity and other religions?

b. Do you think that Christian missionaries should try to convert non-Christians or just provide an example of Christian caring? Give reasons for your answer.

11. " . . . the order of events has been decided on by the evangelists themselves" (p.63).

Do you agree with this statement? Give reasons for your answer.

8
THE DISCIPLES AND DISCIPLESHIP

When we look at how Luke portrays the disciples we must remember that he regarded them as the first members of the church. But that does not mean that he saw them as people who were perfect. Luke had Mark's account of the disciples in front of him and that showed people who continually failed Jesus.

When Luke came to write he made Mark's picture of the disciples less harsh, but he did not idealise them. What he seems to have wanted to say was, here are the first members of the church, they are people like you and me, and like us they have faults. They are typical members of Christ's church. (Compare Mark 4:38-40 with Luke 8:23-25; Mark 8:31-33 with Luke 9:21-23.)

A. HOW LUKE PORTRAYS THE DISCIPLES

i) Luke's portrayal of Peter
(5:1-11; 9:20f; 22:31-34; 22:54-62)

Luke's portrayal of Peter is two-sided. He is shown as someone who has faith in Jesus and at the same time as a sinner. This twofold presentation is first revealed at the time of Peter's call (5:1-11). He has fished all night but at word from Jesus will again put down his nets: "Master . . . if you say so I will let down the nets": faith. When he is confronted with the catch of fish he cries: "Go, Lord, leave me sinner that I am": he realises his sinful nature.

Symbol for Simon Peter

Luke seems to be saying to his readers: Here is the man Jesus chose to be head of the church. He is typical of all Christians. He recognises who Jesus is, 'God's Messiah'(9:20), yet he is a sinful man capable of failing Jesus even though he has faith in him. He denies Jesus three times (22:54-62), even after saying that he was ready to go with Jesus to prison or death (22:33), and in the last moments before Jesus' arrest he, like the rest of the disciples, falls asleep while Jesus prays (22:39-46).

There is another, and even more important, lesson for Luke's readers to learn from his portrayal of Peter. It is that what is required for salvation is faith in Jesus. Nothing more. It does not matter that, like Peter, people fail to live up to what they believe. As long as they have faith they will be forgiven. Peter's faith never wavers, even though he is weak, and after the crucifixion and resurrection Jesus appears to him: Peter's denial of Jesus has been forgiven (24:34).

Luke keeps to the tradition of Peter failing Jesus, but he modifies Mark's portrayal of Peter. Peter makes the great confession (Mark 8:29; Luke 9:20). In both gospels, as soon as he is called 'Messiah', Jesus takes up the title 'Son of Man' and begins to teach about suffering. Mark says, "Peter took him [Jesus] by the arm and began to rebuke him" (Mark 8:32); and Jesus responded by saying to Peter "away with you, Satan"

(Mark 8:33). In Luke's account there is no mention of Peter's protest or Jesus' rebuke. Peter does not understand about the Son of Man having to suffer (Luke 9:44-45), but he has sufficient faith in Jesus to accept what he says without protest.

This is an example of Luke softening the harshness of Mark's presentation of the disciples; not only out of respect for the founders of the church but for his own purposes. Luke wants to emphasise that one should be faithful even when one does not understand.

When news of the empty tomb is brought to the Eleven (24:12), Peter appears to show greater faith than the others.

A Christian mission school in Bolivia. Serving others can take many forms, and much missionary work is routine and undramatic.

ii) Luke's portrayal of James and John (9:49-50; 9:51-56)

Luke portrays James and John as disciples who have not fully understood and accepted Jesus' teaching. They are emotional followers of Jesus but they do not pay attention to what he says. Mark tells us they were called "Boanerges" (Mark 3:17), which means 'sons of thunder', and in Luke's presentation of them it appears to be a good name. They are so busy protesting noisily on Jesus' behalf (or so they appear to believe) that they do not take the time to listen to him properly.

Luke gives two examples of their behaviour. In the first, 9:49-50, John reports to Jesus that the disciples have tried to stop a man, who was not one of them, casting out devils in Jesus' name. Jesus tells John, "Do not stop him, for he who is not against you is on your side."

John appears to be jealously possessive of Jesus. In his view only those who were apostles (i.e. sent out on the missions) should heal in the name of Jesus. John's idea is like that of the Jews. Only those chosen by God could be his people. But Jesus has been teaching that anyone who has the faith to see who he is can become members of the new people of God simply by following him. So the man driving out devils in Jesus' name is defeating evil and doing God's work. He is a true follower of Jesus and should not be stopped.

The other incident which shows James as well as John lacking understanding is at 9:51-56. Jesus and the disciples are travelling through Samaria on their way to Jerusalem. A Samaritan village refuses to accept them. James and John respond not by shaking the dust of the village off their feet as Jesus had taught (9:5, and as Luke shows him repeating immediately after this incident, 10:10-12), but by wanting to call down fire from heaven to burn up the villagers.

Here again James and John seem to be unable to leave behind their Jewish background. This time their suggestion seems to reflect an event in the Old Testament when Elijah the prophet called down fire on the messengers of a king who had turned to a foreign god (2 Kings 1:1-16).

James and John by their demand ignore a whole range of Jesus' teaching. They do not show love to their enemies, 6:27; they pass judgment when they should not, 6:37; they call Jesus 'Lord' but do not do what he says, 6:46; and they forget that the prophets and the ways of the Old Testament have been replaced by Jesus, 9:28-36.

By presenting James and John in this way Luke is teaching his church that it is not enough just to belong to the church. They must also follow Jesus' teaching and welcome everyone who will do the same into the Christian family. We should remember that, in spite of their faults, James and John are members of the inner circle of disciples privileged to be with Jesus at important moments. (See 8:51-56; 9:28-36.)

The way Luke portrays James and John was probably influenced by the people he was writing for. In Acts of the Apostles references are made to 'Gentile worshippers' (e.g. Acts 13:43). These were Gentiles who admired Judaism and attended the synagogues of the Dispersion without becoming full Jews. They would be familiar with the Old Testament and Luke's references to it would have meaning for them. Many of these people became Christians, as did numbers of Jews, and both groups probably contained people who found it hard to let go of old ideas.

Some Christians were no doubt jealous of Jesus in the Old Testament sense. To be a jealous God meant that God demanded his rights (e.g. Exod. 20:5). When the Samaritan villagers refuse Jesus they are refusing God the right he has of worship from all humanity. Jesus rejects the type of attitude displayed by James and John. He offers salvation; he does not *demand* that anyone follow him. It is up to the individual to accept or reject - and it is not for members of the church to judge and to try to punish those who reject.

The fact that it is a Samaritan village which rejects Jesus and that he refuses to condemn it, probably reflects Luke's interest in the mission to Samaria. (See also: 10:29-37; 17:11-19.)

The incident at 9:49-50 seems to mirror an event in the Old Testament. At Numbers 11:24-30 the spirit of God descends on two people who had not been members with Moses of the seventy who had shared in the giving of God's spirit. A protest is made that these two should not be allowed to prophesy. Moses rejects it saying that he wished that all the Lord's people were prophets. Perhaps Luke is pointing forward to the time when everyone will do God's will and work to defeat evil in Jesus' name.

In spite of the poor picture Luke draws of James and John, it is still not as harsh as that drawn by Mark. In Mark 10:35-37 James and John ask Jesus to let them have seats of honour in the kingdom. Luke does not mention James and John when he recounts this incident, preferring to present it as a reward for faithfulness open to all the disciples. Again, Luke has softened Mark's portrayal of the disciples in order to emphasise the point he wishes to make: salvation is for everyone who is willing to follow Jesus.

B. WHAT IT MEANS TO BE A DISCIPLE

(i) Following Jesus (9:18-20)

The first thing that the disciple of Jesus does is to confess Jesus as Messiah. This is the fundamental belief which leads someone to follow Jesus and it is the belief which made Christianity into a separate religion rather than a part of Judaism.

This difference is emphasised by the way in which Luke leads up to Peter's confession. Jesus asks the disciples "Who do people say I am?" The answer they give is the one given by 'the people' i.e.

Christian service. Many Christians provide care, comfort and security for old people

the Jews, and previously by Herod (9:7-8). "Some say John the Baptist, others Elijah, others that one of the old prophets has come back to life" (9:19).

Jesus then asks the disciples for their answer to the question, and Peter answers for the disciples and for all future generations of Christians: "God's Messiah" (9:20).

Why are the disciples, at this point in the gospel, shown as recognising Jesus as Messiah? By his ordering of material, Luke suggests that the feeding of the five thousand (9:10-17) was the final event which revealed to the disciples Jesus' true identity. It was seen by Luke as a messianic banquet, such as would be given in the kingdom of God.

Peter's confession comes immediately after this event. To make the confession follow it Luke has made what is called the 'Great Omission'. That is, he

has left out all the material found in Mark 6:45-8:26. The same connection of events is made in John 6:1-15, where, in addition, it is said that the people wished to make Jesus king. Possibly there was a tradition linking the two events which Mark did not know about.

Immediately after Peter's confession Jesus teaches the disciples about the sort of Messiah he is to be: a suffering, serving, Son of Man; not a king such as nationalist Jews hoped for.

14:7-11, 22:24-27 What does it mean for the disciples of Jesus to confess him Messiah? To be a disciple is to follow a teacher and to try to become like him. For the disciples of Jesus it is to live in 'imitation of Christ' (see chapter 10, theme III, section (c)).

Luke makes it abundantly clear what imitating Christ involves. In the parable of the Wedding Feast Jesus teaches that the way to achieve a worthwhile reward (i.e. entry into the kingdom of God) is by humility not arrogance. Jesus repeats this message immediately after the Last Supper. This is at the end of his mission and on this occasion Luke shows him speaking plainly not in parables: "the highest among you must bear himself like the youngest, the chief of you like a servant" (22:26). The reward for those who act like this, in imitation of Christ, will be places of honour in the kingdom (22:30).

(ii) The disciple's choice (5:11, 27-28; 12:49-53; 14:25-35; 18:28-30)

There is an immediate demand made of anyone who becomes a disciple: he must leave *everything*. The disciple can follow Jesus or pursue wealth - but he cannot do both. Peter, James and John left everything and followed Jesus (5:11); Levi did the same (5:28). They chose discipleship.

The choice is even greater than simply between Jesus and possessions. It might be between Jesus and a person's family (12:52). Jesus has come to announce that judgment is coming and that only those who follow him will be saved. So there is no point in choosing one's family if they reject Jesus. They will be judged and condemned. Only those who choose Jesus will live in the kingdom of God (12:49-53).

Like many early Christians, Luke's readers must have found themselves facing a choice between their family and the new religion in which they had come to believe. Not every member of a family left his pagan ways and converted to Christianity at the same time, so those who did needed guidance. How should they choose - family or Jesus? Luke shows Jesus giving the answer. Jesus and the kingdom of God must come before possessions, family or self. The disciple who chooses Jesus will be repaid many times over (18:28-30).

In English, verse 14:26 reads: "If anyone comes to me and does not hate his father and mother...he cannot be a disciple of mine". It sounds odd to hear Jesus demanding that people should hate others. In the original Aramaic the word 'hate' meant 'to love less' and 'to abandon'. The demand is, therefore, to put Jesus first.

Verse 12:51 also sounds odd at first reading. Jesus says he has not come to bring peace but division. What Jesus is talking about is explained at 12:49-50.

He is to suffer persecution and so will his disciples. The baptism he speaks of represents suffering and death (See Ps. 124:4-8). Those who follow Jesus must expect the same, even at the hands of those closest to them. The peace which Jesus has brought is only present when the kingdom of God is present in Jesus (e.g. 7:50; 8:48). In this world, which is ruled by the forces of evil, there can be no peace for God's people until evil is defeated.

(iii) What is needed is faith not wealth (12:22-34)

One thing which is demanded of the disciples is complete faith in God. This means not worrying about where their next meal is coming from, or how they are to afford clothes (12:23). True disciples must stop worrying about such things and trust in God to provide for them. This is a difficult thing to do; it is opposite to the way people normally behave. The disciples must let go of all their everyday anxieties and set their minds on the kingdom of God (12:31), and have faith in God to meet their needs.

Immediately before this teaching, which is addressed particularly to the disciples, Luke places the parable of the Rich Fool (12:16-21). This teaches about the uselessness of wealth. Now Jesus goes on to tell his disciples to 'sell your possessions and give in charity' (12:33). The only treasure worth having is in the kingdom and the only way there is through faith in God. By worrying about the things of this world one chains oneself to them. Faith and reliance on God are the way to break these chains.

In Acts 2:44-45 and 4:32-35 Luke shows members of the early church following Jesus' instructions to sell their possessions. Luke is always concerned to teach his readers how they should live. He also aims to make clear the rewards of living in this way (12:32). The precise meaning of 12:25 is not clear. It may mean either that you cannot make yourself any taller by worrying, or that you cannot make yourself live longer. In either case the message is that anxiety accomplishes nothing: only faith in God is of any value.

(iv) The privileges and cost of discipleship (9:23-27; 10:23-24; 12:1-12, 35-48; 17:1-10, 20-30)

The disciples of Jesus have to face the possibility that at some time they may suffer for their discipleship. Jesus makes this point when he says, "If anyone wishes to be a follower of mine . . . day after day he must take up his cross" (9:23). The same point is made in 12:1-12: anyone who follows Jesus runs the risk of being killed - just as Jesus was - by the religious and political authorities of the world.

Luke makes it clear that Jesus taught that the risk was worth taking. The authorities in this world could only kill the body; they could not condemn anyone to hell - only God could do that (12:4-5). So the disciple who realised that what was important was eternal life in the kingdom of God would willingly risk losing his life in this world. If he remained faithful to Jesus, then Jesus would save him by speaking on his behalf when he was judged (9:26; 12:8-9).

Although it sounded contradictory, to take up one's cross was the only sensible course to follow. Luke emphasises that the true disciple had to do this *daily*: to follow Jesus had to be a constantly renewed decision. Discipleship could not be habit. It required a deliberate effort to forget about oneself, to ignore one's desires for the things of this world, to conquer one's fears and to follow Jesus.

Jesus' disciples are promised the reward of salvation. But they should not follow Jesus simply for the reward. They should do what Jesus teaches because that is God's wish and it is their duty to obey God. This is the message of the parable of the Servant's Reward (17:7-10). The way of the disciple is humility and service, not an arrogant expectation of glory. (See 14:7-11.)

Jesus preached that the kingdom of God was coming but he never said exactly when. The result was that people wanted to know how they could tell when the time was near (17:20-21). Jesus refused to answer in the way they wanted. It was up to those who heard him to recognise that when Jesus was present then so was the kingdom of God (11:20). They had to have faith to recognise who he was and what his actions meant (12:54-56).

Jesus taught his disciples to be ready at all times for the coming of the kingdom. In the parables of The Burglar and The Man Appointed Steward (12:35-48) Jesus teaches that those who faithfully follow his teaching while they wait for the kingdom will be rewarded.

Luke's source for 9:23 is Mark 8:34. Luke has made one crucial change to Mark by inserting the words 'day after day' into the verse. The disciple is to take up his cross day after day. Luke probably made the change to alter Mark's emphasis on martyrdom. Although the threat of martyrdom existed for Christians for many years after Luke lived, Luke wanted to extend the idea of dying for Christ to mean a dying to the things of this world. So taking up one's cross became a daily activity or an attitude one carried with one permanently.

Luke also alters Mark's emphasis in the prophecy about the coming of the kingdom. (See Luke 9:27 and Mark 9:1.) Mark says: 'there are some of those standing here who will not taste death before they have seen the kingdom of God already come in power'. Luke misses out the phrase 'already come in power' which refers to the establishment of the kingdom in this world. (See Mark 13:26-27 and 14:62 for an idea of how it was thought this was to happen.)

We have to remember that Luke wrote some twenty years after Mark. By his time Christians must have been wondering how much longer it would be before the kingdom would be established. The first generation of Christians had expected this to happen very soon. When Luke came to write his gospel the disciples who had known Jesus during his ministry must nearly all have been dead. So Luke makes sense of Jesus' words by making it possible for them to refer to a seeing of the kingdom other than in power. At 10:23-24 and 11:20 Luke makes it clear that the kingdom is present in Jesus, and what it is like in the kingdom can be seen in the effects of his actions.

Therefore, those who were able to recognise what Jesus' signs meant could indeed see the kingdom.

C. OTHER FOLLOWERS OF JESUS

(i) The women (8:1-3; 10:38-42)

In Luke's gospel women play a more prominent role than in Matthew or Mark. Three who travelled with Jesus and the Twelve are mentioned by name: Mary of Magdala, Joanna the wife of Chuza, and Susanna. There were many others and "these women provided for them out of their own resources" (8:1-3). Two of them, Mary of Magdala and Susanna, are witnesses to the resurrection (23:49-24:11).

The women have been healed by Jesus. Mary of Magdala (Magdala is a town in Galilee) has had seven devils driven out of her. The number means that she suffered from the worst possible state of demonic possession, and it probably indicates some sort of mental disorder. They provide an example of how those healed by Jesus should behave, and how members of the church should also behave.

They give their wealth to support Jesus and the Twelve. Their example is in contrast to the fate which befalls someone who is healed by Jesus but does not change his way of life: his condition in the end is even worse than before he was healed. (See 11:24-26.)

Immediately before the mention of these women Luke places the story of the woman forgiven her sins (7:36-50)[9]. She weeps with gratitude and anoints Jesus' feet with oil. She is another perfect example of how to respond to the salvation Jesus offers.

The reactions to Jesus of the sisters Mary and Martha are also recorded by Luke. Mary provides an image of the perfect disciple who sits at Jesus' feet and listens to his teaching. Martha, in contrast, is an example of the disciple who is distracted by worldly cares. Jesus rebukes her, but gently: "Martha, Martha, you are fretting and fussing about so many things; but one thing is necessary" (10:41). That is, to listen to Jesus' words.

In his description of the role of women in the ministry of Jesus, Luke appears to be setting out a role for women in the church. That role was not the same as the one played by women in Judaism at the time of Jesus. When Mary sits at Jesus' feet to learn, she is doing something which Jewish teachers generally opposed; the study of the Law was considered to be the work of men. In encouraging Mary, Jesus is saying that the word of God is the concern equally of both men and women.

The story of the rebuke which Jesus gave to Martha was probably used in the early church to teach how missionaries should be received. Hospitality should be offered but it should not be extravagant. What was important was the message the missionary brought, not the man himself.

Only Luke tells us anything about Joanna, the wife of Chuza a steward of Herod, and Susanna. Possibly they were known to Luke's church, and the former may have been the source of Luke's information about Herod (this is Herod Antipas who ruled Galilee and Peraea). The mention of Joanna and Chuza tells us that Jesus had followers in the aristocratic circles of Herod's court.

---

[9] The traditional view has been that this woman was Mary of Magdala but there is no evidence in the gospels or elsewhere to support it.

(ii) Zacchaeus (19:1-10)

The story of Zacchaeus sums up the ministry of Jesus. Although Zacchaeus is eager to see Jesus and climbs a tree in order to be able to, it is Jesus himself who takes the initiative in saying, "I *must* come to stay with you today" (19:5).

Zacchaeus is a tax-gatherer, a sinner, one of the "lost sheep of the house of Israel" (Matt. 10:6). Jesus' mission is to such people, regardless of the attitude of respectable Jews whose reaction is noted in 19:7. Jesus has come to offer salvation and the only way to obtain it, even for Jews such as Zacchaeus, is through him.

Zacchaeus' response to the offer is an example of the sort of immediate repentance required of a disciple. He gives half of his possessions to charity. This is far more than the one-fifth normally suggested by rabbis. In addition, the promise to repay four times over any money he had unjustly acquired was far more than that required by the Law (Lev. 6:5). Roman law required the amount taken to be repaid four times over, so Zacchaeus imposes on himself the harsher penalty.

The sayings in 19: 9- 10 summarise the mission of Jesus and its result. The Son of Man came to seek and save the lost, and salvation came to Zacchaeus' house because he accepted Jesus. Zacchaeus demonstrates how the old Israel should have accepted Jesus and become part of the new people of God. By calling Zacchaeus 'a son of Abraham' his Jewishness is emphasised, since Abraham was regarded as the father of the Jewish people.

NOTE ON TAX-GATHERERS

Tax-gatherers were outcasts from Jewish society. They were regarded as sinners by devout Jews because they worked for the Roman authorities.

The Romans were Gentiles, and tax-gatherers often had to mix with them and even eat with them. This meant they could not live according to the Law. Anyone who broke God's Law was automatically a sinner. Tax-gatherers were also unpopular with ordinary Jews because they often took more in taxes than they were supposed to. (See 3:12-13.)

(iii) Would-be followers of Jesus (9:57-62)

The three brief incidents which make up these verses show how demanding real discipleship is.

Verses 57-8 illustrate the sacrifice anyone who wants to follow Jesus on his journey must make. He will have no home until he reaches the kingdom. Luke perhaps saw this as a lesson for the missionaries of his day. The words 'foxes' and 'birds' were both used to refer to Gentiles, so the meaning seems to be that everyone in the world has some home, but the Son of Man (and his followers) has no home except the kingdom where he will reign.

Verses 59-60 repeat the demand to put Jesus before family. The dead who are to do the burying are those who do not recognise Jesus as offering everlasting life. They are as good as dead already, and it is appropriate to leave them to bury their fellows.

Verses 61-2 seem to echo 1 Kings 19:19-20. In that passage Elijah summons Elisha to follow him. Elisha first goes home to kiss his father and mother. By contrast, the call of Jesus is more demanding. The ways of the Old Testament are past. There is to be no hesitation, no looking back to one's former life. Fitness for the kingdom demands immediate, total commitment.

D. DISCIPLESHIP TODAY

Are the teachings about discipleship and the pictures of the disciples found in Luke still relevant to Christians today?

Certainly Luke's portrait of Peter would appear to be for all time. Almost anyone who has an ideal fails to live up to it at some time in his life, and the image of Peter failing, but being forgiven, is one to give hope to every generation of Christians. The figures of James and John must also be familiar to every generation. They represent the 'Old Testament' style of Christian: fierce in defence of Jesus but less zealous in applying his teaching to themselves. Christians can still learn from these disciples: they are mirrors for all time.

Every Christian must start by confessing Jesus Messiah, but are the consequences of doing that today the same as in Luke's day? Do many people still face the choice - Jesus or family? Probably not so frequently today, especially in countries with a long Christian tradition. However, society is becoming increasingly secular and the possibility of rejection by one's family or total lack of understanding by much of society are possibilities that people who take their Christianity seriously have to face. There is generally less danger in being a Christian today than there was for the early Christians, but we should not forget that in some countries Christianity is still seen by governments as a threat and, consequently, Christians in these countries take up their cross in a very real way.

Luke's concern about wealth is probably the one which is most relevant today. Is a Christian expected to sell everything and give the money to charity? Did Luke intend that everyone should do this? The teaching of Jesus which Luke gives does not make things absolutely clear. Certainly, if anyone was going to follow Jesus and proclaim the kingdom, it was expected. But not all Jesus' disciples seem to have given up normal life. Mary and Martha have a house and are not told to sell it. There seem to be two classes of followers: those who become preachers of the gospel full-time and those who support them in their work.

This reflects today's situation. There are ministers, missionaries, nuns and all the people who, in various ways, seek to dedicate their lives wholly to Jesus. Then there is the vast majority of Christians who live in the mainstream of society and are subjected constantly to pressures to conform to values which may not be Christian ones. Trying both to be a Christian and to live in a society which frequently measures success in material terms pulls Christians in two opposite directions. Luke's demand that Christians take up their cross *daily* seems especially relevant to them.

How does one take up one's cross in today's world? Luke provides some of the answers. First, Christians must not be ashamed of (i.e. deny) their beliefs. That is not easy when most of the people they meet may be indifferent or hostile. They must resist the social pressure to hide their beliefs and to conform.

Secondly, they can give to charity. This should be more than a token contribution. When giving Christians should ask themselves which comes first, their own comfort or the needs of those the charities help. Unless they give all they can afford, are they really taking up their cross day after day?

Thirdly, like the women in Luke, they can support the church out of their resources. This should mean more than the local church since the activities are worldwide. By these means the majority of Christians can help to bring about the kingdom in their own lives and throughout the world.

Luke's picture of Mary sitting at Jesus' feet raises another difficulty which many Christians face. What is the role of women in the church? There is no agreed answer from the different denominations. The Roman Catholic and Orthodox churches will not allow women to become priests, while *most* Protestant churches are happy to have women ministers.

A question some people ask is: did Jesus call only men to be members of the Twelve because he intended only men to be priests? We have to be careful not to jump to conclusions. The Twelve were not priests but founder members of the new people of God. We have to remember too that, at the time of Jesus, Jewish society would not accept women in positions of religious authority. There were no female doctors of the Law or priestesses in the Temple. But in praising Mary for listening to his words Jesus is shown to change the role of women.

Exactly what the female disciple of Jesus should do today cannot be decided by referring to Luke's gospel alone. The rest of the New Testament must be considered, and so must the attitudes of the society in which Jesus lived and the one in which we live today.

In different ways, true discipleship today is just as difficult as it was for the members of Luke's church, and the questions he raised are still ones which concern us today.

NOTES ON THE TWELVE (6:12-16)

Simon Peter

In Luke's gospel Simon Peter is the first of the disciples to be called (5:11), the first on the list of the Twelve and the one who identifies Jesus as the Christ (9:20). He is the spokesman and leader of the Twelve (18:28-30) and after Jesus' crucifixion he appears as leader of the church (Acts 1:15).

He had a house in Capernaum (4:38) and a mother-in-law. There is no mention of a wife, though presumably he had one or was a widower. (Note that at 18:29 Jesus, in answering Peter, mentions 'wife' in the list of things given up by his followers - though *not* specifically Peter's wife.) He was a fisherman and worked with James and John. These three are the disciples closest to Jesus and witness the healing of Jairus' daughter (8:51) and the Transfiguration (9:28).

Luke, like Mark, mentions that Jesus gave Simon the name Peter but does not explain why.

Matthew tells us that Peter (the name means rock) was to be the rock on which Jesus would build his church (Matt. 16:18-19). However, his character is not very rock-like and, when danger threatened, he denied Jesus three times (22:54-60). It is possible that Luke means us to understand that it was to Peter that Jesus first appeared after his resurrection (24:34). (See also 1 Cor. 15:3-5: Cephas is Peter.)

According to tradition, Peter died in Rome in the persecution of Christians by the Emperor Nero in about AD 64.

NB: In this book we usually use the name 'Peter' for Simon Peter. You will notice that Luke also calls him Peter most of the time. When he changes to 'Simon' this probably indicates that there has been a change in the source from which the incident was originally taken.

Andrew

Although Andrew was Simon Peter's brother and is placed second in Luke's list of the Twelve, he receives only this one mention in the gospel. Luke does not even say that he was a fisherman and called by Jesus at the same time as Peter. (Compare Luke 5:9-11 and Mark 1:16-18.) Andrew is mentioned three times in John's gospel (John 1:40; 6:8; 12:22).

James the son of Zebedee

James and his brother John were fishermen and were called by Jesus at the same time as Peter (5:11). They were, with Peter, the disciples closest to Jesus. (See 8:51; 9:28.) James and John wanted to call down fire upon a Samaritan village (9:54); this might be a clue as to why Jesus, according to Mark, named them "Sons of Thunder" (Mark 3:17).

John the son of Zebedee
(See note about his brother James.) In addition to the times he is mentioned with his brother, John is the spokesman for the disciples when they try to stop a man exorcising in Jesus' name (9:49), and he accompanies Peter to prepare a room for the Last Supper (22:8). It has been suggested that he was the author of John's gospel, but we cannot be sure of this.

Philip
Although Philip is fifth in the list of the Twelve, he is not mentioned elsewhere in Luke's gospel. In John's gospel Philip is said to come from Bethsaida (John 1:44).

Bartholomew
Apart from being mentioned in the list of the Twelve nothing is known about him.

Matthew
The only mention of Matthew in Luke's gospel is in the list of the Twelve. Nothing certain is known about him. In Matthew's gospel (not, as far as we know, written by this Matthew) he is called "the tax-gatherer". Luke describes the call of a tax-gatherer named Levi (5:27). In Matthew's gospel the tax-gatherer in this incident is named Matthew (9:9). This has led some people to suggest that Matthew and Levi are the same person. Luke does not identify the one with the other and we should be cautious about doing so.

Thomas
The only mention of Thomas in Luke's gospel is in the list of the Twelve. In John's gospel Thomas is called "Didymus", meaning 'the twin', but nothing is known about his twin. In the same gospel Thomas is the disciple who refuses to believe that Jesus has risen until he can see and put his finger in the print of the nails and place his hand in Jesus' side (John 20:24-25).

James son of Alphaeus
We learn of James's father in order to distinguish him from James son of Zebedee. He is only mentioned in Luke's gospel in the list of the Twelve. In Mark's gospel the tax-gatherer, Levi, is also called "son of Alphaeus" (Mark 2:14). Whether James and Levi were brothers, or two names for the same person, or totally unconnected, we do not know.

Simon who was called the Zealot
We are told that Simon was called 'the Zealot' in order to distinguish him from Simon Peter. The Zealots were a Jewish nationalist party who wanted to free the country from Roman rule. It is not certain that Simon was a member of this party since the word 'zealot' means 'enthusiast' and it could simply be a description of his temperament. He is only mentioned in the list of the Twelve.

Judas son of James
We learn of Judas' father in order to distinguish him from Judas Iscariot. In the lists of the Twelve in Matthew and Mark there is no such name, instead there is a disciple named Thaddaeus. Whether there is any connection between Judas and Thaddaeus we do not know. He is only mentioned in Luke in the list of the Twelve.

Judas Iscariot
Judas Iscariot is the disciple who betrayed Jesus to the Jewish authorities and was paid for doing so (22:3, 47-48). Matthew tells us that the sum received was thirty pieces of silver and that Judas hanged himself (Matt. 26:15; 27:5). Luke, in Acts of the Apostles, tells us that Judas bought a field with his money, fell down and died horribly (Acts 1:18).

Judas's betrayal is seen in the gospels as part of God's plan. On the level of human motivation, however, it has been suggested that 'Iscariot' meant 'man of Kerioth', which was a town in Judaea. Judas would, therefore, have been a southerner and probably odd man out amongst Galilean disciples, and this might have had some influence on his actions. Another suggestion is that 'Iscariot' came from the word 'sicarius', meaning 'assassin', which referred to a group of dagger-carrying nationalistic Jews who wanted armed rebellion against the Romans. On this basis it has been suggested that when Jesus refused to lead such a rebellion Judas betrayed him to try to force him to do so. Neither of these suggestions can be found in the New Testament and we should be very careful about accepting them.

Questions for chapter 8

1a. Describe the incidents when
  i) Peter confesses that he is a sinner;
  ii) Peter and the disciples do not understand what Jesus teaches;
  iii) Peter denies Jesus three times.
  b. What lesson might Luke want to teach his readers by his portrayal of Peter?
  c. Do you think Peter was a good choice as leader of the Twelve?

9:49-50
2a. What did John and the disciples try to do?
  b. What reply did Jesus give?
  c. Why do you think the disciples wanted to stop the man?
  d. How might this incident be linked to an event in the Old Testament?

9:51-56
3a. How do the Samaritan villagers behave towards Jesus?
  b. What reason is given for refusing Jesus?
  c. What do James and John want to do?
  d. What is Jesus' reaction to their suggestion?
  e. What teachings of Jesus have James and John forgotten?
  f. How might this incident be linked to an event in the Old Testament?
  4. In what ways might Luke's portrait of James and John be a lesson for the members of Luke's own church?

9:18-22
5a. Who did 'the people' say Jesus was?
  b. Who did Peter say Jesus was?
  c. Why does Jesus use the title 'Son of Man' of himself instead of 'Messiah'?
6a. What does the call of Levi (5:28) teach about following Jesus?
  b. What sort of personal sacrifices may followers of Jesus be expected to make?

12:22-34
7a. What does Jesus teach about faith?
  b. Is this teaching still to be followed by Jesus' disciples today?
8a. How could one take up one's cross 'day after day' (9:23)?
  b. Why, do you think, did Luke alter Mark's teaching about taking up one's cross (Mark 8:34)?
  c. How might a Christian today take up his cross?

8:1-3
9a. Name three women who travelled with Jesus and the Twelve.
  b. How did these women help Jesus?
  c. Does the example of these women have anything to teach Christians today?

10:38-42
10a. What did Mary do when Jesus visited the sisters' house?
  b. What did Martha do when Jesus visited the sisters' house?
  c. Why does Martha complain?
  d. What does Jesus say to Martha?
  e. What might Luke have hoped to teach his church through this incident?

19:1-10
11. "The story of Zacchaeus sums up the ministry of Jesus" (p.76). Do you agree? Explain your answer.
12a. Do you think women should be able to become priests in today's church? Give references to support what you say.
  b. Can you suggest what might count as the privileges and the costs of discipleship in today's world?
  c. Are these privileges and costs the same as when Luke wrote?

9
THE MIRACLES OF JESUS

A. INTRODUCTION

No doubt you would think it strange if someone asked when you last saw or experienced a miracle. After all, we live in a world where we do not expect miracles to happen as part of the daily routine. Yet the idea is not strange to us. We all have a good idea of what a miracle is.

There are people today who claim to have had direct experience of miracles. The Bible contains many miracle stories, though miracles are by no means confined to the Bible. They are common in other religions and cultures as well. In fact it would not be an exaggeration to say that the idea of miracles is as old as humankind.

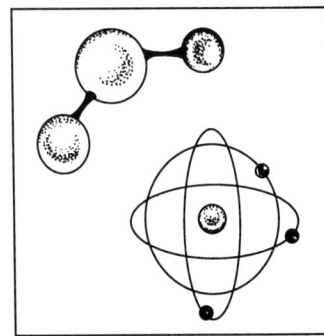

Atoms. Why is it difficult for people today to believe in miracles?

B. MIRACLES AND SCIENCE

Why did Luke find it so easy to believe in miracles, and why do people today find it so difficult? The big difference between the way we think and the way people thought in Luke's day results from the development of science. Science has taught us that the world works in certain ways and that things happen for definite reasons. We even talk of the 'laws' of nature. The common view of miracle is that it is something which goes against those laws. Miracles appear to contradict what we know about the way the world works. Most of us, therefore, are reluctant to accept them. Our normal reaction to a so-called miracle would be to try to find ways of explaining it so that it ceased to be a miracle.

C. CHRISTIANS AND MIRACLES

Many Christians today are confused about the miracles of Jesus. They know what the gospels say, yet, like everyone else in the West, they have been brought up to think scientifically about the world they live in. There are some Christians who claim to have no difficulty in holding both to be true. But many more find it difficult to believe that miracles happened exactly as the gospels claim.

We can perhaps sympathise with that point of view. As we have said, most Christians readily accept science and do not want to challenge its views. Fortunately, because of work done by Biblical scholars, we have come to realise that the gospel-writers were not mainly concerned to give us accurate historical information about Jesus. Their real interest was to tell people that they believed Jesus was a very special person sent by God. One way of doing this was to show that Jesus had special powers. In fact, powers that people would normally only associate with God himself.

D. ASKING THE RIGHT QUESTIONS

We have to admit that we do not really know whether the miracles of Jesus actually happened. It is certainly not the purpose of this chapter to try to prove or disprove them. But we do need to learn to ask the right questions. We shall soon discover that asking the question 'Did it really happen?' about miracles does not get us very far. In fairness to Luke, we need to ask other questions. For example, did the people who lived in the first century AD believe in miracles? Did they know about our 'laws of nature'? Was Jesus the only person in the ancient world who performed miracles? What is Luke trying to tell us when he presents Jesus as a miracle-worker? If we begin to find answers to some of these questions, we shall have a much deeper understanding of what the gospel of Luke is about. We shall also realise that the gospels and science are not in conflict, because they are not about the same thing. And we may also arrive at the conclusion that you do not necessarily have to believe in the miracles as real facts of history to be a Christian.

E. MIRACLES AND MAGIC IN THE FIRST CENTURY AD

(i) A world filled with spirits

If we are to understand anything at all about the miracles of Luke's gospel, we must look at them against the background of the first century AD. Many people then believed that the world was subject to the actions of spirits which might work for people or against them. These spirits were thought to live in the air. The evil ones haunted lonely places such as ruins and tombs (see 8:26-39). People were thought to be under constant threat from spirits because they frequently attacked them and entered their bodies. Any event which could not be readily explained was attributed to the activities of the spirit world.

It is very easy for us to mock this idea because we have been conditioned to a scientific outlook. However, had we lived in the first century AD, we can be sure that we too would have believed in spirits!

(ii) Spirits and illness

When people were ill or suffering in some way, the usual explanation was that it was the work of an evil spirit or demon. The patient was thought to be possessed by the demon. Medicine, as we know it, did not exist. People with the power to heal used a strange blend of medicine and magic in their methods. The object was to drive out the evil spirit which was causing the affliction, and so restore the patient to good health.

Demons were thought to be extremely hostile, and so the job of the exorcist (that is, the person who drives out the evil spirit) was a dangerous one. He had to use force on occasions and, if he was to be completely successful, he needed also to know the name of the demon, or the type he was dealing with, so that he could assert his superiority and authority over it.

In addition to causing physical and mental harm, demons caused people to behave badly and do evil things. They would seek especially to turn people away from God.

Those skilled in the art of healing would use a variety of methods in their cures, including magical words and phrases as well as actions and the application of potions.

Superstition, fear and dread of the unknown were commonplace in the world of the first century AD. Magicians and wonder-workers were held in high esteem, because it was they who could help when the demon struck. Just as we go to the doctor when we are ill, so the people of the first century would seek out a magician to obtain a cure.

F. LUKE AND MIRACLES

When we come to look more closely at the miracles in Luke's gospel, we need to bear these first century AD views in mind. However, Luke is careful not to present Jesus as simply an ordinary wonder-worker. The miracles are not there just for their own sake, but they act as *signs* pointing to Jesus' true identity. Luke, however, recognises that signs have to be *interpreted* to be understood, and that it is possible to interpret them incorrectly. At 11:14-20 there is confusion among the people about the nature of Jesus' power. Some people interpret the sign incorrectly. Interestingly, in this passage, Jesus makes a reference to other exorcists (11:19), which suggests that this aspect of his work is by no means unique. Luke makes it clear that many people do interpret the miracles correctly. Then they respond in the most appropriate way possible by giving praise and thanks to God (see, for example, 5:25-26, and 18:43).

The miraculous was so much a part of Luke's world that he would not have been faced with the same problems of belief that we experience today. He would not have dreamt of asking such a question as 'Did Jesus really perform miracles?' As far as Luke was concerned, if Jesus was God's Son, then of course he must have done so.

Anointing with oil. The boy is holding a small container called a stock, in which is the holy oil used in anointing.

G. SYMBOLISM IN THE MIRACLES

The miracles Luke records are full of symbolism and so we must be careful not just to accept what he says at face value but be prepared to look for deeper meanings.

As we read Luke's gospel, we must keep constantly in mind his belief about the death and resurrection of Jesus. For Luke, the resurrection was *the greatest miracle* the world had ever known. Jesus' death had appeared to be a triumph for evil, but in raising Jesus from the dead God had won the final victory. The resurrection of Jesus was what inspired Luke to write. All that he says is written in the light of this event and is totally influenced by it. The miracles of which he speaks are but reflections of *the great miracle*. Some of them, not surprisingly, are either about or suggest the raising from the dead. For example, the Gergesene demoniac (who lived among the dead), Jairus' daughter (Jesus was told that he was too late, the girl was already dead), and the widow of Nain's son (whose funeral was actually taking place when Jesus arrived at the city), all show the conquest of death.

There is also a great deal of symbolism in the so-called nature miracles. Luke records two examples; the stilling of the storm, and the feeding of the five thousand. Many people find these the hardest of all the miracles to accept. But if they are interpreted symbolically they can be seen to make sense at a deep theological, rather than a straightforward literal, level.

You will see many more examples of Luke's use of symbols when you examine the individual miracle stories and read the detailed Study Notes .

H. JESUS AND THE FIGHT AGAINST EVIL

As we have seen in chapter 6, immediately after his baptism Jesus had to face temptation. The temptation story suggests that Jesus was confronted by the devil - the prince of all that was good had to resist the prince of all that was evil. For Luke, that was the beginning of a long struggle between the devil and Jesus. But it was only the beginning, because, throughout the gospel, Jesus meets up with the forces of evil (represented by the demons). He defeats them time and again and so proves victorious over them. But the struggle ends only when Jesus conquers death at the resurrection.

Luke wanted to ensure that his readers fully understood the significance of Jesus' miracles. They represented the triumph of good over evil.

I. DO MIRACLES HAPPEN TODAY?

There are some people who do believe that miracles happen. Certainly there are things which occur in the world which we cannot explain. We do not have all the answers, and so perhaps we may think it advisable to keep an open mind. However, the majority of people, including most Christians, do not lead their lives expecting miracles to happen as part of the daily routine.

J. THE HEALING MINISTRY OF THE CHURCH

Many Christian churches believe that they have a responsibility to continue the healing ministry of Jesus. Special services of healing are held, at which prayers are said for the sick. The minister may also use the 'laying on of hands' (placing his hands on the head of the sick person). Anointing with holy oil, also known as unction (a little oil poured over the head and hands of the sufferer), may also take place. The practice of anointing with oil in order to cure the sick is mentioned in the New Testament (see Mark 6:13 and the letter of James 5:14-15), which suggests that this was a method used by the church from the earliest times. And, of course, Jesus and the apostles frequently used the method of laying-on of hands when performing miracles of healing.

Today it is not necessarily expected that the sick and suffering will receive sudden miraculous cures as a result of these services of healing. They are intended mainly to help people to cope with their suffering and to give them strength in their time of trouble. Through the laying-on of hands or anointing, the sick are understood to receive God's special assistance and blessing for the problems they face. These actions may help to give sick people the assurance that God loves and cares for them and is involved in their suffering. The ministers usually regard themselves as working alongside doctors and nurses, rather than as providing an alternative form of treatment.

Religious belief may help people to be calm and contented even if they are physically unwell. Services of healing may help them achieve a feeling of peace and well-being.

Questions for chapter 9

1a. What does the word 'miracle' mean?

b. Why do you think people today find it difficult to believe in miracles?

2a. Do you think that a person can be a Christian even if he or she does not believe in the miracles of Jesus?

b. Do you think miracles happen today?

3a. Look at the picture 'Anointing with oil' p.83. What is the purpose of this ceremony?

b. How might a service of healing benefit a sick person?

4. Find out as much as you can about the healing ministry of the church.

5a. What beliefs did people of the first century AD hold about the cause of illness?

b. What is exorcism?

c. How did the exorcist go about his work?

6. What would Luke have considered to be the greatest miracle? Explain why.

7. Do you think there is any connection between sin and illness?

STUDY NOTES ON THE MIRACLES AS TOLD BY LUKE

K. TYPES OF MIRACLE IN LUKE

We turn now to examine the text of the individual miracle stories in Luke's gospel. These will be looked at in three separate categories - the exorcisms; the healing miracles; the nature miracles. We must, however, be on our guard, because in viewing the miracles out of the context of the gospel as a whole we are in danger of overlooking the aim and intention of the writer. It is not by accident that the miracle stories are placed where they are in Luke's gospel, and frequently they serve more than one purpose. For example, the story of the healing of the man with the withered arm (6:6-11) is important in the context of Jesus' conflict with the Pharisees, and it also illustrates the teaching of Jesus concerning attitudes towards the Sabbath. In fact it would seem that these aspects are more important to Luke than the healing itself.

In dividing the miracles into three separate groups we also need to take care. Luke would not have recognised the distinctions we make. For example, it is dangerous to make too clear a distinction between the exorcisms and the healings which Jesus performed. In those days illness in any shape or form was thought to be either the result of demonic possession or punishment for sin. In either case the suffering was the direct result of something evil.

L. THE EXORCISMS

The following passages should be studied in conjunction with this section:

   (i) The man with the unclean spirit 4:31-37
   (ii) The Gergesene demoniac 8:26-39
   (iii) The boy with the evil spirit 9:37-43
   (iv) The dumb man 11:14-26

(i) The man with the unclean spirit (4:31-37)

1. The evil spirit in the man instantly recognises Jesus and calls him by name, "the Holy One of God". Luke is making the point that Jesus operates in a spiritual as well as a human dimension. Whereas the people are astonished and amazed at Jesus, the spirit world immediately recognises him as the Messiah.

2. To gain complete mastery over your opponent in exorcism, it was thought to be necessary to know his name - hence the evil spirit uses both Jesus' earthly title, "Jesus of Nazareth", and a title for the Messiah, "the Holy One of God", but to no effect. This emphasises that the power of God is stronger than the power of Satan.

3. The aspect of violence which accompanied exorcism is made clear in verse 35.

(ii) The Gergesene demoniac (8:26-39)

1. The description of the man and his condition is worthy of attention. He lives among the dead, is unbelievably strong (he broke loose from chains and fetters) and completely insane (the name Legion suggests that he is a very severe case indeed, possessed by many demons).

2. The evil spirits again instantly recognise Jesus and refer to him as "Son of the Most High God". Jesus too asks the man's name, presumably to gain power over the demons.

3. Apart from the horrific description of the possessed man, this story is best remembered because of the loss of the pigs. We miss the point completely, however, if we start to ask such questions as, 'Why did Jesus allow animals to suffer in this way?' The point of this part of the story is to prove that the demons really had left the man and so confirm the miracle. It was also a commonly held belief that exorcised demons would take revenge, and this loss of pigs (demons were believed to live in animals as well as humans) illustrates well their spiteful and destructive nature. They were certainly a force to be reckoned with. Although they pleaded with Jesus not to "banish them to the Abyss" (8:31), in a way this is exactly what happened. The Abyss was thought of as a bottomless pit and the place of demons. In rushing into the lake, the pigs were in a sense returning the demons home to the bottomless pit. No doubt the early hearers of this story would have been led to ask, 'Who is this who has so much of God's power at his disposal?' And that is the question Luke answers time and again in his gospel.

4. Jesus' true identity is recognised by the demons but not by the people who, at verse 37, beg Jesus to leave their district. However, their reaction is one of "great fear", which suggests they were aware that something quite extraordinary had occurred. These people were also Gentiles (from "the Gergesene district", where they kept pigs, a thing Jews were forbidden to do) and, as Luke understands it, the acceptance of Jesus by the Gentiles comes after his death and resurrection. Despite this, Luke remains loyal to his source, Mark, and has Jesus tell the man to spread the news of his cure. After all Luke is concerned with the Gentile mission and here is a story of Jesus' own involvement in this work.

5. Luke probably intended his readers to interpret this story as a raising from the dead. He emphasises that Legion's home is a graveyard - the place of dead people. After the cure, however, the change is remarkable. The man is seated and clothed and wants to be with Jesus, and at verse 39 is found proclaiming the good news. From being under the total influence of Satan he is now actively engaged in the fight against him. He has, in other words, overcome death.

(iii) The boy with the evil spirit (9:37-43)

1. When told that his disciples are unable to drive out the evil spirit, Jesus speaks against the whole generation for its lack of faith (9:41). His words are similar to the description of Israel given in Deuteronomy 32:5. They are also a reminder of the words attributed to God at Numbers 14:11 where God complains that Israel refuses to trust him "in spite of all the signs" he has given them. In a similar way, Jesus is complaining that people do not trust his signs (the miracles he performs) but treat him as a wonder-worker. If they trusted his signs they would recognise who he was and repent.

2. The condition of the boy is described in vivid detail - see verse 39. So serious is this case of possession that Jesus' disciples are unable to drive out the demon. Only Jesus is able to do this.

3. The demon reacts violently to Jesus' presence, presumably indicating that it knows who Jesus really is. But Jesus is more powerful and drives out the demon and so cures the boy.

4. Finally, it is important to notice that this miracle occurs immediately after the transfiguration (9:28-36) in which Jesus' mission and purpose is confirmed. This story provides an acted-out example of what the function of the Messiah is: namely to restore the faithful to life.

(iv) The dumb man (11:14-26)

1. This miracle story is used by Luke to introduce a controversy about the source of Jesus' power (see p.83), and it would appear that this is its main purpose.

2. It is perhaps worth noting that the effects of what was considered to be demon-possession varied considerably. In this case the devil was preventing the man from speaking.

Questions on the exorcisms

4:31-37

1. Where was Jesus when he performed this miracle?

2. On what day did the miracle take place?

3. What did the unclean spirit say to Jesus?

4. How did the people react to the healing?

5. Why did only the demon and not the people present recognise Jesus?

8:26-39

1. Where did this incident take place?

2. Describe Legion and his condition.

3. What happened when the evil spirits left the man?

4. Describe Legion *after* the exorcism.

5. Why, do you suppose, did the people want Jesus to leave their country?

9:37-43

1. Describe the condition of the boy.

2a. What did Jesus say when told that the disciples were unable to drive out the demon?

b. Why did Jesus react so harshly, do you think?

3. How did the crowd respond to the miracle?

11:14-26

1. What was wrong with the man?

2. What purpose does this miracle-story serve?

General questions

1. Do you think that belief in demon possession helped Luke to emphasise the importance of Jesus? Give reasons for your opinion.

2. Why do you think some people today still hold to belief in demon possession?

M. THE HEALINGS

The following passages should be studied in conjunction with this section:

(i) Simon's mother-in-law (4:38-39)

(ii) The healing of the leper (5:12-15)

(iii) The healing of the paralytic (5:17-26)

(iv) The man with the withered arm (6:6-11)

(v) The Centurion's servant (7:1-10)

(vi) The widow of Nain's son (7:11-17)

(vii) Jairus' daughter (8:40-42 & 49-56)

(viii) The woman with the haemorrhage (8:43-48)

(ix) The woman crippled for 18 years (13:10-17)

(x) The man with dropsy (14:1-6)

(xi) The healing of the ten lepers (17:11-19)

(xii) The healing of the blind man (18:35-43)

(xiii) The healing of the ear of the high priest's servant (22:49-51)

(xiv) Mass healings and exorcisms (4:40-41; 6:17-19; 7:21; 9:11)

(i) Simon's mother-in-law (4:38-39)

1. Luke gives only the bare bones of this miracle. He says that Jesus "rebuked" the fever which suggests that this should perhaps be regarded as an exorcism. However, as we have seen, in the first century AD all illness was understood to be caused by Satan.

2. The completeness of the cure and its miraculous speed are suggested by the words, " . . . and she got up at once and waited on them" (4:39).

(ii) The healing of the leper (5:12-15)

1. Sufferers from the terrible disease of leprosy were certain of two things - that they would die a slow disfiguring death, and that they would experience permanent separation from their families and from society once the priest had pronounced them unclean.

2. To touch the man as Jesus did would have been unthinkable, because leprosy is a contagious disease. Luke, however, stresses that Jesus is prepared to help the outcast from Jewish society.

3. Why does Jesus instruct the man not to tell anyone about his cure, especially when it is clear that the good news cannot be contained (5:15)? Luke has taken this idea from Mark. The theme of 'secrecy' plays an important part in that gospel. Luke may have retained it unthinkingly or perhaps because he felt that Jesus would not want the sort of publicity which presented him as a wonder-worker. Luke sees Jesus' healing powers as evidence of his Messiahship, and it is because of *who he is* that people should freely respond to Jesus rather than because of *what he does*.

4. Jesus also instructs the man to obey the Law by reporting to a priest to be pronounced clean and to make sacrifice (as specified in Leviticus 14).

(iii) The healing of the paralytic (5:17-26)

1. Luke uses this incident to show how Jesus came into conflict with the Jewish authorities almost from the start of his ministry.

2. The real point of the story is to do with Jesus' authority to forgive sins. The early Christians believed that Jesus was Messiah and as such had the power of God at his disposal. They believed that sin could be forgiven by and through Jesus. To the Jews who did not accept the Messiahship of Jesus, the claim to be able to forgive sins was simply blasphemous. In their eyes, Jesus was being disrespectful to God by acting as though he was God. They believed that God alone could forgive sin.

3. If sin caused illness, then to forgive sin or to pronounce a cure amounted to the same thing. There is the suggestion in the story that it is easier to say that the man's sins are forgiven than it is actually to get him to walk; therefore, if the latter is achieved, then the former should also be believed.

4. Jesus refers to himself as the Son of Man - a title which here stands for Messiah (*see page 59*).

5. Luke seems to suggest that Jesus has the ability to know people's thoughts. The Pharisees and lawyers express their views to one another but Jesus knows what is in their minds.

6. The faith of the man and his friends is recognised by Jesus, and the completeness of the cure is stressed (he takes up his bed and walks, to the amazement of all).

(iv) The man with the withered arm (6:6-11)

1. The conflict between Jesus and the Jewish authorities on the use of the Sabbath is the main issue in this incident; the miracle itself pays a subsidiary role. Luke suggests that the Pharisees and lawyers are deliberately looking for evidence to accuse Jesus, and the incident ends with them plotting against him. Luke also suggests that Jesus is well aware of what is going on. Jesus has a special insight which enables him to know "what was in their minds" (6:8). (*See also* 5:22.)

2. The Jewish Law would allow help to be given on the Sabbath only if life was in danger. In this case it was apparently not a matter of life or death.

3. The point Jesus makes is that it is more important to do good when the opportunity arises than blindly to obey a law.

(v) The Centurion's servant (7:1-10)

1. The most significant aspect of this incident is the *faith* of the Centurion. Jesus says that he has not come across this degree of faith before, and it is found not in a Jew but in a Gentile. It is, of course, among the Gentiles that Christianity grows, but this comes later. Jesus' ministry is first to the Jews. Perhaps this is why the Centurion and Jesus never meet in Luke's version of the story. In a way the Centurion is perhaps seen by Luke as a symbol of the Gentile church and its relationship to Jesus.

2. The Centurion is presented as someone sympathetic to the Jewish religion. Perhaps Luke has in mind his own Gentile readers, some of whom may have been Romans of goodwill whom he would urge to be sympathetic to Christianity as the Centurion in the story was to Judaism.

3. The faith of the Centurion is such that he believes Jesus can heal his servant from a distance. He knows from his own experience as a soldier that "words" (commands) result in things happening. The orders he receives must be obeyed, and similarly the orders he gives are carried out. Words which are spoken on God's authority cannot fail to be effective, in the view of the Centurion.

(vi) The widow of Nain's son (7:11-17)

1. This is, strictly speaking, a different sort of 'healing' in that Jesus raises the young man from the dead (his funeral is actually taking place when Jesus arrives on the scene). Luke will undoubtedly have seen this as a reminder to his readers of Jesus' own resurrection. It may also be seen as a symbol of the new life that comes to people when they become Christians. From an apparently 'dead' existence, Jesus raises them to a new life even though still in the same surroundings ("Jesus gave him back to his mother" 7:15).

2. This story is found only in Luke's gospel. In telling it, Luke has clearly been influenced by an Old Testament story about the prophet Elijah. This can be found in 1 Kings 17 and it is about a *widow* (whom Elijah meets first of all at the *city gates* v.10) whose *only son* (v.12) *dies* (v.17). Elijah (who is *concerned* for the widow v.20) brings the child *back to life* (v.22) and gives *"him to his mother"* (v.23). Like the people who witness the incident at Nain, the widow acknowledges that Elijah is a *prophet of God* (v.24). In Luke's story, Jesus meets the *widow* at the *city gates*. He is *concerned* for her ("his heart went out to her" 7:13), and brings the *only son back to life* and gives *"him back to his mother"*. The people acknowledge Jesus as a *great prophet*.

3. As well as providing Luke with a source of information for his own story, this incident also enables him to parallel Jesus with Elijah (*see* Note p.50). According to the Old Testament book of Malachi, God will send Elijah before he brings the present world order to an end. In presenting Jesus as Elijah, Luke is perhaps warning his readers that they are living in special times. Jesus has come to tell them that the judgment is coming.

(vii) Jairus' daughter (8:40-42, 49-56)

1. This is another miracle story which shows that Jesus' power extends even to raising people from the dead. Though Jesus says the girl is only sleeping, it is clear that Luke intended the incident as a raising from the dead. Christians of Luke's day often referred to the dead as sleeping, because of their belief that the dead would be awakened at the resurrection.

2. Usually the Jewish religious leaders are in opposition to Jesus, but here Jairus comes to Jesus and begs for his help. The girl is at the point of death, and only someone with supernatural powers can save her.

3. Faith is an important element of the story. Jairus shows faith in coming to Jesus in the first place, and when the news comes that his daughter is already dead Jesus urges Jairus to continue to believe. The messengers do not possess this faith; they suggest that Jesus should not be troubled further. The professional mourners who are at the house do not have faith; they laugh at Jesus.

4. Those who possess faith are a model for Luke's readers to follow. They must have faith that Jesus will return and raise the dead. Those who laugh at this belief should be ignored - it is they who are really "dead".

5. The words Jesus uses when he performs the miracle, "Get up, my child", are similar to the words he used when raising the dead man at Nain.

6. We are made aware that the cure is complete. The girl stands up and is in need of food.

7. Luke retains, from his source Mark 5:43, the command not to tell anyone about the miracle, though in this instance it would seem rather pointless, as the news could hardly be contained.

(viii) The woman with the haemorrhage (8:43-48)

1. It was a common belief in the ancient world that anything associated with a healer had power in itself. The woman believed that Jesus had such great power that simply to touch his clothes would cure her. What she believed actually happened though, in making personal contact with her, Jesus is able to explain that it is her *faith* which has brought about the cure rather than some piece of magic.

2. According to Jewish Law, the woman's illness made her, and anyone she touched, ritually unclean (Leviticus 15:19-30). This would explain why she was anxious to be undetected. However, somehow Jesus knew that the touch had caused power to go from him. Jesus' words to the woman, "My daughter", suggests that he sees her as 'pure', whereas under Jewish Law she was 'impure'.

(ix) The woman crippled for eighteen years (13:10-17)

1. This story is found only in Luke's gospel, though it is similar to other stories which focus on controversy over the Sabbath. It might equally be counted as an exorcism, in that the woman is said to be "*possessed by a spirit* that had crippled her" (13:11).

2. The woman's Jewishness is emphasised at 13:16, where she is described as "a daughter of Abraham". Perhaps Luke intended her to be seen as a symbol of the Jews. They too could be 'straightened' by Jesus, just as was the crippled woman, if they would only allow him to set them free from their narrow religion and their obsession with rules and regulations. Interestingly enough, the same Greek word is used by Luke to describe the freeing of the woman from her illness and the freeing of the ox from its stall. This emphasises that Jesus is the one who is literally able to untie people (especially those who are 'tied' to a narrow way of life) and set them free. (The quotation from the book of Isaiah at 4:18-19 says that releasing prisoners and letting "broken victims" go free is part of the work of the Messiah.) The president of the synagogue is *tied* to a narrow view which prevents him from seeing what is really important. To him Jesus is just a Sabbath-breaker. But Jesus defeats the president and his supporters with their own logic. The 'rules' did allow them to 'set free' their domestic animals on the Sabbath so that they could be taken to water, for without water they would die. Surely, then, a fellow human-being who is a "prisoner" of Satan (13:16) and, therefore, in a sense, 'dead' should be set free and given new life.

3 . Because the Jewish leaders do not recognise who Jesus is, they fail to understand that the fight against evil is under way. This aspect of Jesus' work cannot pause for a moment, not even for the Sabbath.

(x) The man with dropsy (14:1-6)

1. This is another miracle story found only in Luke, but the issue of Sabbath observance is the same as in the previous miracle at 13:10-17.

2. The real point at issue is whether or not a loving response to human need is more important than the Law. Jesus believes that doing good has precedence, and he tries to get the Pharisees and lawyers to give their opinions. The first question Jesus asks proves impossible for them to answer. To say 'yes' would suggest they were lax in their attitude to the Law, which would never do. On the other hand, to say 'no' would show them to be unsympathetic towards the suffering of the sick man. The question about what to do if your ox or donkey falls into a well on the Sabbath fares no better in terms of a response from Jesus' opponents. In *principle* the rabbis were divided in their opinions on this sort of question, but in *practice* if it was *your* donkey or ox you set to and pulled it out! If such an attitude was taken over an animal, how much more should it apply to a fellow human-being. By not answering Jesus' questions they did not qualify to pass an opinion on his healing of the sick man.

(xi) The healing of the ten lepers (17:11-19)

1. Again, this is a miracle story found only in Luke's gospel, though he has already included a story about a leper (5:12-15).

2. Perhaps the most significant point for Luke is that the grateful leper is a Samaritan. The Samaritans were regarded as foreigners and outcasts from respectable Jewish society, and yet it is one of their number who responds appropriately to Jesus. Luke perhaps wants to show his readers how, even during the period of Jesus' ministry, Gentiles responded more readily to Jesus than did his own people, the Jews.

3. Jesus appears to be critical of the nine lepers for carrying out his instructions - they were presumably on their way to show themselves to the priests as ordered. Perhaps, however, Luke wants to make a distinction between being made clean (as all ten lepers were) and being fully 'cured' (which presumably amounts to more than the healing from the disease of leprosy and includes a new relationship to God). Only the Samaritan is spoken of as having faith. It is this faith which sets him apart from the other nine and, as we know from elsewhere in the gospel, it is through faith that people are saved.

(xii) The healing of the blind man (18:35-43)

1. The blind man calls Jesus "Son of David" which is a title for Messiah. According to the passage from Isaiah (quoted by Luke at 4:18-19) the Messiah will give the blind their sight. Here we have a blind man who recognises Jesus as Messiah and who is healed by him. This further confirms who Jesus really is and occurs whilst he is on his way to Jerusalem for the final conflict.

2. Much interest focuses on the blind man himself. He persists in his attempt to gain Jesus' attention, despite being discouraged by the crowd. Jesus tells him that it is his faith which has cured him.

3. The placing of this incident immediately after Jesus has again predicted his coming death and resurrection, and when the disciples have again failed to understand what he is talking about (18:31-34) suggests it may have had symbolic significance for Luke. At this point in the gospel, the disciples are blind - they do not 'see' clearly who Jesus is. The blind man, however, is a model disciple. He is persistent in his desire to make contact with Jesus which indicates, in Luke's view, his great faith. He does not possess sight, yet he can see quite clearly that Jesus is the Messiah. His response to the cure is to *follow* Jesus and give praise to God.

(xiii) The healing of the ear of the high priest's servant (22:49-51)

1. All the other gospels record the cutting off of the high priest's servant's ear, but only in Luke's gospel does Jesus heal the man.

2. Luke is perhaps making the point that, despite the enormous personal strain on Jesus at this crucial time of his life, he could still put the needs of others first.

(xiv) Mass healings and exorcisms (4:40-41; 6:17-19; 7:21; 9:11)

In addition to the individual stories of healing and exorcism, Luke also mentions in four places instances of mass healings. These have been used by Luke to summarise the overall reaction of the ordinary people to Jesus and, apart from 7:21, to act as link passages. Luke is in no doubt that Jesus was popular with the crowds. They recognised his power for what it was, even if the authorities did not. Wherever he went they flocked to see him, and they brought to him their sick in vast numbers. Luke suggests (6:19) that simply to touch Jesus was sufficient for the cure to be obtained instantly.

At 4:40-41, Luke makes the point that the demons recognise Jesus. They are commanded to silence perhaps for two reasons. First, the testimony of a demon is not necessarily the most desirable of testimonies! Second, the only valid response to Jesus is a free response - people must, in other words, make up their own minds about him and not be persuaded by others.

The main purpose of the mass healing at 7:21 would appear to be an acted-out example, for the benefit of John the Baptist, to show who Jesus is.

Questions on the healings

4:38-39

1. Whose house was Jesus in when he performed this miracle?
2. What action did Jesus take?
3a. What do you think had caused the woman's illness?
   b. Does your view differ from the view of Jesus as implied by Luke?
4. What tells us that the cure was effective?

5:12-15

1. What did the leper ask Jesus?
2. After the cure, why did Jesus tell the man to see a priest?
3. Why was the leper also an outcast?
4. Why do you think Jesus told the man not to tell anyone about his cure?

5:17-26

1. Who was present during this incident?
2. What action did the man's friends take when they found they could not get near Jesus?
3. What did Jesus say to the paralytic which offended the Pharisees and lawyers?
4. What is blasphemy?
5. Who does Jesus declare himself to be in this story?
6. How did the crowd react to the healing?

6:6-11

1. On what day of the week did this incident take place?
2. Who was present in the synagogue?
3. What question did Jesus ask?
4. In healing the man, what message do you think Jesus was trying to get across?
5. Why do you think the Pharisees and lawyers were "beside themselves with anger" (6:11)?

7:1-10

1. Where did this incident take place?
2a. Who brought the first message to Jesus?
   b. Why did the messengers urge Jesus to help the Centurion?
3a. Say in your own words what the content of the second message was.
   b. What is the relationship between saying and doing in the view of the Centurion?
   c. Why does the Centurion believe that Jesus can heal his servant simply by saying "the word" (7:7)?

4. What did Jesus say about the Centurion?
5. In what ways might the Centurion be seen by Luke as a representative figure?

7:11-17

1. Where was Jesus when he performed this miracle?
2. What did Jesus say to the widow?
3. What did Jesus *do* and what did he *say* when performing the miracle?
4. How did the people react to the miracle?
5. In what ways is this story similar to the story of Elijah at 1 Kings 17:17-24?
6. Why might Luke have wanted his readers to see Jesus as Elijah?
7. What extra significance might stories about raising the dead have had for Luke's readers?

8:40-42, 49-56

1. Why did Jairus seek Jesus' help?
2. What message came from Jairus' house?
3. How did Jesus react to the news that the girl was dead?
4. What in the story tells you that the miracle was successful?
5. Give examples of faith and of lack of faith shown in this story.

8:43-48

1. Why did the woman touch Jesus' clothes?
2. What was the result of this action?
3. What did Jesus say to the woman?
4. What do you think Jesus meant when he said that "power had gone out" from him?
5. According to Leviticus 15, Jesus would have been made unclean by the woman's touch. Was this of concern to Jesus, do you think?
6. How could the woman's cure be explained today?

13:10-17

1. How long had the woman suffered her illness?
2. What did Jesus say to the woman?
3. How did the synagogue president react to the healing?
4. What argument did Jesus use to show that he was right to heal the woman on the Sabbath?
5. How might the woman be seen as a symbol for the Jews?

14:1-6

1. Where was Jesus when this incident took place?
2. What questions did Jesus ask the lawyers and Pharisees?
3. Why do you think the lawyers and Pharisees did not answer Jesus' questions?

17:11-19

1. Why did the lepers stand "some way off" and call out to Jesus?
2. How many people were healed from the disease of leprosy in this story?
3. What instruction did Jesus give to the lepers?
4. Why did one of the lepers return to Jesus?
5. What do you suppose was different about the "cure" the grateful leper received?

6. What significance might the nationality of the grateful leper have had for Luke and his readers?

18:35-43

1. What special title did the blind man give Jesus?
2. How did the crowd react to the blind man's shouting?
3. What question did Jesus ask the blind man?
4. What was the blind man's reply to Jesus' question?
5. How might Luke have seen the blind man as a model disciple?

22:49-51

1. How did the servant come by his injury?
2. Why do you think Luke records this miracle?

N. THE NATURE MIRACLES

The following passages should be studied in conjunction with this section:

(i) The stilling of the storm (8:22-25)

(ii) The feeding of the five thousand (9:12-17)

(i) The stilling of the storm (8:22:25)

1. To ask, 'Did it really happen?' is to ask the wrong question. This is a story which was undoubtedly popular teaching material in the early church. It is full of symbolism, and many valuable lessons may be learnt from it. It has been so adapted that it is impossible to tell what really happened.

2. Some background information is necessary in order to interpret the symbolism.

(a) In the Old Testament the sea is often used to represent evil and chaos. The sea was terrifying to the Jews, who were not, by and large, a seafaring nation. It was thought to be inhabited by evil powers. The Psalms suggest that God alone was able to control the raging sea (e.g. Psalm 107:28-29).

(b) At times of trouble, when no help seemed forthcoming, the Jews often spoke of God as asleep. There are a number of places in the Old Testament where God is called upon to 'wake up' (e.g. Psalm 44:23).

(c) The ability to sleep peacefully was a sign of complete and perfect trust in God (e.g. Psalm 4:8).

3. Against this background, the meaning of the story begins to unfold.

(a) Jesus is seen to have perfect trust in God - he sleeps during a violent storm.

(b) The disciples wake Jesus from his sleep. They lack faith and the perfect trust which Jesus displays.

(c) In rebuking the storm, Jesus deals with it in the same way that he deals with demons. Luke may be implying that the raging sea was the work of demons. Certainly he meant his readers to understand that Jesus was God's agent - only God could control the sea.

4. This incident may have had particular meaning for some groups of early Christians. The church was often described as a boat, and the world in which it sailed was a sea of persecution and suffering. But Christians knew that even if their faith was weak, Jesus would deal with the evil which faced them.

5. The real point of the story is contained in the question asked by the disciples, "Who can this be? He gives his orders to wind and waves, and they obey him" (8:25). This was the question Luke wanted his readers to face. There could be only one answer for Luke - this is the Son of God.

(ii) The feeding of the five thousand (9:12-17)

1. This story would have been full of meaning for the early Christians, because it calls to mind the Last Supper and the Eucharist. The actions of Jesus in blessing and breaking the bread are the same as those performed at the Last Supper. The story would also have encouraged Christians to put their trust in God to provide for their every need.

2. The story also reminded the early church of its.own responsibilities. When the disciples asked Jesus to send the crowd away he told them to feed the people themselves - that is, he made the people *their* responsibility. The disciples could not see how they could possibly cope with this but, by following Jesus' instructions, they were shown that faith makes all things possible. The "twelve great baskets" of left-overs are presumably a symbol for the church as the new Israel (the old Israel was made up of *twelve* tribes). This new church can and must accept responsibility for the world. It is a frightening responsibility, but if the church has faith and follows Jesus' commands it will be able to meet everyone's needs.

3. The influence of the Old Testament is again apparent in this incident. In the book of Exodus we read how God provided food for the Israelites in the wilderness after they had escaped from Egypt. The prophet Elisha also performed a miracle similar to the one Luke tells (see 2 Kings 4:42-44). These stories would have been familiar to Luke, and no doubt when he wrote about the feeding of the five thousand he wanted his readers to see that Jesus was following in the tradition of the Old Testament. It was yet another way of saying that Jesus was the Messiah.

4. A popular image which Jews had of the future life was that of a banquet in heaven. The Messiah would act as host, and those sharing the meal would be the saved. Luke almost certainly had this in mind when writing his account of this miracle (see Chapter 8 b(i)).

Questions on the nature miracles

8:22-25

1. What beliefs did the Jews hold about the sea?
2. What is the difference between the attitude of Jesus and the attitude of the disciples when the storm threatens?
3. How did Jesus control the storm?
4. Suggest the answer Luke would have hoped his readers would give to the question, 'Who can this be?'
5. Why might this story have particular meaning for early Christians?

9:12-17

1. Where was Jesus when this incident occurred?

2a. What did the disciples ask Jesus to do about the crowd?
 b. What did Jesus reply?
3a. Describe the actions of Jesus when performing the miracle.
 b. In what way are Jesus' actions here similar to his actions at the Last Supper? (Look up 22:17-19)
4a. How many baskets of left-overs were collected?
 b. Why might the number of baskets be symbolic?
5. How might this incident have reminded the early church of its responsibilities for the world?

10
THE TEACHING OF JESUS

A. JESUS THE TEACHER

A Bible-study group. Many Christians meet regularly in small groups to discuss the Bible and to try to understand how it should influence their lives.

Luke makes it clear that from the very beginning of his ministry Jesus was involved in *teaching* the people (4:15). Indeed the first incident of Jesus' public ministry recorded by Luke finds him teaching in the synagogue at his home town of Nazareth (4:16-30). The same is true when Jesus moves on to Capernaum (4:31). He teaches the people who, Luke tells us, are "astounded at his teaching, for what he said had the note of authority" (4:32). This pattern is continued throughout the gospel. Luke frequently depicts Jesus teaching the crowds who followed him, or speaks of him teaching in the towns he visited.

In some ways, Luke presents Jesus in the style of the Jewish teacher, or rabbi, of his day. The rabbis were the teachers of Jewish scripture and they had the right to give judgment when disputes arose concerning the Law. They also gathered round them bands of pupils known as disciples. The disciples would sit at the feet of the rabbi, receiving his instruction and being under his authority. Much of the teaching given by the rabbis arose out of conversation or argument. Their source of authority was the Old Testament.

When we look at Jesus' method of teaching, we can see the similarities. Jesus selected a number of people to be his disciples, he gave them instruction and they were under his authority. Much of his teaching arose out of conversation or argument. Jesus also used the Old Testament to support many of the things he said and did. However, there was something original about Jesus' teaching, particularly the parables and the way he used them. The people recognised that Jesus taught with authority, and his parables were designed to bring them to the point of decision. Many of the central characters in the parables are forced to decide on what is the right course of action, and challenging people to decide this was one of Jesus' aims in telling parables.

B. LUKE AND 'THE TEACHING'

In the preface to his gospel, Luke implies that there was a wealth of material about Jesus available to him when he wrote. Presumably he selected from these written accounts and oral traditions, ("the traditions handed down to us", 1:2) that particular teaching which served his purpose in writing. He also says his purpose was to "write a connected narrative . . . to give . . . authentic knowledge" about Jesus (1:3-4). But the matter is more complicated than that. Luke may have been as much influenced by the needs and concerns of his own church as he was by the information he had about Jesus. He wanted to make the gospel message relevant to their needs. We have also seen (chapter 4 section (a)), how he was concerned to present Christianity as a serious religion worthy of Roman consideration and protection. In order to meet these concerns Luke *adapted* the teaching of Jesus, as he received it, to suit his own purpose. What we are in fact dealing with is Luke's *interpretation* of the teaching of Jesus. This means that we cannot say with any degree of certainty that the words spoken by Jesus in the gospel were actually spoken by him during his ministry. (The situation becomes even more complicated when we remember that Luke did not get his information straight from Jesus' lips anyway. It came to him through the early church and it seems likely that the church too had adapted the message to suit its own needs.) There is no doubt that the teaching reflects the spirit of Jesus' message but we have no cast-iron guarantee that these were his actual words.

C. LUKE'S ABILITY TO TELL A STORY

As we saw in chapter 4 section (e), Luke is generally regarded as the great storyteller among New Testament writers. The best known and most loved of the stories or parables of Jesus - such as The Good Samaritan and The Lost Son - are found only in Luke's gospel. Only a few of the stories he tells have parallels in either Mark's or Matthew's gospels. Most of Luke's own stories have certain features in common. Typical of this is a description of the situation 'before' a crisis occurs (for example, in the case of The Lost Son, the rich living standard). This is followed by a description of the situation 'after' the crisis (in The Lost Son, the return home and the father's forgiveness). At the point of the actual crisis itself, Luke's characters work out for themselves the new course of action their lives need to take (again, in The Lost Son, hunger at the pig farm and coming to his senses). Many of the parables Luke tells also reflect the special interests he has, as we shall see later in the chapter.

Stories were an important form of teaching in ancient times for a number of reasons. In a world of few books, it was important that special teachings should be clearly *remembered*. It must have been discovered very early on that people remember stories more easily than they do abstract teachings. Stories can also communicate a message. Thus, stories are ideal ways of preserving important teachings. Luke knew this. He knew that if he recorded memorable stories which contained important teachings and truths, people could easily call to mind what those important teachings and truths were every time they *heard* or *told* or *remembered* the stories.

D. TYPES OF STORY IN LUKE

(i) Parable

The word 'parable' simply means the placing of one thing alongside another in order to compare or illustrate. At 13:18-19, for example, Jesus compares the kingdom of God with a mustard-seed. Some of Luke's parables are quite short, like the one about the mustard-seed, consisting of only one or two verses. Others are more developed, illustrative stories, like The Lost Son, which runs to twenty-two verses.

Parables are colourful stories designed to challenge people to come to a decision and to make important teachings easier to understand and remember. Because parables use things from everyday experience, people of the first century AD would have had no trouble in relating to them. People today may have some problems with the parables Luke tells because the situations they refer to are unlikely to be part of their everyday experience.

Parables were a common form of teaching in the East. There are a few examples of parables in the Old Testament and, later on, after the time of Jesus, the rabbis frequently used parables in their teaching. In using parables to make his teaching clearer and more memorable, Jesus developed a method which had its roots in Jewish tradition.

(ii) Allegory

The allegory is also a common method of teaching. Allegories too can be found in the Old Testament as well as in other ancient literature. An allegory is a story in code form which uses a number of symbols to stand in place of what it is really talking about (for example, in the interpretation to the parable of the sower, the seed is a symbol for the word). Each point in the story has to be interpreted and to do this you need to know the code, that is, to know what the symbols used mean. To understand an allegory you need continually to ask, 'What does *that* stand for?'

When you examine the parables in Luke's gospel you may find that it is not always immediately clear whether a story is a parable or an allegory. This is because in many of them there is a mixture of both forms. Take, for example, the story of the fig-tree (called by Luke at 13:6 a parable). This can be read as a parable, and people can see the meaning as applying to them. But it can also be seen to have allegorical elements - for example, the fig-tree can be seen to stand for Israel, and the owner's wishes as the coming judgment or destruction of Jerusalem. As a general rule, the term 'parable' is used in this book to refer to the stories Jesus told. But it should be remembered that many of the parables have allegorical elements to them or may be mainly allegorical. The Notes on the Parables will help you to make the distinctions.

E. THE PARABLES REFLECT LUKE'S INTERESTS

As we have indicated, we cannot be entirely sure of the origin of some of Luke's parables. Some, we know, he got from Mark's gospel (for example, The Sower, The Mustard-seed, and The Vineyard). He shares a few with Matthew (for example, The Banquet, The Lost Sheep, and The Talents). This suggests that Luke either had access to Matthew's gospel as he wrote, or that they shared a common source (see chapter 3). But the majority of Luke's parables are his own. It may be that Luke had these passed on to him via the oral tradition of the early church. If this is the case, he presumably had a source of information not available to Mark or Matthew, who would hardly have chosen to leave out such excellent stories. An alternative suggestion is that these stories are Luke's own creations. Whatever the case, it is clear that Luke has stamped on them his own particular mark. And he has used them, along with other pieces of Jesus' teaching, to further illustrate his own interests.

THE THEMES

We have attempted to collect together all of the teaching of Jesus found in Luke's gospel and place it under four main themes. The themes are: (I) True religion and false religion; (II) Seeing things clearly; (III) Life in the new order; (IV) Getting ready for the kingdom. In doing this, the aim is to focus as clearly as possible on some of Luke's main concerns and interests as we see them. Each theme is further sub-divided to make the material easier to handle. It will be necessary to study the specified gospel references alongside the themes. Notes are also included on some of the parables. By adopting this method, the individual parables can either be studied in some depth as they occur in the themes, or can be treated together at a later time. In taking the teaching material out of the context in which it has been placed by the gospel-writer, we run the risk of losing some of its meaning. It is not by accident that Luke has chosen to place the incidents where he has and frequently they serve more than one purpose. So we need to be on our guard, and look also at the context in which a piece of teaching material occurs in order to balance up the method we have chosen to use.

THE TOPICS

As well as the main themes, there are a number of other *topics* in Luke's gospel which have long been recognised as important interests of this gospel-writer. Among these are the following: prayer, the poor and the lost, women, wealth, the journey, Jerusalem, repentance, forgiveness and the reversal of fortunes. Some of these topics are identified as such within the main themes. These are: Wealth in theme II; prayer, service (caring for the poor and the lost), and women in theme III. Repentance, forgiveness and the reversal of fortunes also receive extensive treatment within the Teaching themes, and the journey is covered in section (h) below. The importance of Jerusalem to Luke is commented on in chapters 5 and 12.

F. WHERE THE TEACHING IS TO BE FOUND

There are two main sections in Luke's gospel where the majority of the teachings of Jesus are to be found. These are the Sermon-on-the-Plain (6:17-49), and the long Central Section as it is called (9:51-18-14). The Central Section takes up a large part of the whole gospel (about 30%), and includes some of the *miracles* Jesus performed (see chapter 9), as well as a large number of *parables* and other *sayings* of Jesus. These parables and sayings which make up the teach-ing of Jesus are dealt with in this book under four main themes:

Theme I True religion and false religion;
Theme II Seeing things clearly;
Theme III Life in the new order;
Theme IV Getting ready for the kingdom.

The remainder of this chapter is concerned with how the Sermon and the Central Section fit into the gospel as a whole.

G. THE SERMON-ON-THE-PLAIN (6:17-49)

Luke likes to prepare his readers for important events. He also makes links between the various incidents he retells. It is, therefore, worth looking back a few verses to see what leads into the Sermon. At 6:12 Jesus goes into the hills (or mountain, as most trans-lations have it) to spend the night in *prayer*. What follows makes it clear why Jesus needed to be with God. He has to choose Twelve disciples, the found-ing members of the Church (see chapter 7). This done, Jesus and the Twelve come down from the hills to level ground (the Plain) where crowds have gath-ered to hear Jesus teach and to be healed.

Luke sets the scene for Jesus to engage in one of his most important activities, the *teaching* of the disci-ples. The new Church needs to be taught what to expect, how to behave, and how to react in the situations which it will face in the future. It becomes clear that a whole new set of standards is needed for the followers of Jesus. The things which most people in the world would value are turned upside down (see especially Theme III: Life in the new order). This is why the Sermon is given to the disciples. Luke believes that only those who actually live the new life, which Jesus invites people to share, will under-stand it. To the usual way of thinking, the demands Jesus makes are hard (for example, 'love your ene-mies'!), but those who strive to lead their lives as Jesus taught are promised great rewards.

The influence of the Old Testament is apparent here. At this point in the gospel Luke may have had in mind one of the great characters of the ancient scriptures, Moses. Moses climbed Mount Sinai to speak with God (Exodus 19:20). If Luke does have Moses in mind then the reason for the meeting with God will hardly have escaped him. It was on the mountain that God gave to Moses the Ten Commandments. After Moses had been with God, he came down from the mountain to speak to the people below. In a similar way, Jesus comes down from the mountain (symbolic of a special place), to the people who are on the level ground (symbolic of the ordinary world). The gospel comes literally down to earth and to ordinary people. Just as the Ten Commandments formed the basis of the old way of life, so the Sermon which Jesus gives invites a *new* way of life for a *new* situation.

H. THE CENTRAL SECTION (9:51-18:14)

At first glance, this lengthy section of the gospel seems to be a jumbled mixture of parables, sayings of Jesus and miracle stories. We know, however, that Luke usually works to a plan, so what is he up to here? A distinct possibility is that Luke wishes to develop the idea of a journey.

At 9:51 it is made clear that Jesus sets out on a journey. This journey will take him first to Jerusalem, but his real destination is heaven ("As the time approached when he was to be taken up to heaven, he set his face resolutely towards Jerusalem", 9:51). At other points in the Central Section are to be found further references to the journey. For example, at 13:22 ("He continued his journey through towns and villages, teaching as he made his way towards Jerusalem"), and 17:11 ("In the course of his journey to Jerusalem"). Other references to the journey, found outside the Central Section, include 18:31 and 19:28. At first glance, then, we might assume that Luke is intending to provide us with some sort of travel document, which will trace Jesus' movements and his route to Jerusalem. But closer inspection will soon put us off that idea. We conclude:

·that Jesus had an extremely poor sense of direction (for example, at 9:52 Jesus comes near to a Samaritan village, but at 17:11 he is back on the Samaria/Galilee border);

·that Luke did not know Palestine very well (in which case, an exact description of the route would hardly have been his intention);

·that the idea of the journey is mainly *symbolic* rather than literal.

Strong arguments can be put forward for the idea that the journey is mainly symbolic. We have already seen from 9:51 that Jesus' real destination is heaven. Here is a clue, then, that the 'journey' is a symbol. No route map, however accurate geographically, can lead to heaven. The route to heaven is much more about the way people lead their lives.

So why has Luke presented this part of his gospel in the form of a journey? Most probably the journey of Jesus is a symbol. It looks *backward* to the Old Testament and *forward* to Luke's church.

(i) The 'journey' looks back to the Old Testament

The idea of a journey would have come naturally to Luke from his knowledge of the Old Testament. There the most significant journey in the history of Israel was recorded at length. This was the journey which Israel made from captivity in Egypt to the freedom of the Promised Land. The story of this journey begins in the book of Exodus and ends in the book of Deuteronomy. Deuteronomy was of particular importance to the Jews because it not only told them of God's dealings with his people but also taught them a way of life. One of the matters Luke's church no doubt frequently discussed was how they should lead their lives. Since Jesus, the teaching of the old religion was no longer entirely appropriate. Change had come about and this had to be taken into account. Perhaps Luke saw a way of meeting this need for new teaching. What was required was a sort of Christian Deuteronomy. It may, then, have been his deliberate intention to parallel this section of his gospel with the Deuteronomy of the Old Testament. The first Deuteronomy includes the *teaching* of Moses set in the context of the *journey* of *freedom* to the Promised Land. The second Deuteronomy (the Central Section of Luke's gospel) includes the *teaching* of Jesus set in the context of a *journey* which, in Luke's view, is also about *setting people free*.

(ii) The 'journey' looks forward to Luke's church

As well as looking back to the Old Testament, Luke may also have had in mind his own church members and their 'journey' through life. In telling his story of Jesus, Luke was as much influenced by the needs of his own church as he was by the traditions he had received about Jesus. The situations they faced may have partly determined the presentation of his story. They needed encouragement in their attempts to lead responsible Christian lives.

Some examples from the gospel may help to make this clearer:

1. When Luke's church members read of the appointment of the seventy (or seventy-two) disciples, their mission and their jubilant return (10:1, 17-20) they would have found confirmation for their own missionary work and been encouraged by the promise of success.

2. When they faced open hostility and found themselves in conflict with the authorities, the opposition which Jesus himself faced (for example, 11:14-20) would have helped them to understand that they were only experiencing what Jesus himself had experienced during his life-time.

3. When they needed to understand more about the meaning of discipleship and the importance of prayer, they could find all they needed to know from Jesus' teaching (for example, 10:25-42 and 11:1-13).

In Luke's view, the 'journey' through life of the Christian is, in a way, a reflection of the journey Jesus had to undertake. For Luke, Jesus is the perfect example for every Christian to follow. Therefore, the journey of Jesus is one which Christians should strive to make their own.

We must not, however, allow the symbolic interpretation of the journey to remove our attention completely from the more literal one. Jesus *is* on his way to Jerusalem. We have already noted (see chapter 5) how Luke begins and ends his gospel in the holy city. The good news must come first to Jerusalem (the centre of the Jewish religious world) before being taken from there to Rome (the centre of the political world) by Paul.

Questions for chapter 10

1. How does Luke emphasise that Jesus' main purpose was to be a teacher?

2. What does the word 'rabbi' mean? Write *five* lines on rabbis.

3. What similarities are there between Jesus and the rabbis?

4. Why is it difficult to be certain that the words of Jesus in the gospel were actually spoken by him?

5. Why were stories a valued method of teaching in the ancient world?

6. What is (i) a parable, (ii) an allegory?

7. How does Luke indicate to his readers the importance of the Sermon-on-the-Plain?

8. What is the significance of the *journey* in Luke's gospel?

THEME I

TRUE RELIGION AND FALSE RELIGION
References: 6:39-49; 8:4-15; 10:25-37; 11:37-54;12:1-12; 14:34-35; 18:15-27.

A. DEFINING THE PROBLEM

It is clear that not everything that is done in the name of religion can be called good. Some of the most terrible deeds that people have committed in the world have been done in the name of religion. No one religion has a better record than another in this respect. However, the vast majority of religious people do not engage in hostile activities. Most try to lead decent lives. Even so, in lesser ways, they may be just as guilty of distorting, through their actions, the true teachings of their faith.

We have to be able to recognise whether actions done in the name of religion are good or bad. Or, to put it another way, whether they are examples of *true religion* or *false religion*. This perhaps sounds over-simplified. Of course, all people, whether religious or not are a mixture of good and bad. This is just another way of saying that we are all human. Luke knew this only too well, as we can tell from the way he presents some of the best known characters of his gospel, such as the Lost Son and Zacchaeus. But we are more concerned at the moment with what religious people *do* - their *actions* - rather than with human nature. We want to know whether the way they lead their lives is consistent with the true teachings of their religion.

B. THE EXAMPLE OF THE GOOD SAMARITAN

Recognising what is true religion and what is false religion is not as difficult as it may seem, according to Luke. In the teaching of Jesus we find that a distinction is made between true religion and false religion (though these actual terms are not used). This is perhaps best illustrated in the well known story of The Good Samaritan (10:25-37). On the face of it, it would seem obvious who the truly religious people are in the story. There is the priest who performed the traditional religious ceremonies of Judaism, and the Levite, who would have been a Temple administrator and perhaps a teacher of the Law and Tradition.[10] You could not get much more religious than either of them! But their behaviour towards the injured man shows how false their religion really was. They were only concerned with the ritual details of religion. Their real worry was that if they touched the man they would become ritually unclean and, therefore, be unable to carry out their religious duties. But, for Luke's Jesus, a religion which sets ritual concerns above human concerns is a false religion. And so here we find yet again an example of *reversal*, that favourite theme of Luke's. The Samaritan whose religion, according to the priest's and Levite's way of thinking, would have been false, is, in fact, an example of true religion. From the Jewish viewpoint, the Samaritan was a foreigner with a suspect religion. Yet, by his *actions*, and his concern for the needs of a fellow human being, he is a shining example of religion at its best.

---

[10] To ensure that the Law was never broken, the Jewish religious authorities developed many more rules to safeguard the individual laws. These rules are known as the Tradition.

The Good Samaritan (10:25-37)

1. Jesus told this story in response to the question: 'Who is my neighbour?'.But the story itself shows that this is the wrong question to ask. The question the story answers is: 'To whom can *I* be a neighbour?' This shifts the emphasis. I should not concern myself with who can be a neighbour to me, but rather look to see who needs my help so that I can be a neighbour to them. The theoretical question of the lawyer is turned round by Jesus and presented in such a way that *practical* action is required: Jesus ends up by telling the lawyer to go and *do* the same as the Samaritan had done.

2. A lesson which focused on the goodness of the Samaritan would have been a hard one for a Jewish religious leader to accept. (*See* Note on Samaritans below). To tell a Jew that he must behave like a Samaritan would have been regarded as insulting. And to tell a story which suggests that a Samaritan knows more about God's love than Jewish religious leaders did would have been regarded as doubly insulting!

3. The story demonstrates how concern for other human beings must come before anything else. To the lawyer, the reasons why the priest and Levite "went past on the other side" were obvious. They could not risk making themselves unclean by coming into contact with blood or, even worse, a corpse. Similarly, the lawyer would not have risked coming into contact with a tax-collector or Samaritan or any other sinner or foreigner for that matter. Such contact would render him unclean. That is why the Pharisees and lawyers could not understand why Jesus mixed with such undesirable people.

It is clear, then, that, for the lawyer, the number of people he could be a neighbour to was limited. Through the story, Jesus is trying to show how such concerns are wrong when faced with human need. The Samaritan is like Jesus in that he is quite prepared to risk becoming 'unclean' (in Jewish eyes) in order to help other people.

Questions on 10:25-37 (*see also* p.108 for questions on this passage)

1. What two questions did the lawyer put to Jesus?

2a. What question did Jesus put to the lawyer?

b. What was the lawyer's reply?

3. To which city was the man travelling when he was robbed?

4. What actions did the Samaritan take when he saw the injured man?

5. Why were Jews and Samaritans hostile towards one another?

6. What did Jesus mean when he said to the lawyer: "Go and do as he did"?

7a. What question did Jesus answer through the story of The Good Samaritan?

b. In what way was the story of the Good Samaritan an answer?

8. It seems that Jesus and the lawyer might have disagreed about what they thought was 'good' behaviour. In what ways would their views have differed?

9. Give an example of a modern-day Good Samaritan you have heard of or read about.

10a. What does the organisation called The Samaritans do?

b. Why do you think they chose 'Samaritans' for their name?

c. Was it a good choice?

NOTE ON SAMARITANS

To the Jews, Samaritans were to be avoided at all costs. They were regarded as racially inferior because it was believed that centuries before they had inter-married with foreigners. A long-standing feud developed between the two groups, which had led to the Jews banning Samaritans from Jerusalem. The Samaritans became a separate community (and they continue so today), though their religious roots remained in the law books of the Old Testament.

C. TEACHINGS FROM THE SERMON

In the Sermon-on-the-Plain some of the things Jesus says are concerned with the true religion/false religion distinction. He uses the image of trees and the types of fruit they produce (6:43-45). Good trees do not produce worthless fruit, nor do worthless trees produce good fruit: "For each tree is known by its own fruit." It is the same with people. We know them by the things they *do*.

Two other images are used to show that, although some people may claim to be leading truly religious lives, this is just a pretence. A blind man is not capable of guiding another blind man (6:39-40), nor can you remove the speck of sawdust from your brother's eye if you have a plank in your own (6:41-42)! The point being made here is that we need to examine our own lives before we can comment on others. Even if we claim to be religious and call "Lord, Lord" (6:46), this is false religion, and worthless unless we actually do what God wants us to do.

The story of the two builders (6:47-49) makes clear the distinction. True religion (like the house built on rock) is firmly grounded on the teaching of Jesus and the good actions which follow from it. But false religion (like the house built on soil) is shaky because it is not founded on Jesus' teachings. As soon as this sort of religion is tested (like the river bursting on the house) it is shown to be false.

It is not really a question of having to *judge* what is true religion from what is false religion. (At 6:37, Luke has Jesus advise against making judgments of this sort. It is clear from the blind guide and the man with the plank in his eye that we can only comment on others if we ourselves are free from fault.) This distinction will be apparent to us from a person's actions. As a rough guide we might say that if the consequences of a person's actions are helpful to others this is likely to be an example of true religion. If, on the other hand, an action is harmful to others it is likely to be an example of false religion. For Luke, true religion is acting in accordance with the teachings of Jesus.

D. CONFLICT WITH PHARISEES AND LAWYERS

In the examples of true and false religion so far considered, people, it would seem, are left to make up their own minds as to whether or not what Jesus has to say applies to them. But at Luke 11:37-54, Jesus focuses on two specific groups who, in his view, are practising false religion. These are the Pharisees and the lawyers. Jesus is not attacking the whole Jewish faith. His concern is with the way the leaders of the Judaism of his day have distorted the religion. It is the leaders and teachers of the religion Jesus attacks not the religion itself.

There is no doubt that the gospel writers tend to paint the Pharisees in particular in a poor light. Most of them were devout and sincere Jews, even if some did have narrow views concerning the behaviour God expected of them. It may be that Luke, like the other gospel writers, presents Jesus and the Pharisees as more opposed to one another than they really were. Even so, those who met Jesus, must have genuinely felt that he was encouraging a far too relaxed attitude towards the ritual side of the religion. Indeed, at 11:37-38, the Pharisee who has invited Jesus to a meal is surprised that Jesus does not follow the customary ritual of washing before eating. This leads Jesus into an attack on what he sees as the false religion of the Pharisees and the lawyers. In their inflexible attitude to the minute observance of every detail of their religion, they have gone too far. The real problem was that their desire to stop themselves and others from doing wrong actually prevented them from doing good. (See Note on Pharisees, p.104). They had become obsessed with detail and had overlooked the really important things of life. Their concern to be "clean" on the outside (11:39) meant they had failed to examine themselves on the inside. For Luke's Jesus, a religion which sets ritual concerns above human concerns is a false religion.

E. A WRONG INTERPRETATION OF RELIGION

Jesus attacks the Pharisees and lawyers on a number of specific issues. By examining his criticisms of them, we can understand more about the way the Pharisees and lawyers interpreted their religion. The paying of tithes was a religious requirement. You had to give a proportion of your income to God. The Pharisees were so obsessed with keeping every detail of the law that they even paid tithes on what they grew in their gardens, just to be on the safe side (11:42)! Jesus is critical of them for not having a better sense of proportion. He does not say that tithing is wrong. But he does say that there are much more important issues, such as loving God and being concerned for justice (11:42).

The self satisfied behaviour of the Pharisees seems to have annoyed Jesus. This led them to occupy the important seats in the synagogues. They also wanted others to recognise and acknowledge their holiness (11:43). But Jesus made a rather unflattering comparison when he likened them to "unmarked graves" (11:44). Because it was thought that coming into contact with death made a person unclean, graves were frequently painted white to warn people to stay away. Like unmarked graves, the Pharisees looked innocent enough, but close contact revealed just how dangerous they really were.

Jesus was equally strong in his attack on the lawyers. It was they who were largely responsible for developing the thousands of rules which they expected ordinary people to obey. But it was almost impossible to carry out your daily routine *and* obey the rules, if you were an ordinary working person. Jesus accuses the lawyers of loading people with intolerable burdens (the thousands of rules they were expected to obey) without ever lifting a finger to help them (11:46). He then attacks them for building tombs for the prophets (11:47-48). The view of religion held by the lawyers was the same as the one held by the Jews of the past who had failed to recognise true religion as taught by the prophets of the Old Testament. They had killed the prophets, and now people like the lawyers were building tombs for them. By doing this, it was as if they were approving of the murders in the first place. Jesus warns that they will have to answer for these misdeeds of the past (11:49-51). (Luke probably also has in mind, at this point, Jesus' own death, and may be implying that the destruction of Jerusalem - the event that occurred in AD 70 - is their punishment.) Finally, Jesus attacks the lawyers for misusing their opportunities (11:52). They are the learned people, the teachers, who have a great responsibility and a great opportunity (possession of "the key of knowledge"). But instead of putting people in the way of true religion they have turned them, and themselves, from it. After this attack, Luke notes how hostile the Pharisees and lawyers are towards Jesus (11:53-54). He is preparing his readers for the greater hostilities that are to come.

NOTE ON MARTYRS (11:51)

Abel and Zechariah are the first and last martyrs mentioned in the Old Testament.

Though Jesus appears to think of the prophets as martyrs, there is not much evidence in the Old Testament of prophets being killed for their beliefs.

NOTE ON PHARISEES

The name 'Pharisees' seems to have meant 'the separated ones'. It indicated that they wished to remain apart from those who did not observe the Law (e.g. tax-gatherers), from pagan customs (those of the Romans), and from religious impurity (anyone ritually unclean, e.g. lepers).

They were extremely devout and attempted to keep the Law of Moses in every detail. They also preserved oral traditions which they treated as being of equal importance to the Law. They were probably successors to the Maccabees and the Hasmonaeans, Jewish dynasties which had resisted the spread of Greek ideas in the second century BC.

Unlike the Sadducees, the Pharisees believed that after death there would, at some time in the future, be resurrection to a new life for law-abiding Jews. They also believed that angels and spirits brought men messages from God. Neither of these beliefs is precisely stated in the books of Moses but they were developed later as a result of persecution. Jesus' differences with them arose mainly because of their insistence on sticking to every detail of the Law regardless of the consequences (see 6:1-11); and of extending it into every area of life (see 11:42).

Although some Pharisees were priests, most were laymen who banded together to live by the Law. Modern Judaism is derived from the Pharisees because, unlike the Sadducees, they were not attached to the Temple and, therefore, survived its destruction in AD 70.

NOTE ON DOCTORS OF THE LAW, LAWYERS, SCRIBES

Luke uses two Greek words, *nomikos* and *grammateus*, to refer to this group of people. They are usually described in English as lawyers or scribes and these words sum up very well the tasks they performed. They were scribes in that they made copies of the scrolls of the Law, and lawyers in the sense that they were expert in the Law and acted as judges in the courts. In their training they learned by heart many past legal cases in which the Law had been applied to settle disputes, and when they heard new cases they would give judgment in accordance with tradition. At 12:13-14, Luke shows a man asking Jesus to act in this way, but what follows is a parable about wealth: a challenge to the man, not a judgment.

Lawyers often had their own groups of disciples to whom they passed on their knowledge and in this Jesus resembled them. Jesus was also acting like a lawyer when he interpreted the Law and when he taught in synagogues (6:9; 4:31). But he differed from the lawyers in that he did not refer to past cases but spoke with authority.

The lawyers were respected members of the community and were addressed as 'rabbi', meaning 'teacher'. Being a lawyer was not a paid profession, and unless they were wealthy they worked for their living. The majority of them lived in Jerusalem.

They were not a religious party themselves, and many of them belonged to the Pharisees' party while others were Sadducees. They were represented in the Sanhedrin and sat in judgment on Jesus (22:66). Not all lawyers seem to have opposed Jesus, and at 20:39 one of them is shown to congratulate Jesus on the way he had interpreted the Law.

F. HAVING THE RIGHT ATTITUDE TO RELIGION

Although at 12:1 the scene changes from the dinner party (mentioned at 11:37) to the gathering of a large crowd, Jesus begins on the same note by again denouncing the Pharisees. He describes their actions as "hypocrisy" and he uses their behaviour to teach the disciples a lesson. The use of the symbol 'leaven' is an interesting one. Leaven is like yeast, which you put into bread to make it rise. Here it would seem to be another way of saying, 'What makes the Pharisees *act* in the way they do?', or 'What *motivates* them?' And the saying at 12:2-3 indicates that Jesus sees their lives as a pretence. What motivates them is their desire to lead faultless lives. This may seem an admirable enough ambition, but it had grown like yeast and had got out of hand. They had built into their lives so many 'DO NOTs' that they had deluded themselves into thinking that they were perfect. According to their standards, everyone else was imperfect and should be looked down on. This is the attitude which Jesus calls hypocritical. Jesus was much more concerned with what goes on in people's hearts and minds than with the ritual details of religion. The Pharisees were hiding their real selves behind a thin veneer of religious ritual. They are not even being honest with themselves. But Jesus warns that the truth will be revealed and people will be exposed for what they really are (12:2-3).

The religion of the Pharisees would appear to be false religion, in Jesus' view, for two reasons. First, because it is nothing more than a pretence and, second, because it tries to make God act. The Pharisees believed that if all the Jews followed their example and led faultless lives in accordance with God's rules, then God would send the Messiah. In other words, they were hoping to make God *act*. But, in the sayings which follow (12:4-12) Jesus is teaching his disciples that true religion is not trying to make God act but is simply about *trust* in God. If you trust in God then you will not fear what people can do to you (12:4-

5 and 11-12). Jesus assures his disciples that God cares for them (12:6-7) and all they have to do is to keep their trust and their faith in him (12:8-9). The saying at 12:10 is perhaps the most difficult in this passage to understand. Perhaps it means that even if you are not a follower of Jesus you can still have true religion if you do not deny the influence that God has in your life.

G. DISTRACTIONS WHICH PREVENT TRUE RELIGION

There are a number of other examples in the teaching of Jesus where the true religion/false religion distinction is made. In the Parable of the Sower 8:4-15, for example, it is clear that wherever the gospel is preached it will receive a mixed reception. Everyone present may hear what is said but there are so many distractions in this life which lead us down the paths of false religion or no religion at all. Rather like the saying at 6:43-45, about good trees producing good fruit, so those who are truly religious show themselves by their good actions (see 8:15).

Two more examples of the true religion/false religion distinction are to be found at 18:15-27. In the first part of that section (18:15-17), the disciples have to be corrected by Jesus when they try to prevent people bringing children to him. Jesus says that the kingdom of God belongs to children and it is necessary for everyone to accept the kingdom like a child. True religion, as we have seen, is about trust in God. What is more genuine than the trust a young child has in its parents? It is simple, uncomplicated, trust, that results from the love it has been shown. To add to this, in the ancient world, children had absolutely no rights. They were thoroughly dependent on their parents or those who looked after them. Jesus is trying to get across to his followers that the kingdom of God is for those who know they need it. It is for those who are helpless and have nothing to offer as a means of buying their way in. False religion, for Jesus, is when you think you can buy your way into God's favour. That is why, for true religion, a childlike innocence is necessary.

In the second part of that section (18:18-27), Jesus is asked by a man of the ruling class what he must do to win eternal life. His question is the same as the lawyer's at 10:25 which led Jesus to tell the story of The Good Samaritan. Jesus finds out that the man has always led his life according to the Commandments. However, there is still one thing which stands in the way of true religion and that is the man's wealth. He is told to sell his goods, give the money to the poor and follow Jesus. This the man cannot bring himself to do. Unlike the child, the rich man was independent and self-sufficient. He did not need to rely on others - not even God - for his well-being. His religion, although a genuine attempt at following the Commandments, is still false religion because he put his trust in his own resources instead of in God.

The saying about tasteless salt at 14:34-35 might apply equally well to false religion. If it is no good, throw it out!

The Sower (8:4-15)

1. The story falls into two main parts. Part 1 is the parable (8:4-8); Part 2 is an allegorical explanation of it (8:11-15). It was common in the early church to allegorise the parables of Jesus and it is possible that 8:4-8 may originally have stood on its own. The connecting link at 8:9-10 suggests that the purpose of parables is to prevent people understanding the truths they tell. It may be that Luke has included this last point mainly because he found it in Mark. Jesus would hardly have used this popular method of teaching to confuse people. Mark had definite reasons for stating this idea so starkly, whereas Luke probably did not and, therefore, it fits rather oddly. However, it can still make some sense in that the saying could be taken to mean that some people would refuse to accept the truth even if it was made plain to them. This would certainly link in with the missionary experience of the early Church.

2. This parable is perhaps best understood as a story for the early Church which is designed to explain why it is that so few people become Christians. Imagine how hard it would be for those early Christians to find the gospel message so frequently rejected. They were convinced that Jesus was the Messiah, so why could not everyone see this? They must have felt the same about the crowds who followed Jesus during his life-time. Why had not they understood the truth about Jesus? The story deals with the problem. Just as the farmer spreads the seed knowing that it will not all take root in good soil, so Jesus explains that, though many will hear the gospel, not all will respond to it. The good news for the missionaries of the early Church is that there will be a harvest. Many of those who have the gospel preached to them will become true Christians.

3. The explanation of the story is also a warning to new converts to the faith of all the pitfalls there are in trying to lead a good Christian life. Courage and determination are necessary qualities of the disciple. Those who do not have them will fall prey to evil or give up their faith at the approach of danger (8:12-13), or not grow in faith because they are too interested in wealth and material comforts (8:14). These are the people who "look but see nothing, hear but understand nothing" (8:10).

Questions on 8:4-15
(*See also* p.108 for questions on this passage)

1. Write out the main points in the parable of The Sower.
2. What is the given explanation of the parable?
3. How might this parable have helped the early Church to understand why it was that not every-one who heard the gospel became a Christian?
4. What warnings and encouragement does the parable give to those who would wish to lead a good Christian life?

H. TRUE RELIGION/FALSE RELIGION TODAY

We began this section by pointing out that examples of true religion and of false religion can be found in all the world faiths. Jesus identified and commented on the examples of false religion which existed in the country where he lived, and he tried to teach his disciples the meaning of true religion. It was the leaders of the Judaism of Jesus' day who came in for the strongest criticism. But had Jesus lived today he would, no doubt, have found plenty to comment upon in the Christian Church, and in the lives of individuals. There is no room for complacency, and sometimes the line between true religion and false religion can be a thin one. We do not necessarily have to go looking for examples of false religion but it is important to be able to recognise them when they occur. For example, we may hear on the news about the actions of some so-called religious group, or of something which has been done in the name of religion which has caused harm to other people, or which does not seem consistent with truly religious behaviour. We then need to be in a position where we can say: 'This is not true religion, this is false religion'. Can you identify any current situations which you recognise as being examples of false religion, and ask yourselves: 'What would the Jesus of Luke's gospel have said about this?'

Questions on Theme I: True religion and false religion

6:39-49

1a. What is likely to happen if one blind man leads another, according to Jesus?

b. What sort of fruit do good trees produce?

c. What happened to the house built on soil when the river burst its banks?

d. What does Jesus intend his disciples to learn through the short parable of the speck of sawdust and the plank?

e. Do people have bad thoughts and do good things, according to Jesus?

f. What do you think Jesus meant when he said: "For each tree is known by its fruit"?

g. What do you think is meant by "foundations on rock" in the parable?

8:4-15 (*See also* p.107 for questions on this passage)

2. What does the parable of The Sower teach about the difficulties of being a true Christian?

10:25-37 (*see also* p.102 for questions on this passage)

3a. What was the work of **(i)** the priest, **(ii)** the Levite?

b. Why were they reluctant to help the injured man?

4. Why were the *actions* of the Samaritan superior to the religious *intentions* of the priest and Levite?

11:37-54

5a. Why was the Pharisee critical of Jesus?

b. What were the specific criticisms Jesus made of **(i)** the Pharisees, **(ii)** the lawyers?

c. What was false about the religion of the Pharisees, according to Jesus?

d. What did Jesus mean by the 'intolerable burdens' which he accused the lawyers of loading people with?

6a. If you were a good and honest Pharisee what would you think of Jesus?

b. Why do you think the gospel writers present the Pharisees in such a poor light?

7a. Would you agree that Jesus was angry with the Pharisees and lawyers mainly because they did not use their positions of influence responsibly?

b. Can you think of any modern-day examples where people in positions of power fail to act responsibly?

12:1-12

8a. What does the word 'hypocrisy' mean?

b. Why did Jesus accuse the Pharisees of hypocrisy?

c. Can you describe and comment on an example of hypocrisy you have come across?

9a. Give *two* examples of sayings of Jesus from this passage which are meant to show his disciples why they should put their trust in God.

b. How should the disciple behave if brought before the authorities?

c. What do you understand by the saying: "There is nothing covered up that will not be uncovered, nothing hidden that will not be made known?"

10. What might this passage teach the modern-day Christian about living in the world as a disciple of Jesus?

18:15-27

11a. What did Jesus say to the disciples when they tried to stop people bringing their children to him?

b. What do you think it means to accept the kingdom of God as a child?

12a. What question does the rich ruler put to Jesus?

b. What is Jesus' reply?

c. When Jesus learns that the rich ruler keeps the Commandments, what further action does he recommend?

d. How does the rich ruler react to this advice?

e. Why was the religion of the rich ruler false?

13. Does the teaching of Jesus in this passage mean that if you are wealthy you cannot be a true Christian?

THEME II
SEEING THINGS CLEARLY
References: 8:16-18; 11:14-36; 12:13-21; 12:54-59; 15:11-32; 16:1-15; 18:1-8.

A. SEEING THINGS CLEARLY IN TODAY'S WORLD

Before we look at how Luke deals with this idea, it is worth pausing to think about ourselves. All of us have had the experience of not understanding something even when it has been explained carefully to us. Usually, however, if we work hard at an idea, we can come to understand it. We are pleased with ourselves because we have *thought* the matter through. Thinking carefully about issues and situations is important. This is how we come to see things clearly. In life, however, we do not always think things through carefully enough. Sometimes we allow other things to get in the way. For example, we may be *prejudiced* about something or someone and that prejudice gets in the way of our seeing things clearly. People can be prejudiced about all sorts of things from trivial matters, such as the make of car they drive, to much more serious matters, such as racial or religious prejudice. Prejudice of this sort prevents us from seeing clearly the value in other things or other people.

Prejudice is similar to having *narrow views* which can also stop us seeing things clearly. We saw in Theme I how the views of the Pharisees and lawyers were so narrow that they could not see matters clearly at all. Their narrow views gave them a distorted view of religion and of life. People today who hold narrow views are in similar danger.

There are also many *distractions* in life which prevent us from seeing things clearly. We do not always manage to sort out what is really important, because other things get in the way. It might be worth pausing to ask yourself a few questions. For example, what do I consider to be important in life? Do I always act with this in mind? What things distract me from seeing things clearly?

A final example of something which prevents people from seeing things clearly is *poor judgment*. Some people are easily led by others. Instead of working things out for themselves they allow others to influence them or make their decisions for them. Some people are gullible, always allowing others to get the better of them, or to cheat or fool them in some way. Such people have poor judgment and do not see things at all clearly.

These examples show that 'seeing things clearly' is really about having the right outlook on life. We are not born with this ability. It is something we develop as a result of the different experiences we go through as we live our lives. Sometimes coming to the right decision means *changing our minds* or *changing our way of thinking* about something. This is what seeing things clearly is about. It is having the ability to look at the evidence, think matters through and arrive at the right decision, even if this means changing course.

As we come now to look at Luke's gospel, we shall discover that having the ability to 'see things clearly' is something he encourages in his readers. Many of Luke's characters, such as the Lost Son and the Dishonest Steward, have the ability to think things through and see clearly the course of action they must take. In a way, Luke presents them as examples for us to follow. Luke knows that prejudices and distractions, narrow views and poor judgment, will prevent people from seeing things clearly. He is concerned that his readers should have the right outlook on life and, above all, that they should see clearly who Jesus is.

B. SEEING CLEARLY WHO JESUS IS

A favourite image of Luke's is that of the lamp on a stand (he uses it at 8:16 and 11:33). A lighted lamp makes it possible for people to see things clearly. It does not make sense to put a cover over a light, for that defeats the object. Similarly, knowledge about Jesus enables people to have right understanding - to see things clearly in their mind's eye. This knowledge should not be concealed but be made available to all. Perhaps at 8:16 Luke has in mind the house-church where all are welcome to 'come in' to hear the truth about Jesus. But at 8:17 it is apparent that such truth will eventually be made available to all, so that everyone will have the opportunity to see things clearly if they want to.

Luke makes it quite apparent that, during Jesus' lifetime, many people did not see clearly who he was. The incident at 11:14-26 is an example. Jesus has just driven a devil out of a possessed man. Some of the astonished crowd suggest that Jesus was in league with Satan (Luke appears to use Beelzebub as another name for Satan) and that he was using demonic power to perform miracles. How distorted could their vision become? Their poor judgment means they are unable to distinguish between good and evil.

Others want more proof, and demand a sign from heaven to help them make up their minds. Jesus replies with a parable to show that if he is on the side of Satan then Satan's kingdom must be in a state of civil war and in danger of collapse. ("Every kingdom divided against itself goes to ruin" 11:17). At 11:21-22 another short parable emphasises that Jesus and Satan are on opposite sides. It says that you cannot rob a strong man unless you have first overpowered him and made him defenceless. Here the strong man represents Satan and Jesus is "someone stronger" (11:22). In driving out demons Jesus is robbing Satan

of his power. To be able to do that he must first have defeated Satan and, in so doing, shown himself to be the stronger of the two. The only power stronger than Satan's comes from God. Jesus' question to the people at 11:19 is a clear indication that exorcising demons was a common enough occurrence in the ancient world (see chapter 9), so this alone was not evidence of Jesus' Messiahship. But if these people (11:20) had clear vision they would see God at work in Jesus and realise that the kingdom of God had already come. Jesus challenges his hearers to improve their judgment. They must understand that if they are not for Jesus they must be on the side of Satan (11:23). The parable of the empty house (11:24-26) is a further attempt on the part of Jesus to get his message across. Once a person is cured of demonic possession, clear vision and determination to lead a new life with God at the centre is necessary to avoid even worse things happening. Jesus' reply to the woman who shouts after him (11:27-28) shows that it is an individual's *response* to God's word that is really important.

C. JESUS IS GOD'S SIGN FOR THE WORLD

At 11:16 some of the people demand a sign from heaven. In other words, they want more evidence before they make up their minds about Jesus. At 11:29-32 Luke shows Jesus attacking this idea as wicked because it is tempting God to act. (The third temptation (4:9-12) made clear that God should not be tested in this way.) Jesus wants them to understand that God has already given them a sign (Jesus himself) but they simply cannot see it.

He compares the Jews of his day unfavourably with some foreigners from the past. The people of Nineveh and the Queen of Sheba saw clearly the signs which God gave them whereas the Jews do not. Jesus compares himself to Jonah who warned the people of Nineveh to change their ways. Their clearer vision led them to see in Jonah a sign from God and they responded with a change of heart (they repented). But even though Jesus himself is a sign (and a greater one than Jonah) the Jews of his day still do not see clearly who he is and, therefore, do not respond appropriately. Similarly the Queen of Sheba (the "Queen of the South", 11:31) recognised in the wisdom of King Solomon a sign from God for the people of her day. Jesus is greater than Solomon, but still the Jews cannot see clearly who he is. At the judgment, when the Jews of Jesus' day are on trial, the people of Nineveh and the Queen of Sheba will act as witnesses for the prosecution to ensure that the accused are found guilty for their inability to understand what is going on.

This section of the gospel ends with sayings about lamps and eyes (11:33-36) which leave the reader in no doubt that Jesus is making a contrast between those who do understand who he is and those who do not. If you have good eyes (the ability to think clearly) then you will have light (you will recognise that Jesus is a sign from God) whereas if your eyesight is poor (the inability to think things through) you will have darkness (you will fail to understand who Jesus really is). And what a joy it is to be able to see things so clearly (11:36)!

D. IMPROVING ONE'S JUDGMENT

Luke's Jesus, in various ways, continually urges his hearers to improve their judgment. At 12:54-56 Jesus notes their ability to forecast the weather and wonders why they cannot see what is happening on the human and political front. Perhaps the forthcoming destruction of Jerusalem is implied by 'this fateful hour' (12:56). It may also be a veiled reference to Jesus' own coming death. The following short parable about settling out of court (12:57-59) is an example of the sort of common sense Luke admires. It is sound judgment to sort out matters before you get to court otherwise if the case goes against you and you are put in prison you will never be able to earn the money necessary to pay your debt. Luke is perhaps intending to remind his readers that they are all in God's debt (sin) and, therefore, they need to settle their accounts with God (repent) before the judgment.

E. MAKING THE RIGHT DECISION

Most of the examples considered so far in this theme are about people's poor judgment. They fail to see clearly who Jesus is or what course of action they should take in their lives. In a number of the parables of Jesus Luke shows how those people who *do* take the trouble to think things through carefully see clearly what course of action they should take. Quite often this involves them in a complete change of heart and mind in order to survive. This is exactly what repentance is all about. Repenting is not just about saying sorry, though we often use the word to mean just that. It is much more about making a fresh start and embarking on a completely new way of life, as John the Baptist so forcefully reminded his hearers (3:7-14). A good example of repentance in action is the parable of The Lost Son, 15:11-32.

At the point where the younger son has spent all his money, and is forced to work for a Gentile pig-farmer (what could have been worse for a Jew?), he sits down to think, and he comes to his senses. Until this time the lost son has not seen things clearly at all. He has been selfish and rather stupid. But now common sense prevails. In the face of disaster, he thinks things through and decides on a fresh course of action. His life takes off again; his shrewd judgment has paid off.

Another of Luke's rogue characters is the Dishonest Steward, 16:1-15. He faces dismissal from his job for shady dealing and wonders what he should do to make the best of the crisis situation. Luke lets us in on the Steward's thinking as he reviews the possibilities. This careful thought leads him to see clearly what course of action he must take. His solution is hardly honest (*though see* Note 1, p.113), but even his employer congratulates him on his clear vision and sound judgment!

Yet another example of a bad character Luke includes in his gospel is the Unjust Judge, 18:1-8 (*see* p.118 for Notes on this parable). His crisis situation is a widow who continually pesters him to give judgment in her favour over some matter. Again, Luke lets us into the man's thinking. After carefully reflecting on the problem, the judge decides on a course of action. He sees clearly what he must do in order to resolve his problem.

PARABLES ABOUT LOSING AND FINDING (15:1-32)

The Lost Sheep (15:3-7) and *The Lost Coin* (15:8-10)

It is important to see how 15:1-2 sets the scene for the three parables in this section of the gospel. Jesus is talking with 'tax-gatherers and other bad characters'. The Pharisees and doctors of the Law are critical of Jesus because of his association with these undesirable people. In their view such characters are hopelessly 'lost'. Jesus replies in his usual way by telling stories, the meaning of which his hearers are left to work out for themselves. The main theme of each of these stories is *repentance*. A change of mind and heart can mean that suddenly the 'lost' is 'found'. In the case of the sheep and the coin repentance is only an underlying theme. Animals and objects do not repent. Here the emphasis is much more on God's love for those who, like the tax-gatherers and sinners, are 'lost' in life. Like the shepherd and the woman, God actively seeks out such people. When they are 'found', this is a cause for great rejoicing. Both the shepherd and the woman call their friends and neighbours together for a party to celebrate the lost being found.

The Lost (or Prodigal)[11] *Son (15:11-32)*

1. The theme of repentance is much stronger in this parable because it is about a person, and only people can change their hearts and minds. This is the longest of the parables and probably the best known and most loved.

2. Some elements of the story are probably meant to be understood allegorically. For example, the younger son could be seen to represent the undesirables of Jewish society (the tax-gatherers and sinners mentioned at 15:1-2), whilst the elder brother is like the Pharisees and doctors of the Law. The father would then represent God, who wants nothing more than for the sinner to repent. However, these are really no more than interesting parallels. What is central is the Lost Son's act of repentance and the differing attitudes of the father and elder brother towards him on his return home.

The father He is portrayed as a good man who loves his sons. Like other characters in Luke, the father is a devout Jew who, in obedience to the Law, gives his son his inheritance and allows him to leave home. He also demonstrates the spirit in which the Law should be applied by welcoming his son back unquestioningly. The father is generous and he does not condemn.

The younger son He is impatient and wants the good things of life immediately. (According to Deuteronomy 21:17 the younger son was entitled to one-third of the property on his father's death; the elder son would receive the remaining two-thirds. But it was accepted that at least part of the inheritance might be given to a man's sons whilst he was still alive.) Sadly the younger son does not manage his money responsibly. However, when faced with a crisis, he displays common sense and works out a plan to get out of trouble. His act of repentance is the turning-point of the whole story.

The elder son On the face of it the elder son is loyal and obedient. He is hard-working and presumably a morally upright person. However, he is resentful of the way his father treats his immoral younger brother. The story does not tell us whether the elder son saw his father's point of view or not. Did he go into the party and welcome back his lost brother, or did he stay away? If he went in, he too changed his heart and mind (repented). If he did not, he is the one who becomes 'lost'.

---

[11] The term 'prodigal' refers to the younger son's reckless and wasteful spending of the money he received from his father.

3. The crisis point of the story would have made quite an impact on Jewish hearers. Pigs were considered unclean and Jews were forbidden to keep them. By working with pigs, the younger son became religiously unclean, according to Jewish law. He was a sinner and truly 'lost'. But the parable makes the point that the repentant sinner is accepted by God without any need for ritual sacrifice.

4. This parable may be better named the Parable of the Two Sons, because it is as much about the behaviour of the elder son as it is about the younger one. As with some other of Luke's characters, each proves himself to be a mixture of both good and bad. Another name for it could be the Parable of the Forgiving Father. The younger son knows he needs his father's forgiveness whereas the elder one does not recognise any such need in himself. It is perhaps worth comparing this aspect of the story with another parable of Jesus, that of The Two Debtors (7:36-50). Can you work out why?

5. Twice in the story we are reminded of the resurrection. The father at 15:24 and 32 speaks of the prodigal as having been dead but coming back to life. On both occasions this is related to *celebrating* the happy day. Luke is perhaps reminding his readers of Jesus' own resurrection from the dead and how this is a great cause for rejoicing.

Questions on 15:11-32

(*See also* p.116 for questions on this passage)

1a. What action did (i) the shepherd, (ii) the woman take when they discovered their respective losses?

b. What did they do when the lost was found?

c. In what ways are the shepherd and the woman like God?

2a. How did the lost son acquire his wealth?

b. How did he spend his money?

c. What happened to cause him to work on a pig farm?

3. What common-sense course of action did the lost son decide on when facing his crisis?

4a. How did the father behave on the lost son's return?

b. Do you think the father was right to act in the way he did?

5a. How did the elder brother behave on his younger brother's return?

b. Do you think he was wrong to react in the way he did?

6. What aspects of the parable may be interpreted allegorically?

7a. What other names could be given to the parable of The Lost Son?

b. Explain why these names could be appropriate.

8. What is the Jesus of Luke's gospel trying to teach through these three parables?

9. Which other parables in Luke's gospel are concerned with repentance?

The Dishonest Steward (16:1-13)

1. How can such outrageous dishonesty on the part of the steward lead the master, who has just been so badly swindled, to offer him his congratulations on having such sound judgment? Clearly this is a story designed to shock. Surely Luke does not intend to encourage his readers to be dishonest! It may be that another interpretation of the parable is intended. This minimises the dishonesty of the steward. Usury (that is, the lending of money at a rate of interest) was forbidden in the Old Testament. The Pharisees said that the purpose of this law was to prevent people becoming destitute. They argued that, provided that the borrower did not become poverty-stricken, the lender should be allowed to charge interest. When money was loaned to finance a crop of oil or wheat, the loan was repaid in goods and interest was paid by adding extra quantities. This opens up the possibility of interpreting the parable along the following lines. The steward is dishonest but when caught out repents. A sign of his repentance is that he follows the commandment of God rather than the interpretation of it by the Pharisees. By reducing the quantities of oil and wheat which his master's debtors owe, he is removing

the interest and so following the spirit of the Old Testament. The master is then seen to be praising him for repenting and following God's commandments.

2. The key to understanding the parable is to be found in the idea of the crisis situation, and how to act in a crisis. It is the *method* used by the steward which is important. The steward thinks the matter through carefully and then takes action. This is the method Luke would encourage his readers to follow (a) when they face crisis situations in life, and (b) especially when it comes to pursuing their faith. They must, if necessary, be as *determined* and *ruthless* as the steward, in order to secure their future with God. (The "eternal home" at 16:9 means being with God.)

3. Within the parable are some allegorical elements. For example, the command of the master, "Produce your accounts", is like the *judgment* when each person will have to justify his actions. The master is like God who, according to Luke, is willing to forgive those who, like the steward, get into trouble in life. But this forgiveness is given only *if* people are prepared to acknowledge their problems and *do* something about them. Luke may also want his readers to understand that judgment is not something that happens only at death. Crisis situations occur frequently for all of us in life. We have to make decisions and take positive action in the face of these crises. When we do, we find that life goes on. It may take a different direction (as with the prodigal son) and, if the decision is a good one, it may be a *better* direction.

4. 16:9-13 suggests that Luke wanted to set the record straight with his readers. Just in case they have missed the point of the story, here he tells them that he is *not* encouraging them to be dishonest. They *must* be trustworthy and always put God first.

Questions on 16:1-13
(*See also* p.116 for questions on this passage)

1. Why was the rich man going to dismiss the steward?
2. What action did the steward take in order to secure a future for himself?
3. How did the master react to the steward's actions?
4. What is Luke trying to teach his readers through this story?

5. What aspects of the story may be interpreted as allegory?
6. What reasons would you give to show that Luke is *not* encouraging his readers to be dishonest?

F. MAKING THE WRONG DECISION

Thinking things through carefully does not in itself mean that we will arrive at the right decision.

In the parable of The Rich Fool, 12:13-21, Luke gives us an example of someone who thinks things through but arrives at the wrong decision. Once again we are able to listen in on the rich man's thinking. Unfortunately for him his wealth is a distraction which prevents him from seeing things clearly. In purely material terms his decision would appear to be the right one. But putting money before God is the wrong decision.

The Rich Fool
(12:13-21)

1. Why should a sound businessman be dubbed a fool? The answer lies in the introduction to the parable where Jesus is asked to settle a dispute between two brothers who are squabbling over the family property. The man who asked the question presumably thought of Jesus as a rabbi, and rabbis were frequently asked to give judgments of this sort. But Jesus wants to show that his purpose is the more serious one of showing

how God judges people's lives. Through the parable, which illustrates this, Luke issues a warning to all his wealthy readers that, if they leave God out of the reckoning, they are acting like fools. (A fool in the Biblical sense is one who says "There is no God" (Psalm 53:1).) The rich man was so distracted by his wealth that he did not give God a thought - he acted as if he did not believe in God. This serious lack of judgment earns him the title of "fool".

2. The story has a number of features which are typical of Luke. These include the themes of wealth, common sense and reversal. In a way the rich man's thinking is reasonable enough and makes sound business sense. His problem is that he has put his money before God. He is complacent and believes himself to be self-sufficient. In terms of worldly success he has made it. But Luke shows how people's standards are not God's standards: the rich man is, therefore, judged to be poor in God's eyes. This is a spiritual poverty which has come about because he has failed to put God first in his life. If Luke's own church included some wealthy people, he may have felt the need to warn them of the dangers they face if they allow their money to come before their relationship with God. We might consider that, in a relatively wealthy society such as ours, Luke's message is just as relevant today.

Questions on 12:13-21

(*See also* p.116 for questions on this passage)

1. Why did Jesus tell this parable?
2. Why did the rich man decide to build bigger storehouses?
3. What happened to the rich man at the end of the story?
4. Why was the rich man called a fool?
5. In what sense was the rich man 'poor'?

1 ADDITIONAL NOTE ON WEALTH

The Rich Fool (12:13-21) is an example of someone who puts wealth before God. We saw in Theme I (section g, p.106) how the rich ruler does the same. His money prevents him from putting his complete trust in God. Some of Luke's readers may have been wealthy people. Perhaps Luke felt they too were in danger of being so distracted by their money that God was not coming first in their lives. However, Luke does not want them to feel guilty about being rich. Many of the characters in his stories are wealthy people. For example, the father in the story of the Lost Son (15:11-32); the Centurion (7:1-10) who, according to 7:5 built the synagogue at Capernaum for the Jews; Zacchaeus the tax-collector (19:1-10), and Levi (5:27-32) who became a disciple of Jesus and was wealthy enough to hold 'a big reception in his house' (5:29) in Jesus' honour. There are also a number of references to dinner parties and other similar occasions in Luke's gospel (for example: 7:36; 11:37; 14:1, 7, 12, 17) which suggest perhaps that such activities formed part of Luke's world and the world of his readers. Presumably only those who were reasonably well-off could afford to entertain their friends in this way.

In none of the examples mentioned does Jesus criticise these people for their wealth or say that it is a bad thing in itself. It seems that wealth only becomes a problem when people make it their first priority so that it, rather than God, rules their lives. Luke makes the point that money can be used thoughtfully and considerately to the benefit of others. Indeed at 8:1-3 he makes reference to 'a number of women' who accompanied Jesus on his travels and who provided for him and the disciples 'out of their own resources'. Here is a responsible use of wealth which seems quite acceptable to Luke. Zacchaeus himself, after he had met Jesus, we are told, gave half his possessions to charity. The Centurion, as we have noted, spent much money on building a place of worship for the Jews in Capernaum. It is clear that, for the father of the Lost Son, money was not the first priority in his life. He was quite prepared to share his fortune with his sons during his life-time, and all that mattered to him was that his younger son should return home safely. However, it is also clear in Luke's gospel that single-minded devotion to money and material possessions *does* cut one off from God. At 16:13 he warns: "You cannot serve God and Money." Pretence is of no use because, as 16:14-15 shows, God can see through that. The warning is given clearly at 6:24 that the rich have had their time of happiness and the Parable of the Rich Man and Lazarus (16:19-31) makes the same point in vivid terms. Through the illustration of the poor widow making her temple offering (21:1-4), the point is made that what is important is not how much or how little money people have but how they choose to use it. Their first priority should be to trust in God, as 12:22-34 shows. In that situation money and all other concerns would take care of themselves.

Questions on Theme II: Seeing things clearly

8:16-18

1a. What is the purpose of the lamp?

b. What does the image of the lamp suggest about the spreading of the gospel?

11:14-28

2a. Who was Jesus accused of being in league with?

b. How does Jesus explain that his power comes from God?

c. What decision does Jesus call on people to make in this passage?

11:29-36

3a. Why did Jesus call the people of his generation wicked?

b. Who was **(i)** Jonah, **(ii)** Solomon?

c. What are **(i)** the similarities, **(ii)** the differences between Jesus and Jonah and Solomon?

d. What do the symbols of darkness and light (11:33-36) represent?

12:13-21 (*see also* p.115 for questions on this passage)

4. Why was the decision of the rich man the wrong decision, according to Luke?

12:54-59

5a. What is meant by "this fateful hour"?

b. What common-sense action did Jesus suggest to those involved in court action?

15:11-32 (*see also* p.113 for questions on this passage)

6a. What crisis situation did the lost son face?

b. How did he react in the face of this emergency?

c. What is meant by the term 'repentance'?

Why would this picture be a good symbol for the parable of The Rich Fool? Look up 12:13-21.

d. In what way did the lost son repent and what was the result of his act of repentance?

16:1-15 (*see also* p.114 for questions on this passage)

7a. How did the dishonest steward react in the face of crisis?

b. Do you think that the steward made the right decision?

18:1-8 (*see also* p.118 for questions on this passage)

8a. What crisis situation did the judge face?

b. Why are the actions of **(i)** the widow and **(ii)** the judge good examples for people to follow, in Luke's view?

Additional questions on the topic 'wealth'

9. Name *two* wealthy people in Luke's gospel who use their money in a responsible way.

10. Name *two* wealthy people in Luke's gospel who put their money before God.

11. Is it wrong to be rich, according to Luke's gospel?

12. What does it mean to put your trust in God?

13. "You cannot serve God and Money" (16:13). What do you understand by this saying?

14. What message might Luke's gospel have for rich people today?

THEME III
LIFE IN THE NEW ORDER

References: 5:33-39; 6:20-38; 7:36-50; 8:19-21; 10:21-24; 11:1-13; 12:22-34,49-53; 14:7-14,25-27; 16:16-18; 17:3-10; 18:1-14

A. OLD AND NEW

By the time Luke wrote, the final split between Jews and Christians had occurred. For some decades after Jesus' death Christians had continued to attend the synagogue and worship alongside Jews who did not accept that Jesus was the Messiah. As time went on, it became increasingly difficult for the two groups to continue together because of their differing views about Jesus. Eventually the Christians broke away to form a new religion. However, as we saw in chapter 5, Luke is at pains to show how Christianity is the rightful heir and successor to the Judaism of the past. In a way, for Luke, it is the Jews who have given up their heritage. The new religion of Christianity is not really new at all. It can be compared perhaps with some of Luke's characters who make decisions which start their lives off again in new and exciting ways. Those who have made the decision for Jesus are linked firmly with the old religion but they are now living in the new order of things.

The two short parables at 5:36-39 confirm for the new Christians that the break with Judaism was right. And it must be a clean break if Christianity is going to survive intact. The 'new cloak' of Christianity will be ruined if it is used to patch up the 'old' cloak of Judaism. What is more, the old cloak would look odd anyway because the new would not match the old. Similarly, the new fermenting wine of Christianity would burst the old, brittle and already stretched, leather wineskins of Judaism. In other words, the old religion of Judaism with its own set teachings and practices could not contain the new teaching of Christianity.

The new order, which Jesus has brought about, is made clear also at 5:33-35 where Jesus is asked why his disciples do not practise fasting. Jesus compares his time with the disciples to a wedding-day, when all usual practices are put aside to celebrate the occasion. The wedding-day is the beginning of a new life for the couple involved. In a similar way, Jesus' ministry is a new beginning for all those who follow him. But Luke is realistic, as 5:39 shows. He knows that the old Judaism is still strong with many followers, and that it will take time for the new wine of Christianity to be accepted, for people always prefer mature old wine to new.

B. NEW TEACHING FOR A NEW ORDER

Given the break with Judaism, how are the new Christians going to live their lives? The old religion taught its followers a way of life. How, in the new order, are people to behave? As we noted earlier (p.98), a whole new set of standards are needed for the followers of Jesus. Luke makes it clear that these new standards are not what the world values. In fact, worldly standards are turned upside down as we can see from the examples which follow.

1.) At 10:21 Jesus thanks God "for hiding these things from the learned and wise, and revealing them to the simple". The world would assume that great theological truths are for the scholars to unravel, but God has chosen to reveal them to simple people. Prophets and kings are denied seeing and hearing Jesus, but the ordinary people who are Jesus' disciples have that privilege (10:23-24).

2.) Through the parable about choosing where to sit at a wedding (14:7-11), Luke makes the point that it is the humble who "will be exalted" (14:11). We have noticed before (chapters 4 & 5) how reversal of fortunes is a favourite theme of Luke's. Here he uses it to show how those who have high opinions of themselves (perhaps he has in mind the Pharisees) may be denied the sort of recognition they desire, whereas those who put others first are given the recognition which they did not look for or expect.

3.) The parable about who to invite to dinner (14:12-14) is another example of how Luke's Jesus turns the world's standards upside down. A usual practice would be to invite to dinner your friends, neighbours, or relations. You might then expect them to invite you back in return. But Jesus' advice to the host is to invite those people who are in need who could not possibly repay the invitation. That is a much more rewarding thing to do. The point is being driven home that in the new order there are new standards.

C. IMITATION OF CHRIST IDEA

In his gospel, Luke encourages his readers to lead their lives by following the example of Jesus. The way of life in the new order is to be based on the teaching of Jesus and the example which he set through his actions during his life. In Jesus the kingdom of God was seen to be present, and so it must be in the lives of repentant Christians. Luke wants his readers to imitate the life which Jesus lived. In particular, he focuses on three aspects of Jesus' life which the followers of Jesus should make their own. These are the life of prayer, the life of service, and the life of suffering (for suffering see chapter 8 section (b.iv)).

D. PRAYER

In presenting Jesus as a man of prayer (e.g. 3:21; 6:12; 9:18, 29; 22:41; 23:34, 46) Luke is perhaps urging his readers to follow this example. They too must be constantly at prayer and especially must they be with God in prayer when facing some challenge in life. According to Luke, Jesus told the parable of the Unjust Judge (18:1-8) in order "to show that they should keep on praying and never lose heart". The message of the parable is that Christians should be persistent in prayer because they know that God is the one who answers prayer.

The Unjust Judge (18:1-8)

1. The point of the parable is made clear at 18:1: people should be persistent in *prayer* (see above). Here the focus is on *petitionary* (asking) prayer. Luke is encouraging his readers continually to make their requests known to God. They must be like the widow and never give up. The point is also made, that they must leave the answer to God.

2. A widow in the ancient world was in an extremely weak position. She had few rights and no man to defend her. The only thing she could do was to plead her case before the judge and leave the decision to him. However, Luke also assures his readers that God *does* answer prayer. The judge did not care for the woman but he did respond to her need. Luke's point is that if an unjust judge behaves like that, how much more will God, who *loves* his people, answer their prayers.

Questions on 18:1-8
(*See also* p.116 for questions on this passage)

1a. What action did the woman take to try to get justice for herself?

  b. What problems faced widows living in the ancient world?

2. What sort of character was the judge?

3. In what way is the Christian like the widow and God like the judge in the parable?

4. What is the main theme of the story?

5a. What is 'petitionary' prayer?

  b. Do you think that Christians today should engage in petitionary prayer?

  c. What other sorts of prayer are there?

Jesus, according to Luke, also taught his disciples how to pray. Having watched Jesus at prayer, one of the disciples wanted to be able to imitate him and so he asked, 'Lord, teach us to pray' (11:1). Jesus responded by teaching the best known Christian prayer of all time, sometimes called the Lord's Prayer. It begins, 'Father . . .'. According to Mark's gospel, when Jesus prayed in Gethsemane he called God 'Abba' ('Father', Mark 14:36). It is generally thought that Jesus commonly used this Aramaic word for God. If he did, he was using a term which was normally used only by children when addressing their fathers. In other words, it suggested a close loving relationship between parent and child. It is sometimes said that Jesus taught Christians to call God 'Daddy'. He was certainly encouraging them to approach God in the spirit of a child approaching his or her father.

The prayer continues by first focusing on God himself, before turning to human needs. In the ancient world names meant more than they do to us today. A person's name indicated also what they were (compare Legion at 8:30). So Jesus first prays that God's name should be kept holy because God is holy. He then prays that God's kingdom will come. For the early Christians, Jesus himself was seen as evidence of the kingdom of God. But, in another sense, the kingdom was still to be established on earth and Christians awaited it with great expectation.

Two human needs are then included in the prayer. No one can survive without food ('bread') and, in the Christian view, no one can survive without forgiveness.

Finally, there is an appeal to God's mercy, that he will not make us face any situation ('test') that would prove too much for us to handle (compare Jesus' prayer for Peter, 22:31-32).

The remainder of the section 11:1-13 (like the parable of the Unjust Judge, 18:1-8), is about being persistent in prayer. The parable of The Friend at Midnight (11:5-10) shows that people must continually pray to God. Only when you ask will you receive, when you seek will you find, and when you knock will the door be opened to you. The following illustration (11:11-13) is designed to show that if a human father, with all his weaknesses, only wants the best for his children, how much more will God want the best for those who ask him. The greatest gift of God is the Holy Spirit, which is available for those who know they need it and ask for it.

As well as knowing what to say in prayer, having the *right attitude* is also important. In the parable of The Pharisee and The Tax-gatherer (18:9-14) Luke gives a warning to "those who were sure of their own goodness and looked down on everyone else". The Pharisee had the wrong attitude because he was only interested in himself and not in God. In fact, he did not really pray at all, he just reflected on his own goodness. The tax-gatherer, on the other hand, had the right attitude because he saw himself as God saw him. His was a real prayer. He acknowledged his sinfulness and threw himself on God's mercy.

The Pharisee and the Tax-gatherer
(18:9-14)

1. The idea of reversal is again evident in this parable. It would be unfair to suggest that all Pharisees were as complacent as the one in the story. However, it seems that many of them regarded themselves as superior to ordinary Jews, especially in their religious practices and their observance of the Law. It would, therefore, have been something of a shock to Jesus' hearers to discover that it is the swindling tax-gatherer who is used as an example for them to follow in their prayer-life rather than the devout Pharisee.

2. The story suggests that the Pharisee is so full of himself that he does not think of God at all. His so-called 'prayer' is simply a recitation of his own goodness. The tax-gatherer, on the other hand, is so aware of all his wrong-doings that he can only turn to God in trust and ask for mercy.

3. By his actions, as well as his words, the tax-gatherer indicated that he was sorry for his wrong-doings. He "kept his distance" (perhaps not wishing to contaminate anyone else by his own sinfulness); he "would not even raise his eyes to heaven" (keeping his eyes lowered symbolised his humility); he "beat upon his breast" (an act which symbolised his sorrow for his wrong-doings).

Questions on 18:9-14
(*See also* p.129 for questions on this passage)

1. What did (a) the Pharisee and (b) the tax-gatherer say in their respective prayers?
2. What actions did the tax-gatherer perform which suggest that he was really sorry for his wrong-doings?
3. Which prayer was answered with forgiveness?
4. Why might the Jews of Jesus' day have been shocked to discover that it was *not* the example of the Pharisee they were being urged to follow?

E. PRAYER TODAY

Prayer is important in the lives of Christians today. On nearly every occasion when Christians meet together prayers are said. In services of worship, time is set aside for prayer and frequently the Lord's Prayer (the universal Christian prayer) is recited. A special "prayer-meeting" may be part of a church's weekly programme of activities, when members get together to pray about things of local, national or international concern. Most Christians also pray daily in their own homes, either on their own or as a family. In the case of monks and nuns, their whole lives revolve around prayer. For them, prayer times are the most important times of the day and night, and all other activities (including sleep) have to be fitted around them. Priests and ministers also devote part of each day to prayer.

The Pater Noster church in Jerusalem.
Each of the plaques along the wall has the Lord's Prayer
in a different language. Why is the Lord's Prayer an
appropriate prayer to find in this church?

Prayer is regarded as the way in which people communicate with God. It is, therefore, a common practice in all religions. For example, prayer is just as important to modern day Jews and Muslims as it is to Christians.

Prayer is thought by Christians to be a two-way process. It involves 'listening' to God as well as 'speaking' to him. Through prayer Christians believe they receive guidance from God on how to live their lives, as well as being able to put before God their own needs and the needs of others.

Prayers may be divided into a number of different types. These include petitionary prayers ("asking" prayers), thanksgiving prayers, prayers of confession and prayers of praise. Some Christians today may question whether it is right to ask God for things. They may feel that God knows their needs without them asking, and to ask is like putting pressure on God to act in their favour. As we have seen, Luke has no such inhibitions! His message to his readers is to ask and keep on asking. But what happens when prayers are *not* answered? Presumably, the Christian may also interpret this as an answer! By not meeting the request, God may be viewed as saying that it is not part of his will. In Matthew's version of the Lord's Prayer, the phrase "Thy will be done" (Matthew 5:10) is included. And in the garden of Gethsemane, when Jesus prayed that he might not have to go through with his trial and crucifixion, he said, "Yet not my will but thine be done" (22:42). Following this example, it is likely that, in making their requests to God, Christians will add "if it be your will". This is an acknowledgement that God knows better than they do themselves what is best for them. It is also a recognition that we see things only from our own limited human point of view, whereas God knows and sees all things from his own eternal viewpoint.

F. SERVICE (CARING FOR THE POOR AND THE LOST)

At the beginning of his ministry, when Jesus visited his home town of Nazareth, he read the lesson in the synagogue. It was from the book of Isaiah:

The Spirit of the Lord is upon me because he has anointed me; he has sent me to announce good news to the poor, to proclaim release for prisoners and recovery of sight for the blind; to let the broken victims go free. (4:18)

Jesus' comment was that in him this text had come true that very day. The words he read suggest that Jesus saw the role of Messiah as one of *service*. According to the passage, the gospel is for the poor, the sick, and the lost (the lost being any of those characters who are outside or on the fringe of respectable Judaism, such as the tax-gatherers and sinners mentioned in the gospel). To preach the good news to the poor, to heal the sick and care for the lost are all acts of service. Throughout Luke's gospel, Jesus is constantly engaged in all of these activities, and Luke would urge his readers to follow the example of service by themselves caring for the poor and the lost. To do so is the duty of every Christian as he makes clear in the short parable at 17:7-10. The master is not grateful to the servant when the servant only does his duty. In a similar way, Christians, in carrying out God's orders, are only doing what is required of them. And God is not going to be especially grateful to them for this, as it is their duty to serve and care for others. Through the miracles he performed, through the teachings he gave (for example, the three 'lost' parables of Chapter 15), through the company he kept (for example, 5:29-32 and 15:1-2), Jesus showed that his life was a life of service. Life in the new order requires Christians to strive to follow Jesus and make their lives lives of service.

G. SERVICE TODAY

Many Christians today spend their lives helping others. Some are nuns and monks belonging to religious orders, others are lay people. They care for the sick, run hospices for the dying, look after old people and assist those who are mentally or physically handicapped or unable to care for themselves. Many Christians also work for relief agencies in Third World countries, where they do what they can to ease the suffering of many unfortunate people. One of the main jobs of ordained ministers is to care for the people in their parishes or areas. Some clergy take on special caring responsibilities by working in prisons and hospitals.

Of course, it is not only Christians who care for others in this way. People of other religions do similar work, and Humanists, who claim to have no religion, are equally concerned and involved in the relief of suffering and helping the less fortunate. However, for Christians, serving others takes on a deep meaning because they believe that Jesus was the perfect model of service and that, above all, God wants them to follow Jesus' example.

H. FORGIVENESS

Life in the new order, according to Luke, requires a willingness constantly to forgive people for the wrong they do. However, before forgiveness can be offered, repentance on the part of the wrong-doer is necessary. Repentance and forgiveness are really opposite sides of the same coin. We have already examined the idea of repentance in the previous theme (see section (e): 'Making the right decision'). The right response to repentance, according to Luke, is forgiveness. This is made clear in the parable of the Lost Son where the father forgives his repentant son without question.

Luke at 7:36-50 tells of an incident where Jesus forgives the sins of a woman "who was living an immoral life" (one of the 'lost'). She came to Jesus while he was dining at the house of Simon the Pharisee, and anointed his feet with oil. Simon failed to see what Jesus clearly saw. The woman was sorry for the wrong things she had done and was seeking forgiveness (although in another sense the love she shows indicates that she is already forgiven - see Notes on this incident and accompanying parable).

The Two Debtors (7:36-50)

1. The parable cannot be separated from the incident of the anointing of Jesus by the immoral woman. Indeed its purpose is to make clear to the host, Simon the Pharisee, the meaning of the woman's behaviour towards Jesus, and to teach him something about himself.

2. The detail of the story suggests that Jesus may have been reclining on a couch, which was the customary position when eating at a banquet. Following the fashion of prostitutes of the day, the woman's hair was let down - a thing which respectable women never did in public. Kissing someone's feet was a way of expressing gratitude. The behaviour of the woman towards Jesus is compared with the way Simon had treated Jesus.

3. As with so many of Luke's characters, we are given an insight into the way Simon's mind works. He thinks that if Jesus were a real prophet he would recognise the woman as a sinner. What he fails to understand is that the love the woman shows is evidence that her sins have *already* been forgiven.

4. The parable is told for Simon's benefit. As usual with a parable, the hearer is left to make up his own mind. Can Simon see himself in the story? Does it speak to him?

5. Luke's favourite theme of reversal is again evident in this incident. The point of the parable seems to be that if a person feels truly forgiven this will be reflected in the amount of love shown. In the case of the woman and Simon, it is the woman who, despite her immoral background, has come closer to God than the morally upright Pharisee.

Questions on 7:36-50.

(*See also* p.129 for questions on this passage)

1. Where was Jesus when the immoral woman brought oil to anoint him?
2. What actions did the woman perform?
3. How did Simon react to the woman's treatment of Jesus?
4. Retell in your own words the parable of the Two Debtors.
5. How did the behaviour of the woman towards Jesus compare with the treatment he received from Simon?
6. What lesson did Jesus hope Simon would learn from the incident and the parable?

Jesus, according to Luke, seized the opportunity to teach a lesson to Simon. Through the parable of the Two Debtors, Jesus presumably hoped that Simon would be able to identify himself and the woman. The Pharisee got the answer right but, just to make sure he had understood, Jesus went on to show how the love of the repentant woman was evidence of the forgiveness she had received. Simon's own behaviour towards Jesus, on the other hand, had been less than loving. He had invited Jesus for a meal and had called him 'Master' but, apart from that, had not extended any courtesies. The little love he had shown was evidence that little had been forgiven. This was not because of any unwillingness on the part of Jesus to forgive, but simply because Simon saw no need in himself to repent. It would seem Jesus is saying that without repentance forgiveness is impossible.

Christians living in the new order are also to be constantly forgiving. A Christian is someone who has repented. Repentance has brought God's forgiveness. And because God has been willing to forgive, so must Christians be willing to forgive those who do them wrong. Jesus teaches his disciples at 17:3-4 that, however many times the Christian is wronged, he or she must be willing to forgive the repentant wrong-doer.

An example of Christian worship. Why do these people have their arms raised?

I. HAVING FAITH AND TRUSTING IN GOD

(i) Promised blessings

We have already considered how the world's values are turned upside down in the new order. In the teaching about having faith and trusting in God, Luke's Jesus develops this idea. The Sermon-on-the Plain (6:20-49) begins with the Beatitudes (which means 'promised blessings'). Here a whole new set of standards is put forward. These standards are to be the standards of the new order, and only those living the new life will understand them. To the rest of the world such teaching will not make sense. But Luke makes it clear that Jesus gave this special teaching to the disciples (6:20), who were the first members of the new order. Of course, to live by such standards is demanding, and only those who truly have faith and put their trust in God will succeed. Faith and trust are necessary because the Christian is *promised* blessings (Beatitudes) rather than actually given them. The onus is on the believer to trust that God will keep his promise. In the new order, then, people must lead their whole lives in faith and put their entire trust in God.

(ii) Reversal of fortunes

The reversal of standards is made especially clear by Luke at 6:20-26, where four "blessings" are balanced by four "woes". The needy, the hungry, the sad, and the despised are blessed by the promise of the reversal of fortunes. But the rich, the well-fed, the happy, and the respected have all had their blessings in this life. Their fortunes too will be reversed, just as with the Rich man and Lazarus in the parable (16:19-31).

The Rich Man and Lazarus (16:19-31)

1. This story offers a terrible warning to those who are wealthy and lead selfish and thoughtless lives. The rich man was so wrapped up in himself he failed to notice the suffering of the world even when an example of it existed at his own gate. Luke's readers are urged to take notice of the warning and to use their wealth for the benefit of others.

2. The story offers a clear example of Luke's reversal of fortunes theme because, according to the parable, in the after-life the rich man suffers and Lazarus experiences good things.

3. As with many of Luke's characters, the rich man is a mixture of good and bad. His good point in the story is his concern for his brothers. He asks Abraham[12] if a message can be sent to them so that they might change their selfish life-style. At this point, it is apparent that the story is more about religion than money. The focus is now on Jesus' resurrection and the failure of the Jewish nation to respond even to that. Luke is perhaps trying to explain how blind the Jewish religion has been to the things going on around it. It has ignored Jesus just as the rich man ignored Lazarus. The Jews had received through Moses and the prophets all the warnings they should have needed but they had not understood. Even when someone rose from the dead they still failed to pay attention.

Questions on 16:19-31

1. What happened at death (i) to the poor man and (ii) to the rich man?
2. Who is Abraham?
3. What is meant by Hades?
4. What allegorical elements are there in the story?
5. What does Luke want his readers to learn from this story?

This seems a hard lesson, especially for those who live in the relatively affluent West today, just as it was a hard lesson for wealthy Gentile readers of Luke in the first century AD. But, as we saw in the section on Wealth (p.115), it is not that the apparent good things of this life are necessarily bad in themselves. They only become bad when they prevent people from looking beyond them to more important things. There is a danger that the wealthy and the well-fed, the happy and the respected, become complacent and self-satisfied. They put their faith and trust in themselves instead of in God. So, again, Luke warns his wealthy and respected Gentile readers. Now it is up to them to heed the warning!

(iii) Love

When you have faith and when you put your trust completely in God then all things become possible. You *can*, for example, "love your enemies" and "do good to those who hate you". Again, this is a reversal of the world's standards. But this is what life in the new order amounts to. The pictures of violence and robbery at 6:29-30 are perhaps not meant to be taken literally, but they emphasise what Christian living is like. The Christian must always be prepared to offer more than is asked for or demanded. We find at 6:31 the 'golden rule': "Treat others as you would like them to treat you." This stresses the positive action the Christian must take.

Luke wants to make clear to his readers that life in the new order is based on love. He wants them to see that if they put their faith and trust entirely in God they will lead loving lives. Jesus' life was based on love, in Luke's view, and this reflected God's love for people. Love, in the sense in which Luke uses it here (the Greek word is *agape*), is an active concern for the wellbeing of others. It can be contrasted with the love which results from sexual desire and the

---

[12] Abraham is thought of as the spiritual founder of the Jewish race.

love we have for family and friends. *Agape* always seeks the good of others under any circumstances and without the thought of any reward. It means loving others whatever they might do to you (like Jesus who prayed for the forgiveness of his executioners, 23:34). This love must be a human attempt to love as God loves. God "himself is kind to the ungrateful and the wicked" (6:36). Therefore, it should be the aim of Christians to 'love their enemies' and not seek to retaliate (6:27-31). It should be the aim of the Christian to love without looking for a reward for oneself (6:32-36), and in not looking for a reward one will receive a rich reward (6:35). The picture of the promised blessing at 6:38 suggests a most generous repayment for faithful living. It should also be the aim of the Christian not to pass judgment on others (6:37-38). God is the one who judges and, in any case, as human beings our knowledge is limited and, therefore, we can never be in a position to make judgments about other people. God himself is to be the model for the Christian, as Luke makes clear at 6:36, "Be compassionate as your Father is compassionate."

(iv) Anxiety

Having faith and trust in God also means that people should stop *worrying* about the necessities of life. Luke is aware that money can also be a worry when you have not got any of it! Again, in the new order, such worrying must cease. At 12:22-34 Jesus addresses the disciples. This is significant. This teaching, we need to remind ourselves, is for those who are living in the new order. The world will not understand it. It is only in living the new life that it will be understood. So Jesus tells the disciples that they are not to worry about food and clothing. The images of birds and flowers are used to show how God provides all that is needed for the survival and the beauty and splendour of the natural world. If God looks after nature in this way, how much more will he look after his "chosen" (12:32)? Luke makes the point that worry shows a lack of faith and trust in God (worry is the preoccupation of the "heathen", 12:30). And he points out how little control people have over their physical condition anyway. No one "can add a foot to his height" (12:25) by worry or any other means. God is responsible for the way people are, and for giving them life itself. If God has provided these things then people must trust him to *preserve* life with food and clothing.

Like wealth, then, worry about not having money can be a distraction from the real concerns of life. Luke wants his readers to get their priorities right. The Christian's only concern must be for the kingdom of God and how its standards are reflected in daily living. If that is the case all these matters of lesser importance will work out satisfactorily. So Luke urges his readers to sell their possessions and give to charity (this is evidence of faith and trust) so that they can concentrate on what is really important. Material possessions are subject to decay and theft but the treasure in heaven is "never-failing". And Luke reminds his readers, " . . . where your treasure is, there will your heart be also" (12:34).

(v) Faith

Christians must live by faith, but at 17:5-6 Luke reminds them how fragile and uncertain their faith is. It is certainly nothing to be complacent about. The saying of Jesus about uprooting the tree and replanting it in the sea is not meant to be taken literally, but is to remind the disciples that faith makes the impossible possible. This sums up life in the new order. This life is by faith, and faith is believing that God can and will do what the world thinks impossible.

J. FAITH AND TRUST TODAY

What does it mean to have faith and trust in God today? Should Jesus' teaching, for example, about not worrying where our food and clothing come from really be taken seriously? Should we really give away our money and possessions? What about the concern of parents to provide for their children? What of the sense of responsibility to care for ourselves and our families?

Christians today may have different views about what it means to have faith and trust in God. Some will believe that it is right to give up money and possessions so that they will not be in danger of putting their faith and trust in these instead of in God. Others may consider that as God, in their view, provides all things, they must use what he has given them in a responsible way. They might argue that having a sense of responsibility about money is not the same as letting it dominate one's life.

Given the teaching of Jesus (at 12:22-34) about having faith and trusting in God, what do you think is a reasonable position for a Christian today to hold?

K. THE TRUE FAMILY

(i) The break with traditional family ties

There is no doubt that in becoming Christians many members of the early church had been forced to separate themselves from their families. Some may have been rejected or betrayed, others may have felt that their families simply did not understand or accept their new Christian commitment. Whatever the case, Luke, in his gospel, shows how, in living in the new order, a person becomes a member of *a new family*. When Jesus receives a message that his mother and brothers have arrived to see him (8:19-21), he offers a new definition of the family. The Christian family consists of those "who hear the word of God and act upon it" (8:21). In other words, the new family is a community of people dedicated to listening to God's message and obeying it. In another passage (14:25-27), it is made clear that, for the Christian, God must always be the first priority. Family ties have to take second place as does concern for one's own life. Only two things are important to the disciple; taking up the cross (that is, facing up to the dangers and difficulties of being a Christian) and following Jesus (who will lead the Christian to God). In a passionate outburst at 12:49-53 Luke has Jesus warn that division within families will occur because of the gospel. To those Christians who had experienced similar family strife, these words of Jesus might offer help and encouragement.

(ii) Attitude to the Law and divorce

There is not a great deal of teaching in Luke's gospel about marriage and other formal relationships between people living in the new community. Most of the attention, as we have seen, is focused on the gospel and its implications for Christian living. However, at 16:16-18 we find comment on what is to be the Christian attitude towards the *Law* and *Divorce*. The Law referred to here is presumably understood to be a mixture of the rules found in the Old Testament together with the interpretations given to them by the rabbis and scribes. At 16:16 the suggestion is that the old order (the Law) is over, now that the new order (the period of the gospel) has arrived. The following verse (16:17) may then be seen as an example of humour at the expense of the legal side of Judaism. Jesus pictures a great catastrophe happening to the world, but the rabbis and scribes take no notice because they are too busy making their minor adjustments to the rules! However, another interpretation of this verse is possible. It could be that it is a reflection of the uncertainty the Christians of the early church felt about the Law. They know that being obedient to moral rules does not bring salvation, yet they know the value of these rules for everyday living. The comment from Jesus about divorce at 16:18 suggests that the Christian is required to observe high moral standards. To divorce and remarry is the same as committing adultery according to Luke's view. But because Luke gives this whole matter such brief treatment it was presumably not an issue which interested him a great deal. (His source of information, Mark, for example, spends more time on it and puts the whole issue in the context of God's intentions at creation, Mark 10:2-12).

(iii) Attitude to women

Luke is regarded as having a special interest in the role of women. In the ancient world, women did not have equal rights with men. They were most definitely second-class citizens. It is against this background that Luke's concern for women should be seen. In his gospel he shows the valuable role they have to play. Perhaps he was trying to tell his readers that in *the true family* everyone, regardless of sex, should be treated with respect, and be regarded as of equal worth. At the outset of the gospel, women play a prominent role. Elizabeth, like her husband Zechariah, is "upright and devout" (1:6), and God had a special purpose for her. Gabriel, God's messenger, treats Mary with great respect when he visits her to tell her of the news of her pregnancy (1:26-38). (It is worth comparing this 'annunciation' with Matthew's gospel where it is Joseph who receives the message in a dream - see Matt. 1:20-25.) When Jesus is brought to the Temple as a baby (2:22-38) he is met by Anna, the old prophetess, as well as by Simeon, the old prophet. In Luke's view they each have an equally significant role to play.

Luke also uses women as examples of *faith* (the woman with the haemorrhage, 8:43-48), of what it means to be truly *repentant* and to receive *forgiveness* (the immoral woman, 7:36-50), of persistence in *prayer* (the widow and unjust judge, 18:1-8), and of true *generosity* (the widow's gift at the Temple, 21:1-4).

Women are also counted among Jesus' disciples and followers. At 8:1-3 Luke speaks of the women who accompanied Jesus and used their wealth to support him and the disciples. It is Jesus' female disciples who watch the crucifixion (23:49) and are the first witnesses to the resurrection (24:1-11).

Other women worthy of note in Luke's gospel are Martha and Mary (10:38-42), the widow of Nain (7:11-17) and the crippled woman (13:10-17), and the "Daughters of Jerusalem" (23:27-31) who follow Jesus on his journey to the place of crucifixion.

In a whole variety of ways, then, it can be seen that Luke stresses the importance of the role of women in the life of the new community. They are of equal significance to men in the true family. Indeed, in some instances, in the gospel, they can be seen to be even more privileged than men. Perhaps Luke's point is that if God gives them such privileges and responsibilities, they must be treated as important members of the new community.

We should not make the mistake of seeing Luke as putting forward arguments for the equality of men and women. That would be to transplant modern ideas back to the first century AD. However, Luke is consistent with the Old Testament, where women frequently have important roles to play (e.g. Deborah (Judges 4-5), Ruth, Esther). It may have been that the Jews of the first century AD had chosen to ignore this fact of their past. Luke reminds them and his Gentile readers that God uses women as well as men to forward his purposes.

L. LIVING AS A CHRISTIAN TODAY

Christians aim to live their lives following as closely as possible the example of Jesus. Jesus' example influences them in their praying, and in their care and concern for others. Jesus' teaching about forgiveness is vitally important to the lives of Christians today. They feel confident that God forgives them repeatedly for their wrong-doings and so, in turn, they are willing to forgive those who do them wrong.

Christians also aim to reflect God's love, by living loving lives themselves. Part of this love will involve treating all other human beings of whatever sex, nationality, religion, or social class, with proper respect. Another aspect of this love should also be obvious in the church itself, where the spirit of community (the true family) should be evident. Here all members should be of equal worth and a common purpose found. These are examples of what is meant by the New Testament idea of *agape* (see section (I.iii) above).

On issues of importance today Christians have to make up their own minds how to act. The particular issues which the gospel-writers claim Jesus dealt with during his life-time may be different from the ones Christians face today. However, the gospel-writers themselves give the Christian a model to follow in this matter of decision-making. They may not always have been certain exactly what Jesus said on a particular occasion, but they were so convinced that Jesus was the Messiah, and they had heard so many stories about him, that they felt they did *know* what Jesus would have said or done in any given situation. Christians today can follow this example by working out for themselves, from their knowledge of Jesus, what their response as a Christian should be to a specific problem. The need to apply the spirit of Jesus' teaching means that individuals are *responsible* for making their own decisions. Many people would argue that this is preferable to following blindly someone else's instructions, even if that someone is Jesus. And we know, that in Luke's view, thinking things through carefully is absolutely crucial (see Theme II).

It is clear that living as a Christian today is no easier than it was in Luke's day. The clash between the world's values and the Christian's values remains the same.

In this church a woman is allowed to distribute the bread to the congregation at Holy Communion.
Is there any denomination which would not allow this?

Questions on Theme III: Life in the New Order

4:16-20

1a. For whom is the gospel intended?

b. Why should the life of the follower of Jesus be a life of *service*?

5:33-39

2a. What reply did Jesus give when asked why his disciples did not practise fasting?

b. What did he mean by his reply?

3a. What did Jesus say about the new and old cloaks and the new and old wineskins?

b. What message do you think he was trying to get across to his hearers?

6:20-38

4a. What does the word 'Beatitude' mean?

b. Why are the needy, the hungry, the sad and the despised fortunate?

c. Who are the people who are to be pitied?

d. How might Luke's point about the reversal of fortunes be explained to people today?

5a. What does it mean to 'love' in the Christian sense?

b. Why should love be the basis of Christian action?

c. Why should Christians love their enemies?

d. Why should Christians not judge other people?

7:36-50 (see also p.122 for questions on this passage)

6a. How does the woman's behaviour suggest that she has already been forgiven?

b. Why was Simon's behaviour towards Jesus less than loving?

c. Why is repentance necessary before forgiveness, according to Luke's gospel?

8:19-21

7. How would Jesus describe the true Christian family?

10:21-24

8a. Who are the privileged ones in this passage?

b. How does Luke's idea of reversal of fortunes work in this passage?

11:1-13

9a. What name is given to the prayer which Jesus taught his disciples?

b. What should Christians say to God when they pray, according to Jesus?

c. What does "thy name be hallowed" mean?

10a. What short parable does Jesus tell in order to encourage his disciples to be persistent in prayer?

b. How does Jesus compare a father with God?

12:22-34

11a. What examples does Jesus give to show his disciples that they should not worry about food and clothing?

b. Why does 'worry' suggest a lack of faith and trust in God?

c. What does the saying " . . . where your treasure is, there will your heart be also", mean?

d. How literally should Christians today take Jesus' teaching about not worrying over food and clothing?

12:49-53

12. Jesus warned of a split in families which the gospel would bring. How might his teaching have given encouragement to some of Luke's readers?

14:7-11

13a. What advice does Jesus give to wedding guests about where they should sit at table?

b. "For everyone who exalts himself will be humbled; and whoever humbles himself will be exalted." What do you understand this to mean?

14:12-14

14a. Who, according to Jesus, should the host invite to his dinner-party?

b. Why should the Christian be concerned for the poor and needy, according to Luke?

14:25-27

15a. What surprising thing does Jesus say to show that Christians must put God first in their lives?

b. What does it mean to "take up the cross"?

16:16-18

16. What should be the attitude of the Christian towards divorce, according to Luke?

17:3-4

17. What does this passage teach about forgiveness?

17:7-10

18. What does this parable teach about *duty*?

18:1-8 (*see* p.118 for questions on this passage)

18:9-14 (*see also* p.120 for questions on this passage)

19. What is the right *attitude* to prayer, according to this parable?

Additional questions on the topic 'prayer'
1. What different types of prayer are there?
2. Why is prayer important in the lives of Christians today?
3. Why might Christians end their prayers with "thy will be done"?

Additional questions on the topic 'women'
1. Why is it sometimes said that Luke has a special interest in women?
2. How does Luke use women in his gospel to illustrate the following important themes:
    a. repentance and forgiveness
    b. persistence in prayer
    c. use of wealth and true generosity.

Additional questions on the topic 'service'
1. In what ways do Christians today follow the example of Jesus by leading lives of service to others?
2. Why do some Christians today think it important to lead lives of service?

Essay question
What do you consider to be the main problems in living a truly Christian life today?

THEME IV
GETTING READY FOR THE KINGDOM

References: 5:29-32; 12:35-53; 13:1-9,18-30; 14:15-24,28-35; 17:1-2,20-37; 19:11-27; 20:9-18.

A. THE DELAY OF JESUS' RETURN

As far as we can tell the early Christians expected Jesus to return to earth within a short space of time. They believed that, after his resurrection, he had ascended to heaven where he was ruling with God. It would not be long, however, before the present situation on earth came to an end. Jesus would return and then the kingdom of God on earth would begin. It was believed that all this might happen within the lifetime of some of his disciples. The time between Jesus' departure and his return was thought to be a very special time and Christians had to be in a constant state of readiness for the Second Coming.

As time passed, and the people who had known Jesus began to grow old and die, Christians became less certain about the idea that Jesus' return would be soon. Luke was probably one of those Christians. We have seen in his gospel how important history was to him. Clearly there is little point in writing history if you believe the present world is coming to an end. Some scholars argue that one of Luke's main aims was to show how the imminent-return-of-Christ idea held by the early church was a mistaken one. For Luke, Christianity has a future in this present world order. However, even if this view of scholars is correct, it seems likely that Luke believed that the *parousia* (a term used to mean the return of Jesus at the Second Coming) would occur eventually. He may have assumed that Christians had misunderstood when it would happen. Certainly we can find evidence for this in his gospel. He urges his readers, as we shall see, to remain alert so that they will be ready for the kingdom when God decides the time is right.

B. BEING WATCHFUL AND BEING PREPARED

In the passage 12:35-48 there are a number of short parables which urge Christians to be watchful and prepared for the Parousia. They are to be in a constant state of alert and "ready for action" (12:35). The time before Jesus' return is in one sense a time of *waiting* (for example, to let the master in when he returns from the wedding-party, 12:36). Patient waiting and watchfulness is rewarded according to 12:37, when the roles of master and servant are reversed; the master will wait at table while the servants eat. The warning that the time of the visitation is unknown and unpredictable comes at 12:39-40, where the image of the burglar is used to suggest that Christians must be constantly on their guard so that they are not taken by surprise.

But waiting expectantly is only part of being prepared for Jesus' return. Life goes on and it must go on in a way which reflects the specialness of the things which are about to happen. Peter asks at 12:41 whether the parable is just for the disciples or for everyone. Luke is perhaps here using Peter's question and Jesus' response to address the church of his own day. Jesus does not in fact answer Peter's question but, through an allegory (12:42-46), explains the heavy responsibility the church has in these special times.

Allegory

The sensible *steward* is appointed by his *master* to run his affairs while he is away.

If the steward uses his position responsibly and treats the other servants well, he will be rewarded.

But if he abuses his position because the master is away for a long time, when the master eventually returns the steward will be severely punished.

Explanation

The *church* is appointed by *Jesus* to spread the good news.

The church must live up to the example set by Jesus.

The church must not lose faith if Jesus' return appears to be delayed.

Jesus will return (the Second Coming).

Jesus will pass judgment on the church.

The further short parable at 12:47-48 adds to the point, in case it has been missed and, in some ways, provides part of an answer at least to Peter's question (12:41). The church is, or should be, the servant who knows his master's wishes. If it makes no attempt to carry them out it will be severely punished. Those outside the church (the non-Christians) whose lives leave much to be desired (who do not know the master's wishes) will be less severely punished. The church has had a great deal entrusted to it and, therefore, much is expected of it. Luke does not want the church to be any less faithful to Jesus because of the delay of the Parousia.

Elsewhere in his gospel, Luke urges his readers to watch their own behaviour. He records at 13:1-5 two incidents which do not receive mention outside this gospel: Pilate's massacre of some Galileans, and the collapse of the tower at Siloam. The most common explanation for suffering in the Old Testament was

that it resulted from sin. But Luke's Jesus warns his hearers that the people who suffered these terrible fates were not worse sinners than anyone else. It is too easy to jump to that conclusion and to fail to see one's own wrong-doings and, therefore, one's own need for *repentance*. The context in which this passage occurs also suggests that Luke may have had another terrible disaster in mind - the destruction of Jerusalem in AD 70. Many Christians interpreted this event as God's punishment on the Jews for their failure to repent.

A further warning comes from Jesus at 17:1-2 when he tells his disciples, "Keep watch on yourselves". It is not entirely clear who the "little ones" are - the reference is most probably to children or to those who, like children, have no rights and are, therefore, particularly open to abuse. However, the point is that the Christian's behaviour must be beyond reproach.

Part of being prepared is weighing up the cost of being a disciple (a Christian). It is very easy to get carried away on a wave of enthusiasm without thinking enough about what is really involved in being a follower of Jesus. As Theme III (Life in the new order) shows, a high degree of commitment is necessary on the part of the Christian disciple. Through two short parables, Luke urges his readers to think carefully about what they are letting themselves in for *before* they become followers. The parables of the Tower Builder and the King Considering War (14:28-35) provide two examples of the sort of serious thinking that is necessary for the would-be Christian. Following their example, would-be disciples must make a realistic assessment of the situation and only go ahead if they can in all honesty meet the commitment.

Part of this realistic assessment may include the warning of Jesus at 12:49-53 that divisions in families will occur because of the gospel. Unless people are willing to put God first in everything they cannot be considered to be well enough *prepared*. Presumably we are meant to understand from this passage that Jesus himself, even though prepared for his task, is under a great deal of strain. The fire he speaks of is probably a symbol for the coming judgment (in Acts fire is also a symbol for the Holy Spirit) and baptism is a symbol for his coming death. Luke knows that the gospel will give rise to conflict because so much of the world is not in tune with its thinking. Perhaps, even in Luke's church, there is evidence of the division brought by the gospel. The true disciple must be prepared and able to face this.

C. WHO WILL BE SAVED?

This is a question which must have exercised the minds of the early Christians, and it is of particular concern to Luke. In a way it is also partly at least a question about the relationship between Jews and Christians as well. Christians must have often reflected on why it was that there was hostility between the two groups when they had so much in common. The Jews, after all, believed themselves to be God's chosen people and, therefore, the ones to be saved. We have seen on numerous occasions how loyal Luke is to the Old Testament. This was his Bible and he knew it thoroughly. There was no mistaking God's intentions here - the Jews were clearly the 'chosen' ones. However, as Luke and the early Christians saw it, the Jews had been given their chance but they had rejected the promised Messiah and, therefore, the idea of the 'chosen' had been redefined by God. In Luke's view, it was not that God had excluded the Jews from salvation, the Jews had excluded themselves. Of course, not all the Jews had done so. The first Christians (the disciples and other followers of Jesus) were Jews, just as Jesus himself had been a Jew. But, the organised religion of Judaism had shut out Jesus and in so doing, Luke believed, had excluded itself from God's salvation. The 'chosen' were now those people, Jews or Gentiles, who *responded* to the gospel. To show how Jesus himself was aware of this, Luke has Jesus tell two parables about people who choose to exclude themselves from the kingdom: the parable of The Dinner-party (14:15-24) and the parable of The Vineyard or Vine-growers (20:9-18).

In the parable of The Dinner-party, the host invites many guests but, in turn, they make excuses as to why they cannot attend. In other words, they exclude themselves. This is clearly not what the host wants, but it leaves him no choice. The dinner-party is now open to other people, and all who want to can come in. As for the 'chosen', they have made their decision and, therefore, they will not share in the feast.

The Dinner-Party (14:15-24)

1. It was a custom to send out servants to fetch honoured guests when the meal was ready. The inclusion of this sort of detail is typical of the parables and shows how they were rooted in everyday life and, so, quite vivid and realistic to the hearers.

2. Each of the guests gives a reason for not being able to attend the dinner-party. We have seen before how Luke's characters think things through for themselves, and they do not always arrive at the right decision.

3. It is clear that this story is about "the feast in the kingdom of God" (14:15). The heavenly banquet was a common symbol of the future life with the chosen gathered round the table.

4. There is an important allegorical side to the story. Those who were first invited and refused the invitation are the Jewish religious leaders. They excluded themselves by refusing to accept Jesus and so sealed their own fate in Luke's view. The poor, the crippled, the blind, and the lame are the "lost" of Judaism (we have noted before Luke's concern for the outcasts of respectable Jewish society). Finally, the search for guests is widened ("the highways and along the hedgerows") to include the Gentiles (the people to whom the invitation is extended in Acts).

Questions on 14:15-24

(*see also*: p.140 for questions on this passage)

1. What is the symbolic significance of the "heavenly banquet"?
2. How might this story be interpreted allegorically?

3. Does this parable have anything to teach people today?

The theme of self-exclusion is even more evident in the parable of the vineyard. This is really an allegory about Jewish history:

Allegory	Explanation
The Vinegrowers	The Jewish leaders
The Owner	God
The Servants	The Old Testament prophets
The Son	Jesus

According to the allegory, the vine-growers are given every opportunity to respond to the owner (he sends his servants to them and even his son) but they freely choose to ignore the invitations. In this way they exclude themselves from the good fortune which is rightfully theirs, and it is, therefore, given to others (the Gentiles). This veiled summary of Jewish history perhaps helped to explain to the early church why Christianity had grown among the Gentiles rather than the Jews. It might also have helped with the question, 'Who will be saved?', even if the answer was negative. Those who will *not* be saved are those who choose to exclude themselves from that possibility.

Luke does provide a more positive answer to the question, 'Who will be saved?', at 13:22-30. Here someone asks Jesus, "... are only a few to be saved?" In typical fashion, Luke's Jesus does *not* answer the question he was asked, but responds with a parable which focuses on the question he wishes to answer. Presumably the number of the saved is only for God to know. The point is that the door (of the kingdom) *is* open and the opportunity to enter exists. Entering may prove to be a struggle. It is something to be worked at, and those less than determined will not make it. The parable also suggests that the door will only be open for a certain length of time and then it will be shut. Those who miss the opportunity will find that no amount of pleading will gain them access. The idea of reversal of fortunes is never far away in Luke. Those the master of the house has eaten and spoken with he claims not to know, whereas foreigners "from east and west", "from north and south" will be welcomed to the feast. Most probably this is another veiled reference to the exclusion or self-exclusion of organised Judaism, and the welcoming of Gentiles into the church.

It is easy to get the feeling that, according to Luke, the Jews are 'out' and the Gentiles are 'in'. In one sense this is a false impression. However, because of the situation in which the church found itself in relation to Judaism, it must have been hard for Luke not to interpret things in this way. The real evidence of Luke's gospel, taken as a whole, however, is that salvation is for those who need it and know they need it whether they be Jew or Gentile. This is summed up in the incident at 5:29-32 where Jesus is at a reception given in his honour by Levi. The Pharisees and lawyers ask why Jesus eats with tax-gatherers and sinners and Jesus replies, "It is not the healthy that need a doctor, but the sick; I have not come to invite virtuous people, but to call sinners to repentance." The so-called 'healthy', as so often in Luke's gospel, believe themselves to be self-sufficient and do not feel the need for God, whereas the 'sick' know they are inadequate and know that only God can save them. The faith and trust that this leads to does, according to Luke, bring them salvation.

The Vineyard (or Vine-growers) (20:9-18)

1. The vineyard is a common Old Testament symbol for Israel (e.g. Isaiah 5:1-7) and so it would have been clear to the priests, lawyers and elders (mentioned at 20:1) that this was a parable about them. The other important allegorical elements (*see* p.134) would have fallen quickly into place.

2. The reaction to the story ("God forbid!", 20:17) suggests that its meaning had been grasped by the people (though Luke does not make it clear whether they are horrified at the prospect of Gentiles being included in God's kingdom or whether they recognised this as a forecast of the destruction of Jerusalem). To make quite sure they have understood correctly, Jesus quotes from Psalm 118:22-23. Jesus may have been rejected by the representatives of the old Jewish religion (the builders) but he is the cornerstone on which the new religion of Christianity will be built.

Questions on 20:9-18

(*see also:* p.140 for questions on this passage)

1. What does the symbol of the vineyard represent in the Old Testament?

2. Why do you think the people said, "God forbid!" (20:17)?

D. WHEN WILL THE KINGDOM OF GOD COME?

This is the question which the Pharisees asked Jesus, according to Luke 17:20. The reply which Jesus gave (17:20-37) is by no means easy to understand. Perhaps the key to understanding it is to recognise that in style the reply is *apocalyptic*. The word 'apocalypse' means a 'revelation' or an 'unveiling'. Apocalyptic books claim to reveal things which are normally hidden, or to reveal the future. In view of the question, the style of the reply would seem to be an appropriate one. However, Luke is anxious to keep links with history and so part of Jesus' response appears to be concerned with the forthcoming destruction of Jerusalem (although for Luke this would be a past event).

The first point Jesus makes is concerned with the present rather than the future. He tells the Pharisees that the coming kingdom of God will not be observable in the way they imagine it, for it is "among" them. Because the Greek word which is translated in the New English Bible as 'among' can also be translated as 'inside' or 'within', the exact meaning in this context is not clear. Luke may be saying that in Jesus the kingdom has become a present reality. He may also be saying that the kingdom of God is not to be understood as another form of government, but is rather an inner experience or a spiritual condition.

As so often in the gospel, the important teaching of Jesus which follows is given to the disciples. He warns them not to be misled by false claims. When the kingdom comes it will be absolutely clear to all ("like the lightning-flash that lights up the earth from end to end", 17:24). But before this happens, Jesus warns that he must suffer and be rejected (17:25). The suddenness with which the kingdom will occur is then compared by Jesus to two events of the Old Testament. This is also a further warning that Christians must be *prepared*, because when the flood came in Noah's day it caught everyone but Noah unprepared. Similarly, the destruction of Sodom caught its inhabitants completely unaware of their terrible fate. Verse 31 is puzzling, and may be a reference to the attack on Jerusalem by the Roman army in AD 70. When the enemy advances it is best to escape as swiftly as you can. There must be no hesitating or turning back. Lot's wife looked back and turned into a pillar of salt! (See Genesis 19:1-28). The reference to vultures at 17:37 may also be a reference to the Jerusalem massacre, though it could be another way of stressing the importance of being prepared: vultures sense the presence of food almost before the animal dies. Luke may have seen Jesus' words at 17:31-37 as referring both to the fall of Jerusalem (which was a foretaste of judgment) and to judgment day itself. With the coming of the kingdom comes judgment, as 17:34-35 warns. Judgment will be swift and will involve separation from friends and work-mates. The idea of reversal of fortunes is evident yet again at 17:33: "Whoever seeks to save his life will lose it; and whoever loses it will save it, and live."

E. WHAT IS THE KINGDOM OF GOD LIKE?

This is Jesus' own question. He answers it with two short parables: the parable of The Mustard-seed (13:18-19), and the parable of The Yeast (13:20-21). These help to explain how the kingdom is both present now and a hope for the future. The two parables here make the point that it has come in Jesus but still has to develop into full maturity.

The main point of the parable of The Mustard-seed is to contrast the smallness of the seed with the greatness of the tree. What seems an insignificant beginning (the ministry of Jesus which was largely rejected) can develop into something spectacular and enormous (the kingdom of God). Luke perhaps intends his readers to identify with the birds who come to roost among the branches of the tree.

The parable of The Yeast makes a similar point. A small amount of yeast mixed with a large quantity of flour ("half a hundredweight") will change the dough in a remarkable way. Although you cannot observe the yeast working, through a process which appeared mysterious to people who did not know about enzymes, it causes the mixture to expand and rise. Similarly, the influence of the kingdom (present in Jesus) may not be recognised immediately but it will eventually grow in an unbelievable way.

F. FACING JUDGMENT

With the coming of the kingdom comes judgment. Luke does not include as much teaching on this subject as does Matthew. We have seen how, for Luke, judgment is something which may come in the course of everyday living. The Lost Son and the Dishonest Steward are two examples of Luke's characters who are judged during their lives. They have to make decisions and, as a result, their lives take on new meaning. However, judgment is also something that all people will have to face at the end of time, in Luke's view, and he includes some teaching about this. The parable of The Pounds (19:11-27) is a parable about judgment. Its main theme focuses on how people use the gifts they have been entrusted with. Those servants who exploit their gifts to the full are rewarded, whereas the servant who hides away his gift is punished. The message of the parable is presumably that, at the judgment, those who have taken risks for the gospel will be rewarded, whereas those who have done nothing to promote God's kingdom will be punished.

The short parable of The Unfruitful Fig Tree at 13:6-9 is another reminder of the need to be responsible and work positively for God's kingdom. The fig tree in the story has not borne fruit for three years and the order is to cut it down. The gardener persuades the owner to give the tree just one more chance before judgment strikes.

The Pounds
(19:11-27)

1. There are two main themes evident in this story: the nobleman who became king, and the money-making activities of the servants. Luke has combined these in his retelling of this parable.

2. There may be an historical core to the idea of the nobleman who became king (19:14). Archelaus went to Rome in 4 BC, after the death of his father, King Herod, to be given the kingdom of Judaea. The Jews did not want him to be their king and sent a delegation to Rome to protest. Their plea was not successful. However, another, more allegorical, interpretation is possible: the nobleman could be Jesus, who was appointed by God as king (Messiah). Jesus' fellow-citizens, the Jews, rejected him and, in so doing, brought judgment (19:27) on themselves.

3. If the period between the king's departure and return is meant to represent the period between Jesus' ascension and his second coming, then the meaning of the second theme of the parable seems clearer. Christians have been given special tasks and responsibilities (the pounds) which they must undertake with enthusiasm. They must not be like the Pharisees, simply trying to preserve for the Jews alone what God had given them (the servant who kept his pound wrapped in a handkerchief), but take risks by carrying the gospel into the Gentile world (the servants who traded with their pounds and made a great deal of money).

Questions on 19:11-27

(*See also* p.140 for questions on this passage)

1. Why did the nobleman go abroad?
2. What responsibilities did he give his servants while he was away?
3. Why was the king pleased with the first and second servants but angry with the third?
4. How might this story be interpreted allegorically?
5. To what extent is this a story about judgment?

The Fig Tree
(13:6-9)

1. In order to understand the significance of the fig tree and the vineyard it is necessary to go back to the Old Testament, where both are used as symbols for Israel. Luke, then, is making clear to his readers that this parable is about the Jews. The lack of fruit represents the negative response of their leaders to Jesus. One final chance is offered (while Jesus is with them they can still change their minds about him) before judgment strikes.

2. The passage which comes immediately before this (i.e. 13:1-5) may be a veiled comment on the fall of Jerusalem. If so, the parable here could also have this catastrophe in mind. A last chance was offered to the Jews but they did not take it. Therefore, judgment (the fall of Jerusalem) is the consequence.

Questions on 13:6-9
(*See also* p.139 for questions on this passage)

Questions on 13:6-9

1. What hints does Luke give us that this is a story about the Jews?

2. What other stories in Luke's gospel suggest that people can respond positively   when given a second chance?

G. GETTING READY FOR THE KINGDOM TODAY

The idea that this world will suddenly come to an end and be replaced by the kingdom of God is not an idea which most Christians hold today. They accept that death brings the world to an end for many people every day. This is, in a way, when the kingdom of God comes for them. As none of us knows when or how we may die, there is a sense in which Christians will want to lead their lives in a state of readiness and preparedness for the kingdom.

Christians, however, do take seriously the claim of Jesus that the kingdom of God is "among you" (17:21). They understand this to mean that God's kingdom is a *present* reality in this world. It is not something that has to be waited for but can be enjoyed here and now. As a result of that belief, they may be encouraged to try to make this world a better place in order to reflect more accurately the heavenly kingdom.

There is also an understanding that, at death, each person may face judgment. The belief that this may lead to some form of reward or punishment is probably less popular today than in the past. Most Christians would probably find it difficult to believe that a God of love would dole out permanent punishment (such as the idea of Hell symbolises) even to the worst offenders. The belief in purgatory as a state to which human beings pass at death, is held by some Christians. In purgatory, it is believed, people's souls are gradually made fit to be with God.

The question, 'Who will be saved?', has taken on a new and important significance for Christians today. This is because there is a much greater awareness of the other religions of the world. Many Christians will recognise the value of the teachings of these other faiths for those who follow them. The vast numbers of good people of other religions forces the Christian to ask: 'Will they be saved?' Although there is no agreed answer to this question, an increasingly popular view among many Christians is that God has a purpose for the people of other religions and that they too will receive God's salvation. (See also chapter 7 section (g)).

An Easter Sunday in an Orthodox church.
The priest is declaring 'Christ is risen'.

*A blind Nigerian girl learning to use a
Braille tape measure. Can the Kingdom of God be
"a present reality in this world" for her?*

Questions on Theme IV: Getting ready for the kingdom

5:29-32

1a. Who hosted the reception given in Jesus' honour?

b. What complaint did the Pharisees make to the disciples?

c. Who do you think Jesus means by "the sick"?

12:35-48

2a. Why must the disciple "be ready for action" (12:35)?

b. How should the servants behave while the master is away?

c. What does the saying about the householder and burglar mean?

d. How should the steward treat the other servants?

e. Why will the servant who did not know the master's wishes be punished less severely than the one who did?

f. What important lesson would the church of Luke's day have learnt from 12:41-48?

12:49-53

3. What do you think Jesus meant when he said he had "come to bring division"?

13:1-5

4a. What, according to Luke, happened at Siloam?

b. What is the most common answer of the Old Testament to the question, 'Why do people suffer?'?

c. Do you think Jesus agreed with this view?

13:6-9 (see also p.138 for questions on this passage)

5a. Why does the owner want the fig tree cut down?

6. What important lesson did Luke intend his readers to learn from this story, do you think?

13:18-19

7a. How does the parable of the mustard-seed help to explain that the kingdom of God is both present and future?

b. Why is yeast a good example of the way the kingdom of God works?

13:22-30

8a. What did Jesus reply to the question, "Are only a few to be saved?"?

b. What is the door, and why do you think it is described as "narrow"?

c. What evidence is there that this parable may be in part about the exclusion of the Jews?

d. Who are Abraham, Isaac and Jacob mentioned at 13:28?

14:15-24 (*see also* p.134 for questions on this passage)

9a. What reasons did three of the invited guests give for not being able to attend the dinner-party?

b. Whom did the host invite to the dinner-party in place of the original guests?

c. What lessons might this parable have taught the members of Luke's church?

14:28-35

10a. Why should the person who intends to build a tower count the cost before commencing the project?

b. What should the king considering war do if he thinks his enemy likely to defeat him?

c. What sound advice do the parables of the tower-builder and the king considering war offer the person who is thinking of becoming a Christian?

17:1-2

11. Why must the disciples keep watch on themselves?

17:20-37

12a. What reply did Jesus give to the Pharisees' question, "When will the kingdom of God come?"?

b. What do you think is meant by the saying of Jesus, "the kingdom of God is among you"?

c. How will the disciples know when the kingdom of God is coming?

13a. Who was (i) Noah (*see* Genesis 6-9), and (ii) Lot (*see* Genesis 13 & 19)?

b. Why are Noah and Lot given as examples of the need to be *prepared*?

c. What happened to Lot's wife?

d. What teaching is there about *judgment* in this passage?

19:11-27 (*see also* p.137 for questions on this passage)

14a. What is the main theme of this parable?

b. How does the parable suggest that promoting God's kingdom may be a risky business?

20:9-18 (*see also* p.135 for questions on this passage)

15a. Who do the following represent: the vine-growers, the servants, the owner, the owner's son?

b. Why is the parable of the vineyard better described as an allegory?

c. Why might this parable have been understood by the early church as an abbreviated version of Jewish history?

11

THE PASSION NARRATIVE
(19:28-23:49)

Luke's gospel began in the Temple in Jerusalem, the centre of the Jewish world. When Jesus enters Jerusalem at the climax of his ministry, Luke's account of the good news completes a full circle.

At the end of his gospel Luke looks forward to the history he will write in Acts of the Apostles, the history of the Christian church. The Temple's time is coming to an end. Jesus weeps for the city which will suffer judgment and cleanses the Temple which was being used to pursue wealth. The old order is ending and the way to salvation will be by following Jesus, not through Temple rituals.

The topics of conflict, reversal, the poor, the lost, women, the fulfilment of prophecy, the need for constant readiness for judgment, prayer and the kingship of Jesus all occur in the Passion narrative. At the Last Supper the new covenant which is being established is explained and so are its symbols.

One of Luke's aims in writing was to show that Christianity, contrary to widespread belief, was not a threat to the Roman Empire. The guilt of the Jews, the innocence of Jesus and the reluctance of the Roman authorities to execute him are used by Luke to demonstrate this and to set the scene for Acts.

For Luke, the Passion narrative does two things. It completes his account of the ministry of Jesus and looks forward to the resurrection and the next stage of God's plan for humanity's salvation. In Jerusalem, the offer of salvation is made to the Jews one last time and is again rejected. In Acts the offer of salvation goes out from Jerusalem to the Gentiles. Acts ends in Rome, the centre of the Gentile world. The places where the two books begin and end symbolise for Luke the fulfilment of God's plan. The gospel was sent first to the Jews (Jerusalem) and then to the Gentiles (Rome). The progress of the gospel from Jerusalem to Rome is the history of God's offering of salvation to all humanity.

A. JESUS' TRIUMPHAL ENTRY INTO JERUSALEM
(19:28-40)

Jesus enters Jerusalem as a king. Luke has several times shown Jesus teaching about the sort of king he is (e.g. 9:22) and in the temptations shown him rejecting popular ideas of kingship (see chapter 6 section F ii). Now Luke presents Jesus acting as a king, as a heavenly not an earthly one. Luke's description of Jesus' entry into Jerusalem combines the account in Mark 11:1-11, with his special material (L).

Jesus approaches Jerusalem from Bethany, which is on the east side of the city. Luke obviously saw something significant in the fetching of a colt for Jesus to ride, since the incident is described at length. The important point seems to be that the animal had not previously been ridden and so was ritually pure. Animals for royal or religious use could not be used for any other purpose. The colt was therefore a fitting mount for the Messiah to use to enter Jerusalem.

The description of the scene recalls Zechariah 9:9:

. . . for see, your king is coming to you,
his cause won, his victory gained,
humble and mounted on an ass,
on a foal, the young of a she-ass.

The early church certainly saw Jesus' entry into Jerusalem as that of a king coming to claim his kingdom. The description of the cloaks on the colt and on the road recalls 2 Kings 9:13, where the same action was a symbol for the people accepting the kingship of Jehu. Today, putting out a red carpet for royalty is a similar type of action.

In the Passion narrative Luke is constantly directing our attention back to incidents earlier in his gospel. His account of the disciples singing,

Blessings on him who comes as a king in the name of the Lord!

Peace in heaven, glory in highest heaven!

uses words from Psalm 118:26 with which pilgrims were greeted as they approached the Temple. However, Luke adapts them to emphasise Jesus' kingship. It then becomes a song of welcome for the king. In the second part of the verse the meaning of Jesus' coming is made clear, and this echoes the angels' words of 2:14: "Glory to God in highest heaven, and on earth his peace for men on whom his favour rests." Jesus is the Messiah and the bringer of God's peace.

Jesus has prophesied his own fate, now Luke shows him predicting the destruction which will fall on Jerusalem when it refuses his message (19:41-44). For Luke and the early Christians the fall of Jerusalem to the Roman legions in AD 70 was seen as God's judgment on the Jews for their rejection of Jesus. This way of interpreting historical events is the same as that found in the Old Testament. There the prophets warned that God would send destruction on the people if they failed to keep God's commandments. Jesus weeping for the city seems to answer a question that Jeremiah, one of the Old Testament prophets, asked: "Who will take pity on you, Jerusalem, who will offer you consolation?" (Jer. 15:5). This was asked by Jeremiah after the people were told that God would destroy them because they had followed false gods.

This point is driven home by Jesus' first action when he enters the city. This action is usually called 'the cleansing of the Temple'. Jesus goes straight to the Temple and drives out the traders. They are an example of false religion. They deal in the things of this world and pursue worldly wealth. The Temple authorities allow this, and so judgment and destruction follow.

Jesus' action is seen by Luke as a symbol for the sweeping away of the old order. The way to salvation is through following Jesus, not through Temple sacrifices, which had become associated with profiteering by Temple traders. When Jesus preaches in the Temple he is putting it to its proper use: the word of God is being spoken there. By noting that the chief priests and lawyers "were bent on making an end of him" (19:47), Luke reminds us that the devil is still biding his time (*see* 4:13) and planning Jesus' death.

The elaborate procedure for obtaining the colt (19:30-35) suggests some prior arrangement which involved a password (19:34). Jesus was well known in Bethany according to Mark 14:3-9 and John 11. (Similar mysterious arrangements appear to have been made for finding a room to celebrate the Passover, 22:7-13.) Alternatively, Jesus might simply be using his authority as a noted rabbi to make a request which could not be refused. Luke would probably have seen the response of the colt's owner to Jesus' request as an

example of true discipleship.

Jesus' words in 19:46 are a quote from Isaiah 56:7: "My house shall be called a house of prayer for all the nations." This passage in Isaiah reflects a belief that one day all the peoples in the world would come to Jerusalem to worship God. Luke saw this prophecy being fulfilled not through the Temple, but through Jesus and the Gentile mission of the church.

Jesus' authority is questioned: 20:1-8. Anyone who wished to teach in the Temple had to have permission from the Temple authorities. Jesus' authority comes from God and the incident brings to mind the time when Jesus was twelve years old (2:46-49). The passage from 19:45 onwards is the first time since then that any mention has been made by Luke of Jesus being in the Temple. The amazement he caused that first time by his answers is echoed in the disputes which follow (20:1-40), but now the result is hostility. The Temple authorities are obsessed by worldly things, such as who gives permission to teach in the Temple, and are unable to recognise that Jesus is in his father's house and preaches with God's authority.

Those who challenge Jesus' right to teach are the three groups who make up the Sanhedrin which in a little while will bring about Jesus' death. Luke includes the incident to show the whole people rejecting Jesus, just as they had rejected John the Baptist and their forefathers had rejected the prophets of the Old Testament. (See 11:47; 13:34.)

B. RENEWED CONFLICT

Jesus' enemies are, from this point until the crucifixion is over, in direct conflict with him. The parable of the vineyard or vine-growers (20:9-18) is used by Luke to set the scene for what follows. The rejection of Jesus by the Jews is illustrated in allegorical terms (*see* pp134-.135 for notes on the parable).

(i) Taxes to Caesar (20:19-26)

The lawyers and the chief priests are the first to try to trap Jesus. Their aim is to hand him over to the Roman Governor (20:20). In order to do this they need to provoke Jesus into making a political statement which the Romans would find treasonable. This leads to the question about taxes. If Jesus said that they were not to pay taxes, it would amount to rebellion. His way out of the question is to appeal to the custom of his time. Anyone who used coins with Caesar's head on them was considered to be accepting Caesar's authority. In addition, the coin was thought to belong to the person whose head it bore. Jesus, therefore, says that they should give to Caesar what belongs to Caesar, that is, his coins. At the same time people should not forget their duty to God, that is, become so concerned about wealth in this world that they forget about the true wealth of the kingdom of God.

The saying at verse 25, "pay Caesar what is due to Caesar and pay God what is due to God", shows that Jesus, and therefore his followers also, were not a threat to Rome. This was an important matter for the early church which might suffer persecution at any time. The story also shows that the Jewish authorities later lied to Pilate (*see* 23:2).

(ii) A question about the resurrection (20:27-40)

The next group to challenge Jesus are the Sadducees. They try to make a mockery of belief in the resurrection which they did not believe in but which Jesus taught (e.g. 9:22). Jesus' teaching is that life after the resurrection will be different from that at present. Those who are judged worthy of resurrection "are like angels: they are sons of God . . . " (20:36). There will be no death and no marrying. Human relationships as we know them will be at an end and questions which imagine them continuing after the resurrection are foolish. Relationships will be of a completely different type and will be like those of angels because there will be no more death. We are told no more than this and it is perhaps impossible for human language to describe something beyond human experience. The important point for Luke is that Jesus silences those who oppose belief in the resurrection.

In this dispute Jesus argues like a lawyer, quoting from the Old Testament (20:38 = Exod. 3:6). A lawyer congratulates him, and because of Jesus' power of argument no one dares to ask him any further questions. This reminds us that Jesus speaks with God's authority and is unconquerable by those who represent evil. (*See* 4:31f.).

NOTE ON THE SADDUCEES

The Sadducees were the aristocratic party. Their name might have meant 'the righteous ones', or, since many of them were priests, may have been connnected with the name Zadok, a priest who lived at the time of David and Solomon. (See 1 Kings 1 and 2.)

The High Priest was appointed from among their number, and they controlled the Sanhedrin and the Temple. They were only able to exercise this power because they co-operated with the Romans. Ever since the party had arisen during the second century BC, the Sadducees had favoured a policy of compromise with pagan ideas. The ruling dynasty of that time, the Maccabees, had opposed pagan customs and this policy was continued in Jesus' time by the Pharisees.

The Pharisees and the Zealots were not popular with the Sadducees, because both criticised them; the former for not being strict Jews, the latter for not resisting the Romans. The Sadducees possibly saw Jesus as a source of trouble in their dealings with the Romans and as a threat to their authority.

The Sadducees based their beliefs firmly on the books of Moses, with none of the Pharisees' additions such as resurrection, angels and spirits. They believed in a shadowy after-life for all men in *Sheol*. This is why they are shown to ask a question about resurrection when trying to trap Jesus (20:27-38).

When the Temple was destroyed in AD 70 the Sanhedrin ceased to exist and the Sadducees' party came to an end.

(iii) True and false religion (20:46-21:4)

Once Jesus has silenced the opposition and, by so doing, established his authority to teach in the Temple, he proceeds to give examples of true and false religion. The doctors of the Law are shown as hypocrites who care only for earthly glory and ignore the needs of the helpless members of society. Their long prayers, which it was the custom then to say loudly enough for all to hear (see 18:11), would be of no help to them. In contrast, the offering by a widow of all she had to live on (one might say, she offers her life) was a far greater gift to God. This is true religion. The result will be a severe sentence for the doctors of the Law and reward for the widow. Once again Luke shows that the conditions of this world will be reversed in the kingdom.

(iv) The Messiah and King David (20:41-44)

This brief section continues in the style of legal argument practised by the doctors of the Law. In this case it is about the status of the Messiah with regard to David. The Messiah was expected to be a descendant of David and so subordinate to him. However, Jesus, as Messiah and Son of God, is subordinate to no one. How can these two beliefs be reconciled?

Jesus quotes from Psalm 110:1 to show that David acknowledged that the Messiah would be more than an ordinary human descendant. This is another comment on the nature of Jesus' kingship. The passage sounds like a Christian answer to arguments by their opponents that Jesus must be inferior to David and so could not be everything Christians claimed.

(v) Teaching about the future (21:5-38)

This is the last section of Jesus' public teaching. It is apocalyptic (see p.135 for an explanation of this term) and is concerned with signs of the end, the difficulties of remaining faithful and the coming of

the Son of Man. This style of prophecy reflected first century beliefs about the way in which the present world would end. Wars, earthquakes, famines, plagues, portents in the sky were all anticipated. But Jesus had already rejected the idea that one would be able to predict the end by signs (11:29). It would happen suddenly. The same was the case for the appearance of the Son of Man (17:22-24) and the coming of the kingdom (17:20-21).

These two passages appear to reflect the difficulties Christians of Luke's generation had with the gospel tradition they inherited. Within the tradition were sayings, either from Jesus or formed by the early church, which contained prophecies that Luke could not ignore about the end time (21:25) and about the nearness of the end (21:32f.).

Luke appears to accept that these signs will occur before the end, but he wants to separate the signs from the end time. The Son of Man *will* return to bring this world order to an end. This final event will happen *after* the signs - but how long afterwards was not known.

So the 'present generation' (21:32) will already (by Luke's time) have seen the fall of Jerusalem in AD 70 (one of the signs), but it will still be waiting for the appearance of the Son of Man. Christians, therefore, had to be prepared at all times (21:34-36; also 17:20-37).

The sequence of historical events, as Luke saw it, was:

1. Jesus prophesies signs and end of world.
2. Signs occur: fall of Jerusalem.
3. But Second Coming and end of world are still in the future.

Luke has to re-examine the Christian understanding of Jesus' words as he received them. Jesus' words cannot be wrong; the way they are understood can be. Luke, therefore, reinterprets their meaning: there will be signs - but the end will follow at an *unknown* time after them.

C. THE LAST SUPPER (22:1-23)

(i) Symbols of the new covenant

Since the very beginning of the gospel, Luke has shown Jesus approaching the moment when a new *covenant* will be made between God and humanity. The time has now arrived and the event is marked by renewed activity by the powers of evil. Luke makes it clear that the death of Jesus is brought about by Satan (22:3). The powers of evil appear to triumph at last, but in fact the opposite is the case: their actions fulfil God's purpose. How this is accomplished is explained by Jesus at the Last Supper.

The preparations for this meal remind us of the way a colt was obtained (19:30-35). There is again the suggestion of some secret arrangements for obtaining a room, or of supernatural knowledge on Jesus' part. A man carrying a jar of water would be an unusual sight since fetching water was women's work. Such precautions for time spent away from the safety of the crowds were perhaps necessary because of the authorities' hostility to Jesus (19:48).

At the festival of the Passover Jews look *back* to and relive the time of the Exodus, the great salvation event of the Old Testament, when God rescued their ancestors from slavery in Egypt. They also look *forward* to the coming of God's kingdom. At the time of Jesus' transfiguration (9:31) there was a discussion of the departure ('exodos' is the word used) which Jesus is to accomplish in Jerusalem. This moment has now arrived. Jesus looks forward to the next Passover meal which will be the messianic banquet that he will eat in the kingdom of God (22:16). His words appear to mark the end of the old order of Judaism and the establishment of a new covenant. Now the way to the kingdom will be through communion with Jesus.

Jesus acts as a typical Jewish host at a Passover meal, giving thanks for (i.e. blessing) the wine and the bread. But he gives a new meaning to the bread: "This is my body" (22:19). Those who celebrate the Passover are members of the old covenant. The Twelve are the first members of the church and become, through sharing the bread and wine, members of a new covenant.

The linking of the Last Supper with the Passover would bring to mind for Luke's readers various symbolic actions connected with the festival. The old covenant was sealed by the sacrifice of a lamb and membership of it was shown originally by the people having blood sprinkled on them (Exod.

24:8). The sacrifice of Jesus on the cross established a new covenant, and membership of it is shown by sharing bread and wine in the Communion meal. When Jesus looks forward to the fulfilment of the Passover meal in the kingdom, it is a promise of salvation to his followers who will share it with him.

The account of the meal ends on a note of danger and with a prophecy of betrayal. Jesus refers to the Son of Man, the title associated with the idea of suffering, and suffering is the recurring theme until the resurrection.

Luke mentions two festivals: Unleavened Bread and Passover (22:1). They fell on consecutive days not on the same day, as Luke appears to think. It is difficult to know, historically, on which day Jesus ate the Last Supper with his disciples. In John's gospel it is on the earlier of the two days (John 13:1), in Mark it is on the later of the two (Mark 14:16). The important point for understanding the meaning of the Last Supper is that Luke saw it as a Passover meal and its symbolic significance relies on its connection with the Passover.

(ii) Jesus' farewell to his disciples (22:24-38)

It was customary, at the time when Luke wrote, for an author to give his central character a farewell speech. This is what Luke does for Jesus. He alters the order of events in Mark 14:26-31 by expanding Jesus' speech to his disciples and by putting it at the time of the Last Supper, rather than on the Mount of Olives. By doing this Luke shows what it means to be members of the covenant Jesus has just established.

The disciples are warned against worldly glory (22:24-27): true religion requires humble service to others. Those who stand firm will be rewarded with places in the kingdom (22:28-30). This is true wealth, unlike earthly glory.

Jesus prophesies Peter's denial, which will be caused by Satan, but he looks forward to the time when Peter has come to himself, that is, repented of his denial, and is able to lend strength to his brothers (22:31-34). Peter is affirmed as leader of the church which will face the same suffering that Jesus faces now (22:35-38). From the crucifixion to the parousia (Second Coming), without Jesus' physical presence, things will be different (22:36). It will be a time of suffering when Satan will test God's people.

NOTE ON PETER'S ACTS OF REPENTANCE

Peter makes three acts of repentance. Each marks a stage in the development of the church.

1. At 5:8, at the time of his call, he recognises his sinful nature: this marks the beginning of the church.

2. At 22:32 Jesus looks forward to Peter's repentance for his denial of Jesus: this marks Peter's appointment as head of the church on earth after Jesus' crucifixion.

3. At Acts 10 Peter accepts a Gentile into the church and lays the foundation for a Gentile church.

(iii) The Last Supper today

Holy Communion, Lord's Supper, Eucharist, Mass, Breaking of Bread: these are some of the names given to the church service which commemorates the Last Supper that Jesus shared with his disciples before being crucified. For many denominations it is the most important act of worship. By joining in the Communion Service, Christians show their faith in the promises made by Jesus.

The celebration of Holy Communion today. Can you tell which denomination this is?

The words spoken by the priest when the Prayer of Consecration or Thanksgiving is said over the bread and wine echo the words of Jesus at the Last Supper (22:17-20). In the Church of England service the priest says:

'Take, eat; this is my body which is given for you;
do this in remembrance of me.'
In the same way, after supper
he took the cup and gave thanks;
he gave it to them, saying,
'Drink this, all of you;
this is my blood of the new covenant,
which is shed for you and for many for the
forgiveness of sins.'

The priest takes the place of Jesus, and those receiving the bread and the wine take the place of the disciples whom Luke saw as the founder members of the church. By taking part in the service, they put themselves at one with each other and at one with God. The Communion meal is a sacrament. Those taking part in it are made one with Jesus and draw from it the strength necessary to live as he taught.

After the crucifixion, and before the disciples know about Jesus' resurrection, Luke uses the Eucharist to express the idea of knowing Jesus. When Jesus breaks bread and offers it to the disciples they recognise who he is (24:30f.). After this Jesus vanishes and what is left behind is the symbol of the bread. This represents Jesus' presence. Those who share the sacred meal declare themselves to be the people of God who hope for a share also of the deliverance Jesus offers.

NOTE ON 22:19b-20

You may find that in your version of Luke there is no mention of the wine being Jesus' blood or that the breaking of the bread is to be done as a memorial to Jesus. This is because in some ancient manuscripts the words at 22:19b-20 are missing. Some people think that they were added to Luke's original account of the Last Supper to bring it into line with Mark 14:24 and 1 Cor. 11:25.

D. THE ARREST OF JESUS
(22:39-65)

The final battle with evil begins on the Mount of Olives, where Jesus and the disciples have been in the habit of spending the night (21:37). The momentous events of Jesus' last hours are introduced by prayer. Jesus prays to know whether he must suffer. The Old Testament image of a cup is used to represent suffering (see Ezek. 23:33). His prayer is answered by an angel who brings him strength from God for the coming ordeal. The disciples have fallen asleep instead of praying and the result is that they, unlike Jesus, have not received the strength to remain faithful when tested (22:54-61).

Jesus tells them to pray that they may be spared the test, but immediately Judas and a crowd appear. Jesus asks Judas whether he is going to betray him with a kiss, the greeting of a disciple. (Note: Luke's gospel does not say that Judas does kiss Jesus.) Suffering will follow the betrayal and this point is emphasised by Jesus using the title Son of Man (22:48). The disciples fail their first test by using violence. Jesus forbids resistance because this would be to resist God's plan (22:51). The people who have come to arrest Jesus are the leaders of the Jews. Luke has altered Mark's account to emphasise their guilt (Mk. 14:43; Luke 22:52). They are wholly in the power of evil (22:53).

After the arrest, Peter follows Jesus at a distance, but then fails his test. When he is accused of being a disciple he refuses to admit it. Possibly Luke had in mind 9:26 and 12:8-10. where he had included teaching about being ashamed to admit to being a follower of Jesus. To be ashamed of Jesus meant that one denied being his follower, especially at a time of persecution. However, Jesus has already made clear that Peter will be forgiven when he has come to himself (22:32), so all is not lost for those who fail the test in moments of weakness, provided that they repent and turn back to Jesus.

The importance of the Mount of Olives (22:39)

It is from the Mount of Olives that Jesus begins his triumphal entry into Jerusalem (19:29), it is where Jesus is arrested (22:54), and from where Jesus ascends to heaven (24:50; Acts 1:12). Luke probably identifies this mount with the mountain mentioned at Ezekiel 11:23, because it was to that mountain that the glory of God went when it left Jerusalem. The reference to the Old Testament event shows what will happen when the Jews bring about Jesus' execution. The Temple will no longer be God's house on earth, the torn curtain will signify his departure (23:45), and Jesus will ascend to heaven. The pattern of events gains meaning from and mirrors those in the Old Testament.

At 22:45 Luke softens Mark's picture of the disciples (Mark 14:32-42). Mark says that they fall asleep three times, Luke just once; and Luke gives them an excuse. Luke also spreads the failure to all the disciples, not just the three closest to Jesus, as in Mark.

NOTE ON ELDERS

When Luke refers to the elders he means one of the three classes of people who made up the Sanhedrin (the others were priests and lawyers.) They were laymen who were respected by their communities.

NOTE ON PRIESTS (2)

Priests were in charge of the Temple in Jerusalem and it was their job to offer prayers and sacrifices on their own behalf and that of the whole people in accordance with the Law of Moses. They conducted the daily offerings and the large annual festivals such as the Passover to which thousands of people came. The leper healed by Jesus was told to show himself to the priest and make the offering laid down by Moses (5:14).

The High Priest was the only person allowed to enter the Holy of Holies, the most sacred place in the Temple, and then only once a year on the Day of Atonement. He held the position of president of the Sanhedrin and it was his and the council's duty to see that the religious and national laws were obeyed. When Jesus is brought before the council or court it appears to be on religious grounds (22:66-71).

Luke takes the reference to 'chief priests' from Mark 15:1. It probably means priests from important families who were members of the Sanhedrin. There was no class of priests with that precise title.

E. THE TRIALS OF JESUS

(i) The trial before the Sanhedrin (22:66-71)

The Sanhedrin was the ruling council of the Jews. Its intention is to find Jesus guilty of blasphemy. Jesus is asked if he is the Messiah. His answer is not direct and he changes to talking about the glorification of the Son of Man. Either there is a deliberate misunderstanding by the Sanhedrin or they believe Jesus is admitting the charge, because they then change to using the title 'Son of God' and treating it as an alternative title for 'Messiah' (at that time it need not necessarily have meant Messiah - see p.64). Jesus is then said to have admitted that he is the Messiah and is therefore guilty of blasphemy.

Luke does not make it clear what he thinks the Sanhedrin really believed about Jesus' words, and that is not important to him. The main point Luke wants to make is that Jesus is innocent for two reasons. First, Jesus never claims the title 'Messiah' because he does not want his mission to be misunderstood. Second, if he did claim the title, it would not be blasphemy but the truth. None of this matters to the Sanhedrin, who are in the power of evil and intent on Jesus' death.

NOTE ON THE SANHEDRIN

The word 'Sanhedrin' means 'council'. It was the Jewish ruling council and was also a court which enforced Jewish laws. It had a force of Temple police at its service and the right to arrest people. Three classes of people belonged to the Sanhedrin - priests, doctors of the Law and elders. Since these people also belonged to the Pharisees' and Sadducees' parties and many came from aristocratic families, the Sanhedrin contained all the groups opposed to Jesus.

The Sanhedrin came to an end with the destruction of the Temple in AD 70.

(ii) The trial before Pilate: first part (23:1-6)

There are two possible reasons for the Sanhedrin bringing Jesus before Pilate. They may have wished to transfer blame for his death to the Romans and so avoid unpopularity with the people, or, at that time, they may have lacked the right to impose a death sentence.

The charge of blasphemy is not mentioned to Pilate, instead political charges are brought. Jesus is falsely accused of turning the people against Rome, of opposing the payment of taxes (*see* 20:25) and of claiming to be a king. Again Jesus does not answer questions directly. Pilate finds him innocent. This point is important for Luke's generation of Christians because it shows that Jesus and, therefore, they themselves are not a threat to Rome.

> **NOTE ON PONTIUS PILATE**
>
> Pontius Pilate was Procurator of Judaea, AD 26-36. His headquarters were in Caesarea, but he would be in Jerusalem in case of disturbances during the Passover festival. He is reputed to have been a cruel and inflexible man. It was the custom for Roman governors to hear court cases early in the morning, so the various trials could all have been completed in time for a crucifixion the same morning. (Although Pilate is often called 'Procurator' his title was in fact 'Prefect'. The change of title to Procurator took place in AD 41, some years after the time of Pilate and Jesus.)

(iii) The trial before Herod Antipas (23:6-12)

None of the other gospels mentions this trial. Luke probably included it since it showed a Jewish king (the only Jewish authority not so far involved) also under the influence of evil and mistreating Jesus, even though he did not find him guilty of anything (23:15). It also showed how Jesus brought together Jew and Gentile, even when they were his enemies and previously enemies of one another (23:12).

Luke has prepared for the meeting of Jesus and Herod by telling us that Herod was anxious to see him (9:9). At 23:28 we are told that Herod wanted to see a miracle. This identifies him as one of the wicked generation which demands signs (11:29). Jesus ignores him. The source of Christian information about Herod was possibly Joanna (8:3; *see* p.75).

(iv) The trial before Pilate: second part (23:13-25)

In the first four verses of this section Luke emphasises the innocence of Jesus and Pilate's wish to release him. The responsibility for Jesus' death is placed fully on the Jewish authorities, who are all said to be present (23:13). The Jews reject God's Messiah and demand the release of a political rebel, Barabbas. In leading a rising Barabbas has tried to obtain worldly power, which was the second of the temptations refused by Jesus (4:5-8). Barabbas is, therefore, in the power of evil and those who demand his release also serve evil.

Luke has Pilate declare Jesus innocent for the third time (23:22). The number three means that there can be no doubt. In spite of this, Jesus is sentenced to death.

The trials of Jesus are extremely brief. It may be that Christians had no sources of information to provide details. On the other hand Luke's interest was in showing that Jesus was innocent, that his death was the responsibility of the Jews and that Christianity was no threat to Roman rule; he was not interested in additional details.

The trials of Jesus have provided biblical scholars with a rich field for disagreement. The following are examples of some of the arguments and counter-arguments which have been put forward about the trial before Herod.

It has been suggested that the trial before Herod was not historical. Luke is said to have constructed it on the basis of Psalm 2:1f. It is also doubted whether Pilate would have sent a prisoner to Herod. The giving of a robe is transferred from Mark 15:17, which shows the Roman soldiers in a bad light: this, Luke did not want to do.

Against this it is argued that since both Pilate and Herod are shown to find Jesus innocent the event does not reflect Psalm 2:1f.; that Pilate might have been seeking advice from an expert in Jewish affairs; and that there might have been more than one occasion on which Jesus was mocked.

F. THE CRUCIFIXION OF JESUS

(i) On the way to crucifixion (23:26-31)

This section is filled with references to the Old Testament. Luke's intention is to show that what happens is God's will and a part of God's plan for mankind's salvation. He also emphasises again Jesus' innocence.

It was common practice to select someone from the crowd to carry the cross if the condemned person was too weak. Simon appears as a model disciple following Jesus with his cross (see 9:23). Cyrene was on the North African coast. Possibly Simon was a pilgrim in Jerusalem for the Passover.

Luke presents the traditional, ritual mourning of Jerusalem women for one condemned to die as a fulfilment of Zechariah 12:10-14: "... the inhabitants of Jerusalem ... shall wail over him ..." They provide the cue for Jesus to be shown to call for repentance and to illustrate the horror of judgment. To be barren was a woman's greatest shame, yet at the day of judgment those who were barren would be happier than those who saw their children perish.

The saying at 23: 31 is probably an allegorical reference to Ezekiel 20:47: "... fire will consume all the wood, green and dry alike ..." The green is Jesus who is innocent; the dry stands for the people of Jerusalem who are guilty. It is asking people to think what will happen to them if one who is innocent faces such suffering.

(ii) The mocking of Jesus (23:32-38)

The place of execution was outside the city. Jesus gives an example of how to respond to one's persecutors: pray for their forgiveness (23:34). Luke shows the martyr Stephen behaving in the same way (Acts 7:60). The mockery of 23: 35 shows once again the failure of the Jews to understand what is happening. They challenge Jesus, if he is the Messiah, to save himself. But it is just because he is the Messiah that he must die. He is not an earthly king, and those who expect him to behave like one do not understand the type of king he is or the nature of the kingdom he is going to establish. By dying he is departing to establish this kingdom and at the same time accomplishing the salvation of humanity.

The casting of lots for Jesus' clothes echoes Psalm 22:18. It is not clear in Luke who casts lots. In Mark it is the Roman soldiers (Mark 15:24), but Luke has so reduced their role in things that 23:25 does not even make it clear that they are carrying out the crucifixion. This was a Roman punishment and soldiers would have executed it. Following Mark, Luke says that the soldiers offered Jesus sour wine and joined the Jews in mocking Jesus. The offering of sour wine, which was drunk by the common people, might have been an act of charity to a dying man (which the offering of drugged wine in Mark is), but Luke interprets it as mockery perhaps thinking of Psalm 69:21: "... and gave me vinegar when I was thirsty."

(iii) The two criminals (23:39-43)

Luke makes use of the two criminals to show that salvation is available to anyone who repents. Jesus saving the lost is one of Luke's favourite topics (see 7:36-50; 18:9-14; etc.). Even though Jesus is suffering Luke shows him still to be completely confident that he is doing God's will and that he will be raised from the dead. He is also thinking of others (serving: see 22:24-27), even at that time, and promises the repentant criminal a place in Paradise[13]. Despite the enormous difficulty in breathing, records exist of conversations taking place between those being crucified.

In Mark's account of the crucifixion the two criminals are mentioned in only two verses (15:27 & 32). Luke has enlarged their roles in the narrative to illustrate, for the last time, the teaching on repentance. The first criminal repeats the mockery of the Jews and is rebuked by his companion. Possibly the use of the word 'rebuked', which was used in mastering evil spirits, is intended to tell us that he is in the power of evil. The second criminal accepts that he deserves his punishment. When anyone did this, it was taken as a sign of repentance. This is confirmed by his words to Jesus (23:42).

(iv) The death of Jesus (23:44-49)

Darkness can stand as a symbol both for God's displeasure and for the grip of evil on the land. The whole people has rejected God's Messiah and God is about to offer salvation to all humanity through Jesus and no longer through the sacrifices made in the Temple.

As a symbol of the destruction of the Temple which is to follow, the Temple curtain is torn. This event also symbolises the Christian belief that God is available to everyone everywhere and is not found in one particular place which is open to only a minority of people. Jesus has torn aside the barrier between God and humanity.

Jesus' final words are an example of how a faithful Christian should die. Luke pictures the first Christian martyr, Stephen, dying with similar words on his lips (Acts 7:59). Jesus says, "Father, into thy hands I commit my spirit" (23:46). The centurion in charge of the execution praises God which, in Luke, is a typical reaction to being in the presence of divine power (e.g. 2:20; 5:26). The centurion also repeats that Jesus was innocent, so emphasising that Rome (first represented by Pilate and now by the centurion) found Jesus innocent. The responsibility for his death is placed by Luke firmly on the Jews.

23:44-5: The darkness and the torn curtain seem to be a fulfilment of Joel 2:31. Darkness is said to be a portent of judgment to come and the torn curtain an illustration of what that judgment entails. The curtain hid the holiest part of the Temple, without it the Holy of Holies was no longer sacred, atonement for sins could not be made and Temple rituals became useless. The torn curtain symbolised the coming end of Judaism and the opening of a direct relationship between God and people.

It has been suggested that the darkness was an eclipse of the sun. This could not happen at the time of the full moon, which was when Passover was held. Other suggestions, such as a sandstorm, have been made, but they all miss the point: darkness is a symbol.

23:46: Jesus' final words are very different from those given at Mark 15:34. Luke quotes Psalm 31:5. These words give a more fitting display of faith (one of the topics Luke is interested in) than do the despairing words in Mark.

23:48: It is difficult to say why the crowd beat their breasts. It was probably a formal display of sorrow for one who has died, rather than a show of repentance.

23:49: None of Jesus' disciples has been near the cross. The Roman soldiers would not have allowed it. Luke probably wishes to use the disciples' witness to confirm that Jesus did indeed die - just as the women (23:55) confirm which tomb Jesus was laid in. Both then support Christian claims about Jesus' resurrection.

---

[13] 'Paradise' was a Persian word meaning 'park' or 'pleasure-garden'. It was used by Jews to suggest a perfect place, like the Garden of Eden.

NOTE ON CRUCIFIXION

Crucifixion was a Roman punishment used on the worst criminals. Jesus was condemned to death by Pontius Pilate, the Roman Procurator of Judaea, and the execution was carried out by Roman soldiers.

The condemned person (man or woman) was made, as part of the punishment, to carry the cross-beam to the place of execution. If he or she were too weak, the soldiers would choose someone from the crowd of spectators to carry it. The condemned person was nailed through the wrists to the crossbeam. This was fixed to the upright, and the cross was lifted with the victim on it and slotted into a hole in the ground.

Some crosses had a ledge to stand or sit on. This was provided not out of kindness, but to make the victim's agony last longer. By propping himself up on a ledge he took the strain off his arms and chest. In the end he died of suffocation, because the strain on his chest made it impossible to breathe.

Crucifixion was a humiliating form of execution. The naked victim, was put on display to discourage others from committing the same crime and was mocked by those who had come to enjoy the spectacle.

G. THE CROSS OF JESUS TODAY

How do Christians today view the death of Jesus? A popular old hymn contains the words, 'He died that we might be forgiven; he died to make us good.' These words sum up a complicated idea which links Jesus with the story in Genesis of Adam and Eve.

In that story Adam and Eve are created perfect by God, but they are tempted and eat the fruit from the tree of the knowledge of good and evil which God has forbidden them to touch. Because of their disobedience, God sends them away from him. This story explains why people live in a world in which evil, suffering and death exist. It tells of the fall of man: that is, how humanity fell out of favour with God. Some Christians believe that since that time all people have been born sinners, however good they may appear to be. This is because they regard the sin of Adam as having been passed on to the whole human race.

As a result, human nature is seen as fundamentally sinful and this places humanity in the power of evil. People cannot free themselves from their slavery to Satan, only God can do that. Luke makes it plain at the start of Jesus' ministry that this is what he sees Jesus as doing. In the reading from Isaiah 61:1-2, Jesus declares that he has come 'to proclaim release for prisoners' (4:18). Jesus is to bring about humanity's deliverance from the powers of evil. The proof that he has overcome evil is his resurrection: the defeat of death means freedom for humanity because until that moment death was evil's final victory.

Over the centuries many Christian thinkers have tried to explain exactly why Jesus *had* to die, and how his death helps people. Their explanations have not always been entirely satisfactory, and for those today who regard the Adam and Eve story as a myth[14], rather than as something that actually happened, these explanations seem even more unsatisfactory. What is more, most people today do not think of themselves as sinners.

Is there, then, another way of viewing the death of Jesus? More recently some Christians have interpreted Jesus' death as God's wish to identify himself with a suffering world. Although, for many people living in the West, suffering often seems remote, we are all aware that in some parts of the world people are dying from disease and malnutrition. In our country, too, we know of tragic deaths from road accidents, heart disease, cancer, and so on. We call such suffering *innocent suffering*, because the people it happens to have done nothing to bring it on themselves.

---

[14]The word 'myth' means a story which, while not necessarily historically or scientifically true, expresses through striking imagery truths about man's existence. The story about Adam and Eve is, therefore, called a myth.

Christians believe that God cares about all the suffering in the world. They may not be able to explain *why* God allows it to happen, but they can see that God had a part in the suffering and death of Jesus. In sharing in the pain of Jesus' death on the cross, God was identifying himself with the whole of the suffering world. In this view, God is trying to tell people that he is not remote from them, but involved in all the tragedies in the world. Jesus' death on the cross can be seen, then, to stand as a symbol for all the world's suffering.

Questions for chapter 11

19:28-48

1a. What instructions does Jesus give in order to obtain a colt?

b. From which hill (or mount) does Jesus approach Jerusalem?

c. What do Jesus' disciples sing as he approaches Jerusalem?

d. How does Jesus react when he comes within sight of the city?

e. What does Jesus say will happen to Jerusalem?

2a. What is the signficance of Jesus riding into Jerusalem on a colt?

b. How does the song that the disciples sing (19:38) link up with incidents earlier in the gospel?

c. **(i)** What is meant by 'the cleansing of the Temple'? **(ii)** What is the importance of this event?

3. Why was it important to Luke to show that Jesus fulfilled prophecy? Give examples to illustrate your answer.

20:19-26

4a. Who asked the question about taxes to Caesar?

b. How were they trying to trap Jesus?

c. What does Jesus reply?

d. Explain the meaning of Jesus' reply.

20:27-40

5a. What is the imaginary situation described by the Sadducees?

b. What question do the Sadducees ask?

c. Why do the Sadducees ask a question about resurrection?

d. What does Jesus reply?

e. Why does a lawyer congratulate Jesus on his reply?

20:46-21:4

6a. How does Jesus describe the doctors of the law?

b. Why are they hypocrites?

c. How much does the poor widow offer?

d. How do the lawyer and the widow illustrate the difference between true and false religion?

20:1-8

7a. Why is the question of authority important?

b. (20:41-44) Why is the question of the relationship between the Messiah and King   David important?

21:5-38

8a. What is meant by 'apocalyptic'?

b. List three of the prophecies Jesus makes.

c. **(i)** Why did the prophecies in verses 25 and 32-3 cause difficulties for Luke's generation of Christians? **(ii)** How did Luke resolve these difficulties?

22:1-13

9a. What two festivals does Luke mention?

b. Who were trying to do away with Jesus?

c. Who betrays Jesus?

d. What is the reason for Judas' betrayal of Jesus

e. What arrangements are made for finding a room in which to celebrate the Passover?

22:14-23

10a. What event does the Passover celebrate?

b. When does Jesus say he will next celebrate the Passover?

c. What does Jesus say about the wine (verses 17-18)?

d. What does Jesus say about the bread (verse 19)?

e. Why is it important to Luke that the Last Supper was a Passover meal?

22:24-38

11a. What is the disciples' dispute about?

b. What does Jesus teach in response to the dispute?

c. What will be the cause of Peter's denial of Jesus?

d. For what purposes might Luke have altered the order of events in his source, Mark 14:26-31?

e. How does Luke link Peter's three acts of repentance with stages in the development of the church?

22:39-46

12a. Where does Jesus go to pray?

b. What words does Jesus speak in prayer?

c. What is the meaning of the word 'cup' as used in this prayer?

d. How is Jesus' prayer answered?

e. Why did the disciples fall asleep?

f. What does Jesus tell the disciples to pray for?

22:47-53

13a. Who leads the crowd to arrest Jesus?

b. Why does Jesus use the title 'Son of Man'?

c. Which groups come to arrest Jesus?

d. Why does Jesus say that their hour is 'when darkness reigns'?

e. Why does Jesus *not* resist arrest?

22:54-65

14a. Where was Jesus taken after his arrest?

b. How many times does Peter deny Jesus?

c. What might be the significance of Jesus looking at Peter when the cock crows?

d. What other occasions in the gospel does the use of the word 'prophet' (22:64) bring to mind?

e. What does the use of the word 'prophet' tell us about the people using it?

22:66-71

15a. What is the Sanhedrin?

b. What groups are members of theSanhedrin?

c. What does the Sanhedrin ask Jesus?

d. What does Jesus reply?

e. What does the Sanhedrin find Jesus guilty of?

f. Is Jesus guilty of these charges? Explain your answer.

23:1-5 & 13-25

16a. Who was Pilate?

b. What charges are brought against Jesus?

c. How are these charges different from the one brought against Jesus when he was before the Sanhedrin?

d. How many times does Pilate state that Jesus is innocent?

e. Whose release do the people ask for?

f. Who demands Jesus' execution?

g. Why was it important to Luke to show that Pilate found Jesus innocent?

23:6-12

17a. Why does Pilate send Jesus to Herod?

b. What does Herod want from Jesus?

c. How did Herod and his troops treat Jesus?

d. In what way might verse 8 be connected with 11:29?

e. What might be the reason for Luke including verse 12 in his gospel?

f. Does Herod find Jesus guilty or innocent?

g. Why might Luke have included the trial before Herod in his gospel when the other gospels do not mention it?

23:26-31

18a. Who carried Jesus' cross?

b. Why is Simon of Cyrene an example of a perfect disciple?

c. What is odd about the phrase 'Happy are the barren' (23:29)?

d. Explain the meaning of verse 31.

e. Why does Luke include references to Old Testament prophecy?

23:32-43

19a. Who is executed with Jesus?

b. Where does the crucifixion take place?

c. What does Jesus say in prayer (23:34)?

d. What inscription was on the cross?

e. How does this passage show the Jews' lack of understanding?

23:39-48

20a. Describe the different attitudes towards Jesus of the two criminals.

b. What does Jesus promise the repentant criminal?

c. For how long was the land in darkness?

d. At what time did Jesus die?

e. What are Jesus' final words?

f. What is the centurion's reaction and what is its significance?

21a. What is the significance of darkness in Luke's account of the crucifixion?

b. What does the torn curtain in the Temple signify?

22. Give two or three examples of occasions when Luke refers to the Old Testament in the Passion narrative and explain their importance.

23. Look at the picture 'The celebration of Holy Communion today' on p.147.

a. What event in the life of Jesus does this service commemorate?

b. What do the bread and wine represent?

c. What is the symbolic significance of this meal?

d. Do you agree that Holy Communion 'is the most important act of worship'? Explain your answer.

24. How is the story of Adam and Eve connected with the cross of Jesus?

25. Why did Jesus have to die?

Jesus after his Resurrection. The soldiers asleep by the tomb are mentioned in Matthew 28:4.
What is the connection between the resurrection and the kingship of Jesus?

12
THE RESURRECTION

The resurrection of Jesus is the climax of the gospel. When Christians make a public statement of their faith, such as by reciting one of the creeds, they confess their belief in Jesus as the Messiah and in his resurrection. That is, their belief that God raised Jesus from the dead. The resurrection confirms that the good news preached by Jesus was the word of God, and it also confirms the promise that there will be a new life for all those who follow Jesus.

Christians believe that on Good Friday Jesus died and his body was placed in a tomb. However, something miraculous occurred between then and the following Sunday morning because, *somehow*, Jesus stopped being dead and came back to life. They understand this miracle to be the action of God.

The event is not something which can be explained scientifically. There is not enough of the appropriate sort of evidence to provide material for a scientific analysis of it. The result is that the most important event in the Christian religion is also the one which provokes the most disagreement - both among Christians themselves and with their opponents.

We need to keep these points in mind when we examine Luke's account of the resurrection. We must also set aside, for the time being, any opinions we may have about whether Jesus was resurrected to a physical or a spiritual existence.

A cave tomb with stone to block the entrance. This is the type of tomb in which, according to Luke., Jesus was buried, See 24:2.

A. THE EMPTY TOMB

(23:50-24:11)

The burial of Jesus is arranged by Joseph of Arimathaea, not by one of Jesus' close disciples. We do not know very much about this Joseph. He was a member of the Sanhedrin who had disagreed with those who wanted Jesus killed. Luke describes him in terms similar to those he uses of Zechariah and Simeon (1:6; 2:25), indicating that he considered him an example of a truly devout Jew.

Joseph obtains Pilate's permission to remove Jesus' body from the cross (a brave action since it was not wise to associate oneself with a criminal), and lays it in a new tomb. The newness of the tomb is perhaps noted to show that it was pure enough to contain the body of the Messiah (see 19:30). He did this because the Sabbath was about to begin (23:54), and to leave the body unburied would have defiled the holy day (Deut. 21:23). The Sabbath began at sundown on Friday.

Luke is careful to stress that there is no mistake about the tomb in which Jesus is laid. Women who knew Jesus well "took note of the tomb and observed how his body was laid" (23:55). There had evidently been disputes with the Jews about the reality of the resurrection, though Luke does not mention this in his gospel. (See Matt. 28:11-15.) Although Luke is following Mark, he omits to say that the tomb was closed with a stone, but he assumes this at 24:2.

The women, who carefully note Jesus' tomb, do not go to anoint the body until the Sabbath is over because to do so would be to work, and work of any sort was forbidden on the Sabbath. However, they find the tomb open and the body gone. The two men who appear repeat what Jesus himself had taught about the suffering and the resurrection of the Son of Man (24:6-7). The two men are later described as angels (24:23). However, 'angel' simply meant 'messenger', and it was their dazzling garments which suggested divine messengers. Their message is from God and reminds us of the voice from the cloud at the Transfiguration (9:35). They should listen (or, now, remember) what Jesus told them. Everything Jesus said has happened: God's plan has been fulfilled. Evil has not won. Jesus is alive.

Luke gives the women's names at 24: 10. We already know two of them (see 8:1-3), but there is only this one mention of Mary the mother of James and we know nothing else about her. The women carry the message to the Eleven (i.e. the Twelve minus Judas Iscariot), but they have not listened to Jesus, any more than the women have, and they do not believe.

Luke largely follows Mark 16:1-8. He has changed the young man in the tomb, Mark 16:5, to two men, Luke 24:4. Their words vary considerably, and Luke has probably developed their message in Mark to make clear the significance of the empty tomb. He has also dropped the reference to Galilee, and this appears to reflect his interest in Jerusalem as the place where the Messiah appears and from where the church will go out to offer salvation to the world. The two dazzling figures bring to mind Moses and Elijah, who were seen 'in glory', i.e. of dazzling appearance (9:31). At that time they talked with Jesus about the deliverance which he has now brought about.

B. THE RESURRECTION APPEARANCES

In his account of the resurrection appearances of Jesus, Luke shows the disciples coming to believe in the resurrection, their joy in it, and their realisation of what it means for the future.

(i) The road to Emmaus (24:13-32)

This story of the encounter with the resurrected Jesus on the road to Emmaus is found only in Luke. It takes place on the day of the resurrection (Easter Sunday). Jesus joins Cleopas and another, unnamed, disciple as they are walking but is not at first recognised. 24: 16 tells us that "something kept them from seeing who it was". The suggestion is that their blindness is caused by divine action (see Isaiah 44:18). Later, however, 24:32 tells us that they felt their hearts on fire as he talked.

The resurrection, like the miracles of Jesus, is a sign and only those who have faith can recognise its meaning. To begin with the disciples lack faith. They had been hoping that Jesus "was the man to liberate Israel" (24:21), i.e. bring salvation; but they had not listened carefully enough to his words or had sufficient faith to understand what his deeds meant. So now they, like the women and the Eleven, believe that Jesus is dead and do not recognise him. This is the third time that Luke has said this. There can be no mistake: no one expected the resurrection of Jesus.

As part of the process of opening their eyes to what has happened, Jesus explains why the Messiah had to suffer and refers to the prophecies of the Old Testament. It was all a part of God's plan. But it is not until Jesus breaks the bread that the disciples' blindness is removed (24:30-31). The message that Luke wants to give his readers is that Jesus is known through the eucharist.

It is when Jesus repeats the actions and words of the Last Supper that he is recognised. Luke believed that it was through the same actions, repeated in the Holy Communion service, that every succeeding generation of Christians also met Jesus. The same idea is given solid expression today in Roman Catholic churches where there is an object called a monstrance in which the host (bread) is put on display so that worshippers may 'see' Jesus.

NOTE ON CLEOPAS

Nothing is known about Cleopas. His only mention in the gospel is on the road to Emmaus. The Jewish form of the name appears at John 19:25, but whether it is the same person is not known.

The blindness of the disciples, in the sense of their lack of understanding, parallels the dumbness of Zechariah (1:20). They have all doubted the word of God.

The Christian explanation of what the scriptures meant was believed by the early church to have come directly from Jesus (24:25-27). This interpretation was vitally important. If Jesus was indeed the Messiah, then his life should reflect the prophecies of the Old Testament. The Jews had an alternative interpretation of scripture and of the nature of messiahship. Christians had to show, if they were to convince people of the truth of their claims about Jesus, that there was scriptural authority for what they said.

(ii) Appearances in Jerusalem (24:33-53)

The disciples who met Jesus on the road to Emmaus discover, when they return to Jerusalem, that since their departure Jesus has appeared to Peter. This appearance is also mentioned by Paul (1 Cor. 15:5-7), and Luke *perhaps* wishes to make the point that this is the first of Jesus' appearances after the resurrection. It confirms the importance of Peter, which has been emphasised throughout the gospel. (Note: 24:12)

Jesus' third appearance is sudden and terrifying. At that time it was believed that those who died by violent means returned to haunt those who had known them. The disciples immediately think they are seeing a ghost. Jesus invites the disciples to touch him. This proves that the resurrection has really happend. Jesus was a person of flesh and bones and still is. As final proof he eats some fish.

For Luke the resurrection is undoubtedly physical. But Jesus' sudden appearance suggests that his resurrected body possesses more than normal abilities. Apparently, without any of the normal sounds or movements which tell us that someone is entering a room, Jesus was suddenly "standing among them" (24:36).

The resurrection proves that Jesus has God's authority for everything he has said and done. He entered Jerusalem as the Messiah and now he will rule in the kingdom of God. The kingship of Jesus is beyond doubt.

In 24:44-49 Luke pictures Jesus presenting the message of the Christian church:
verse 44: Jesus fulfilled Old Testament prophecy;
verses 46-47: because Jesus rose from the dead those who repent will be forgiven their sins;
verses 47-48: the good news is to be proclaimed to all the world, starting from Jerusalem;
verse 49: the Holy Spirit which was in Jesus will be sent to the church.

After this there is no more to say. The good news has been proclaimed for one last time. From then onwards it is the responsibility of the church: and Luke will write about the church accepting that responsibility in Acts.

Jesus' arrival amongst the disciples was mysterious and his departure is equally mysterious (24:50-53). Luke presents Jesus' departure as taking place at Bethany. It was from here that Jesus made his kingly entry into Jerusalem; and it is from here that he departs to claim his kingship in the kingdom of God.

Luke describes more fully how "he parted from them" in Acts 1:9-11. The last four verses of the gospel and the first eleven of Acts overlap.

The resurrection appearances in Luke's gospel take place in or near Jerusalem. His appearance on the road to Emmaus is on Easter Sunday, 24:13, and we assume that the others were on the same day, though no further note of time is given. Luke has dropped the hint in Mark 16:7 (which Matthew retains and develops, Matt. 28:16f.) that the disciples will see Jesus in Galilee. Luke does not want any distraction from Jerusalem.

Luke had no information in Mark to provide him with information about the resurrection appearances of Jesus, but Q (see Matt. 28) provided the tradition of the physical reality of the resurrected Jesus.

Jesus' final speech to the disciples (24:44-49) has probably been framed by Luke on the basis of church traditions. (Compare Matt. 28:16-20.) The church would have wished to show that Old Testament prophecy was fulfilled in the mission of the church (24:47) as well as in the mission of Jesus. In 24:25-27 it was Jesus' suffering which was said to be a fulfilment of prophecy. In 24:44-49 the mission of the church is also seen as the fulfilment of prophecy.

The last four verses of the gospel do not go into detail about how Jesus parted from the disciples. It seems likely that Luke intended 24:50-53 to refer to the ascension of Jesus to heaven, since it makes an appropriate ending to the gospel, but there is a lack of continuity between the end of the gospel and the same event which is described in more detail in Acts 1:3-11. Luke may be summarising in a way which makes a fitting conclusion to the gospel knowing

A monstrance. In the centre is a glass door behind which is placed a consecrated wafer. The priest is holding up the monstrance so that the people may 'see' Jesus.

that he can expand on the event later. The ascension in Acts occurs forty days after the resurrection (Acts 1:3); in the gospel the impression is given that it occurs on Easter Sunday (see above).

Luke is the only gospel writer to picture a physical ascension to heaven, and this is in keeping with the style of his imagery, which is always solid: for example, messages are brought by angels which have a very real presence.

The final verse brings the gospel back to where it started: in the Temple. God's plan is fulfilled.

C. RESURRECTION TODAY

Did the resurrection really happen? Was it a trick worked by Jesus' followers as the Jews tried to claim? If there was a resurrection, was it physical or spiritual?

The resurrection is often called the greatest miracle in the New Testament. It is also the central mystery of the Christian faith and cannot be explained in neat, scientific terms. If it could be, then Christianity would not be a religion, because no faith would be required.

We already know from considering the other miracles Luke records that the question to ask is not 'Did it happen?' but 'What did it mean to Luke?' To him it was a demonstration that everything Jesus had said was true. For Christians today the same is the case. The resurrection justifies faith in Jesus.

What bothers people today are questions which Luke, living in a different world, would not even have understood. For him there were no laws of nature. It was God's will which kept the world existing in the way it was. So, if God chose, at the day of judgment, to transform the world into his perfect kingdom he could do so. Likewise, if he chose to bring back to life someone who had died, or to transform the mortal remains of someone who had been crucified into an imperishable body he could do so.

Luke, in keeping with his usual way of thinking, is perfectly content to think of a physical resurrection in which the risen Jesus has the ability to appear and disappear at will and to ascend to heaven. When we try to visualise this event today, a physical ascension to a heaven just above our heads does not make sense because our picture of the universe is not the same as Luke's.

If you ask Christians today what they believe about the resurrection you will receive a variety of answers. Some will be happy to share Luke's view of things. Others will prefer to think of a spiritual resurrection. This is what Paul appears to have in mind (1 Cor. 15), and he does not seem to know the tradition of the empty tomb, at least he does not present it as evidence.

Other present-day Christians prefer to treat the resurrection as a sign which points to how they should live their own lives. In this view repentance and resurrection go together. Christians accept Jesus' call to repentance and their resurrection is to a new life in Christ. They find the personal relationship with Jesus which he promised on the cross (23:43), by living as he taught, and they strive to create the kingdom of God in their own life in this world.

Christians today, like Luke in his day, have to develop their own understanding and discover for themselves what the resurrection means to them. There is no one right answer to any of the questions about resurrection. It is up to individuals to decide for themselves.

Questions for chapter 12

23:50-54

1a. What does Luke tell us about Joseph of Arimathaea?

b. How do we know that Luke approved of Joseph?

c. Why was it brave of Joseph to ask Pilate for the body of Jesus?

d. What did Joseph do with Jesus' body?

e. On which day did these events occur?

f. Why might Luke have included the information that no one had previously been laid in the tomb?

g. For what reason might Joseph have asked for the body of Jesus?

23:55-24:12

2a. Name the women who went to the tomb.

b. What do we know about these women?

c. Why do the women wait until Sunday morning to go to the tomb?

d. Why were the women terrified (24:5)?

e. What message are the women given?

f. What are the reactions of (i)The Eleven, (ii)Peter, when given the message?

3a. What is the connection between verses 23:49 and 55, and why does Luke include them in his gospel?

b.(i) What changes does Luke make to his source, Mark 16:1-8?
(ii) Why might Luke have made these changes.

24:13-32

4a. What do we know about Cleopas?

b. Where are the two disciples going when Jesus joins them?

c. What do the disciples tell Jesus they are talking about?

d. What does Jesus tell them in reply?

5a. Why do the two disciples not recognise Jesus?

b. What does the phrase 'to liberate Israel' mean?

c. Why is Jesus' explanation of the scriptures important (24:25-27)?

d. Explain the importance for Luke's readers of the actions which led to the disciples recognising Jesus.

24:33-43

6a. Why was Jesus' appearance to Peter important?

b. Why were the disciples terrified when Jesus appeared among them?

c. What does Jesus say and do to prove that he is not a ghost?

24:44-53

7a. List the points that Jesus makes in this passage.

b. What important events are connected with Bethany?

c. How does Luke describe Jesus' departure?

d. What do the disciples do after Jesus has parted from them?

8. Does Luke think Jesus was resurrected to a physical or a spiritual existence? Quote verses to support your answer.

9. Has God's plan been fulfilled? Give references to support your answer.

10a. Would Christianity be a religion if everything it claims could be scientifically explained?

b. Why is belief in the resurrection of Jesus more difficult for many people today than in Luke's time?

c. Explain what is meant by saying that the resurrection is a sign.

d. How important do you think is a belief in the resurrection for Christians today?

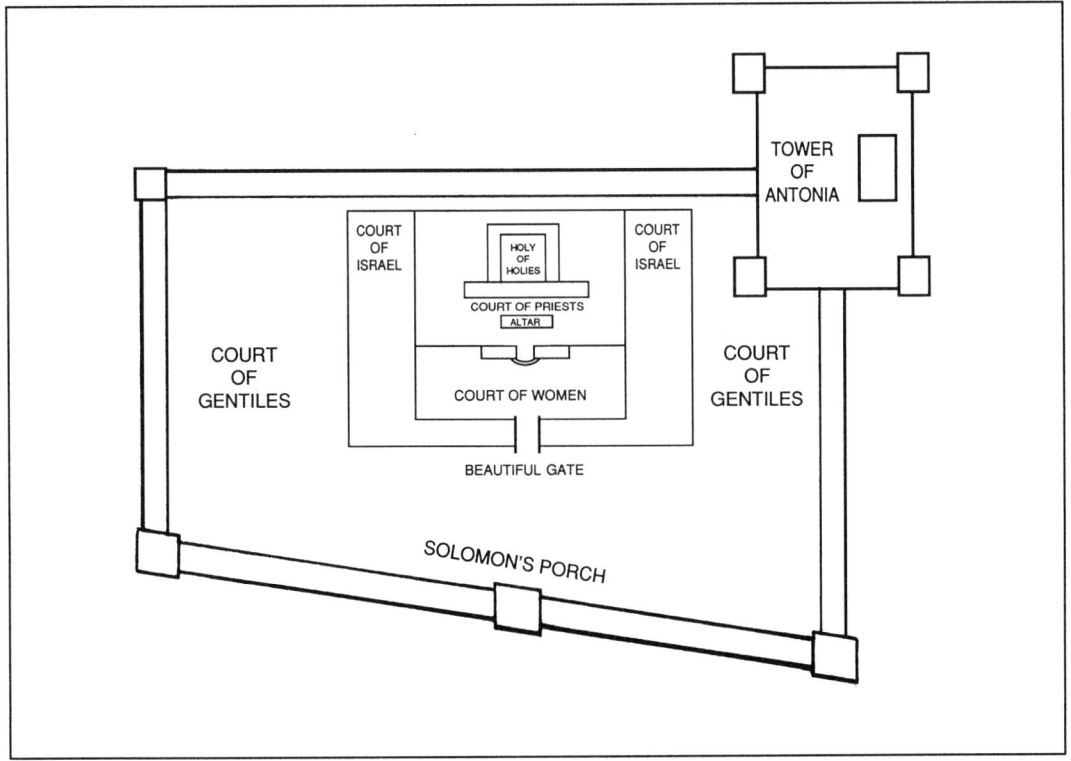

Plan of the Temple of Jerusalem

NOTES ON THE TEMPLE

The Temple shown on the plan was the third to be built on the same site. Solomon had built the first temple, which was destroyed by the Babylonians in 586 BC. The second had been built after the Jews had returned from the Exile in Babylon about 520 BC.

Herod the Great began the building of the third Temple in 20 BC. Work was not finally completed until AD 63 - just seven years before the Temple was completely destroyed by the Romans.

The Temple was a place of sacrifice. (It was the only place where Jews made sacrifice. There were many synagogues throughout the country, where the Jews held their Sabbath day worship, but only one Temple.) Animal sacrifices were made morning and evening each day by the priests.

The Temple was also a place of pilgrimage - devout Jews were expected to visit the Temple sometime during the great religious festivals.

The Holy of Holies - the innermost shrine of the Temple, visited only once a year on the Day of Atonement by the High Priest.

The Court of Priests - altars were placed here, on which priests made sacrifice.

The Court of Israel - only Jewish men were allowed to enter.

The Court of Women - this area was open to any Jew.

The Court of Gentiles - this was open to anyone, Jew or Gentile. Gentiles were not allowed to go beyond this point into the temple itself. The penalty for doing so was death.

Index of Biblical Reference

Subject Index